HOLDING ON TO GOD

A Memoir

FUTOUN HADDAD

CONTENTS

PART I

HOW IT ALL BEGAN

PART II

GAINED IT ALL. LOST IT ALL

PART III

THE FIGHT

PART IV

MOVED ON, BUT TO WHERE?

PART V

IT IS ALL IN YOUR HANDS

PART VI

A JOURNEY THAT NEVER ENDS

INTRODUCTION

Cast Out: Holding On To God, is an account of the struggle for self-realization and for reaching inner peace after a mother is ravaged by the agony of estrangement from her two children, ages 15 and 17, because of infidelity and subsequent divorce. It is a tale of childhood traumas resulting from unintended parental neglect, from phantom love and civil wars, culminating in a love affair and the alienation of children perpetrated by the other parent. It is a journey that started in war-torn Lebanon and carried on over to the U.S., bringing with it stories of loss, of abandonment, and of cultural transitions that could not be bridged within the fierce loyalty of the family she had left behind. Guided by her faith, and her unwavering love and resilience, she carried through thirteen years of suffering in order to reconnect with her children—a journey of hope and never-ending grief.

AUTHOR'S NOTE

All the names given in this book, including the author's, are pseudonyms. This is due to the cultural divide between East and West that makes a public display of one's life story the subject of shame and disgrace, potentially strengthening, if not permanently solidifying, the basis for the alienation or estrangement. Furthermore, it is done with the intention of protecting the privacy of the individuals' intimate correspondence or of their mental or physical well-being to which the book alludes. They are: Anwar, Celina, Fadwah, Futoun, Hassan, Jamileh, Nizar, Nour, Patrick, Rameh, Sabira, Salha, Sam, Sami, and Yelena.

About The Artist

I commissioned this amazing artist, Nizar Ali Badr, after I saw his work on Facebook sent to me by a friend. I was taken by the profound imagery he had created from the rough stones of Jabal Safoon in Syria, where he is from. Badr resides in Lattakia, a Syrian coastal town. He has been creating masterpieces since he was fifteen. His work includes many themes: political, religious, love, empathy, suffering, resilience and poverty, to name only a few. After briefly telling him my story, he created a perfect piece for my book cover which truly depicts what my journey has been all about. I am forever thankful to his heartfelt contribution. You may follow him on Facebook and Instagram. He may also be reached through his agent on Facebook: Adbulrahman MA Joud.

PART I

How It All Began

CHAPTER 1

First Ride

Anwar had had sweet boyish features as a baby and later as a child, even after I had kept his thick brown hair long and curly, bouncing as he walked. Never did I think he would end up with a receding hairline early in his twenties, as is the case for most Middle Eastern young men. His eyes were gorgeous and typically Arabian, wide, and densely lined by their long, dark eyelashes. His mouth was wide, too, never ceasing to laugh and giggle, and his nose, bold and angular, gave him character, as I always told him later in his youth.

MAY 2, 2008

He looked so handsome, and his eyes were as beautiful as ever. He looked up to me and into my face and said, "You know I don't respect you." I looked up to him, my eyes shimmering, for there he was, two feet away on his bike, yet not a touch, not a hug, and not a kiss would dare escape a mother's aching heart. I trembled, there on the curb next to my car, composed myself and said, "I don't expect you to respect me, but I do expect you to treat me with respect." He said he would not raise his voice or call me names because it would be immature. I thanked him and stood like a fool, trying to talk to him as though I had met him for the first time, a stranger, an acquaintance I perhaps once knew. The pain was indescribable. Ten months had passed without a word and without a glimpse, spare the precious moments on January 23, 2008 in that hallway, seated a few feet from one another and stealing a gaze or two until the court was in session and he was ordered to leave the courtroom. As he left, I looked at him: expressionless face; upset eyes laid on me the fear that my son no longer cared for me.

It was only seven months earlier that the divorce documents had been filed by my ex-husband, Rameh, asserting joint custody of our two children, Nour, seventeen, and Anwar, fifteen. It was a chaotic time filled with disbelief, anger, distress, uncertainty, and despair for the looming dissolution that was to separate me from my children, not knowing if and when they would ever decide to reunite with me. The dissolution documents were drafted by Rameh after he realized that my decision to divorce was inevitable and that I was on my way out of the house. I signed the papers that decreed that both of us would have joint physical and legal custody, but that "the children will be living with the husband for now. However, they remain free to elect living with either parent at any time in the future, and for whatever time duration they freely choose." I agreed to the terms because the children wished to stay at home, and I did not want to disrupt their lifestyle. Beyond what I anticipated a reasonable and short time, my children needed to absorb their reality before reconnecting with me. Never did it occur to me for a moment that what was decreed for them to choose "freely" would be stripped from them through manipulation and parental alienation orchestrated by their father, having started months prior to the actual filing.

The courtroom door opened. The judge was about to read the recommendation of the court-appointed mediator regarding my petition to modify the divorce agreement, allowing for visitation and family/individual therapy for my son. Rameh rushed to enter first. Anwar, as would an obedient pupil, followed behind. I sat on one side of the court room, and they sat on the other. The judge ordered, "Rameh and Futoun, you may rise now." I made the case before the mediator for the dire need of an underaged teenager to have as normal a relationship with his mother as possible after it had been severed. I hoped that the court would approve the mediator's recommendations.

My decision came after several failed attempts to connect with my son and my daughter, and fearing that my son's emotional and mental well-being would be gravely compromised by not being allowed to speak to or to see his mother with whom he had lived for fifteen years, filled with limitless love, affection and nurturing. The thought that he would be deprived of all that and of the closely knitted bond he enjoyed so much and the possibility of continuing to live his teenage years without a mother's support and guidance, worried me immensely. I knew better than to believe that a father, well intentioned or not, could assume the role of the mother and the father, comments Rameh had made in several postings on his social media profile. I knew well the fallouts of having grown up without a present father and a mother who did her best to absorb the loss to no avail. I surely did not want my young man to suffer the loneliness, the insecurity and the deprivation that had permeated my existence.

With the opening of the preliminary hearing, Rameh requested that my son be allowed to speak with the judge. Stating that his presence "would be too much pressure on him due to his young age," the judge denied his request and ordered my son to exit the courtroom. In my petition, I had requested that the court order visitation rights as well as conjoined or individual therapy with a social worker to monitor my son's progress. Realizing that my children's judgment had been seriously impaired because their father, playing the victim to win their support, was defaming my character and informing them of every aspect of our failing marriage, I also requested that the court order a cease and desist order barring Rameh from discussing any aspect of our relationship or of my love affair with my partner, Patrick, which had brought up the reality of a broken marriage, of unfulfilled dreams and disappointments that I thought I had sealed twenty one years before.

The judge adopted the recommendations of the mediator as a temporary order and set the matter for a hearing, not having yet considered Rameh's 31-page response to my petition (**I call Manifesto**) for reciting incessant and fallacious accusations that I was someone who was a "pathological liar," who had had several affairs with "other men" and thus lacked tangible credibility to be a good mother. In that same Manifesto, Rameh further attempted to alienate my children from me by enclosing letters from Nour and Anwar outlining the same basis why they did not want to have any relationship with me and requesting the visitation order be dismissed.

The order mandated child therapy to address issues of "feelings following divorce and separation, current estrangement from the mother and interfamilial conflict." Rameh was to enroll our son in therapy within thirty days from the court order, and my once-a-week visitations with my son were to begin on Friday, May 1, 2008 from 6 p.m. to 9 p.m. (I was attending graduate school and working during the day), the exchange to take place at the home of the custodial party or at any other location of mutual agreement. Each parent was to actively receive individual therapy regarding issues of the impact of divorce on the children as recommended by the therapist. The court further ordered that "Neither party shall make derogatory or disparaging remarks about the other parent and shall protect the child from hearing such remarks from the other party." In the months that followed, I actively participated in therapy, and I complied with all the provisions. Sadly, however, not only did Rameh continue to inject poison into my children's minds and hearts, but he also objected to the order, and he submitted two letters from two licensed clinical social workers stating that neither him, nor my son, needed to undergo therapy, against conventional wisdom.

One counselor, in the letter addressed to Rameh, stated that Anwar "Denied depression or anxiety and that there was no evidence of auditory or visual hallucination. Anwar also denied having any suicidal thoughts. He also denied any history of alcohol or drug abuse...Since there are no conflicts between you and your son, family therapy for the two of you is not indicated...This is more about a loss of respect and a violation of familial moral principles than any situational conflict between the (son and his mother). Anwar also does not wish to participate in individual therapy as he does not feel he has any presenting problem."

In the other, the counselor stated: "You stated contentment and enjoyment of the close relationship with your children, family, and friends, comfort in your orderly home and productive employment and community service. While you were willing to come for ongoing counseling, I do not recommend any at this time....While you have reported consistent effort to have the children maintain a relationship with their mother; you have respected their refusal to have any contact with her. Any external pressure to force a sixteen or nineteen-year-old to make them see their mother would also prove fruitless in changing their feelings; in fact, it would likely worsen the situation."

Furthermore, Rameh requested in his appeal that I report any "positive or negative occurrences" to the court during our meeting, and if they were deemed "contentious, then supervised meeting should be recommended in the presence of a court appointed mediator." "My son," he added, "should not be forced against his will, by my ex-wife, to be in the company or in the presence of anyone else whom he does not wish to be with, or to be taken to any place which he does not wish to go to."

It was obvious from this letter that Rameh was attempting to do whatever he could to disrupt our visitations. He was worried I might bring Patrick with me or take my son to his home, all of which would be unfathomable, given whatever precarious relationship I now had with my son, if any at all.

Rameh did not show up for the hearing set for March 19, 2008. Instead, the court clerk read a statement that a call was received on behalf of Rameh that he was undergoing surgery; therefore, he would not be able to attend. The hearing was postponed to the following month.

As I waited in the courtroom to hear the judge decide my visitation trial with Anwar, I looked to my left and saw Rameh slowly approaching the podium, weak as though defeated, pushing a walker; an old man succumbing to his injuries. I fought to hold back my tears watching this man, once so proud, once the center of everyone's attention, a grand presence, reduced to the humility of human frailty, sick and lonely. Still, he pled his case as I did mine, and we each went our separate ways. A few weeks after that, the decision was issued affirming most of the temporary order, adding that the "mother may communicate with Anwar by telephone or e-mail with reasonable frequency." I still reserved the right to visit my son once a week for three hours while the court ruled his primary residence should be with his father.

Anxiously and excitedly, I waited for our first reunion after the temporary order. It was 6:10 p.m. that day. My heart was racing as I waited for that phone call. Would he meet me? Would he talk to me? What would I say? The call came with heavy breathing as he rushed to meet me biking his way from work to the drug store near the house. He said he would be there in five minutes. He came as expected, but remained on his bike and refused to get into the car with me or to go to dinner. He wanted to be sure to send the message that he was not going to give me neither the luxury of his company, nor the pleasure of his accepting me or of anything I owned. To him that would mean that he was acquiescing. We talked about grades, about drugs, his bike races and yes, his fractured rib that no one had told me about. I told him how proud of him I was that he did not take drugs, still hated smoking, and was still a good kid.

Grand ideas Anwar has; me rushing to get married, attending to Patrick's kids, enjoying the million dollars his father had given me with all the pain and suffering I've put Rameh through, including the breakup of the family and the abandonment of my children for the sake of getting involved with another man. His rambling feelings were suppressed by a father's selfish injection of poison into his young, innocent mind. How would I respond without stirring more anger and frustration? I told him I put him and Nour under God, and no one would ever come before or after them. I swallowed my pain and my pride as I listened to him accusing me of being selfish, of my not having considered how much he did not want to see me and of how I was ruining his life and how I was a cheater who should have divorced two years ago before having three, four, or many more affairs.

He said that I did not even admit that I did anything wrong. "Yes, I did, Anwar; it was wrong," I said. "The past has passed, Anwar. All we have is today and tomorrow. You probably hate me, I know." He said he did not know hate. I smiled because he, like his mother, can forgive, and above all, he can love. He said he was leaving at 7:45. "Three hours is what I got,

Anwar," I said. "I carried you nine months and gave you fifteen years…
and you cannot give me 3 hours a week?" He is a teenager who needs to
assert himself. I understand. But I did have these three precious hours, and
I intended to use every second of them to be next to the joy of my life, my
amazing son.

Careful not to provoke him, but trying to assert my right to see him as
his mother who loved him more than the world, I said, "I advise you not
to leave." He then said, "So you are going to lie like you always did and tell
the judge my father grabbed me and took me home!" I said that I had three
hours, and that I was going to do what it took to see him. He said he did
not care about the judge's orders, that he was doing me a favor by coming
in the first place and that he was not going to see me next Friday. I tried in
vain to stop him, but he was determined. He said that I was making him
angry, and he took off on his bike.

I sat in the car for ten minutes in shock, tears frozen on my cheeks.
I turned the engine, drove off, and went home. In my loneliness, I cried
and cried, and then I smiled, for I had finally been able to see my handsome son. Somehow, I had seen in his eyes a child's desire for his mother's
affection. He was too proud to express it, hidden and fed by a wicked,
wicked selfish man who cared only to fulfill his own narcissistic desires
at anyone's expense, flesh and blood included. I slept in the hope that the
next day I would get the court's help to enforce its order and hold Rameh
in contempt.

My brush with joy ran dry as I was advised by the mediator that I was
on my own. The court could not enforce the execution of its orders against
the will or wishes of a sixteen-year-old. I left defeated and without hope. I
prayed for God to give me the strength and the will to carry on and never
to allow me to lose my faith in Him. I wondered would my son ever talk to
me? Would I ever see him again? I fought to bear my pain, the cross that

I had carried for ten months. I asked God to help me and to have mercy on me.

JUNE 26, 2008

My journey came to an end. The end that never had a beginning, and not a chance to pave its first step. It was as aborted as is a fetus before it kicks its first heart beat. I took to my pen, wanting to record my journey with my children, though mostly with my son, since my daughter was over eighteen by then and was legally considered an adult. Writing down my thoughts and feelings allowed me to pour my pain from the solitude of my inner self, shared only by my bare walls in my two-bedroom apartment. My keyboard strokes echoed through the tiny hallway that opened to the second bedroom I had chosen for Anwar when he came to visit me. I had furnished it with a small desk and the single bed I had brought from home, identical to the one he had slept in where every night I tucked him in and lay many butterfly kisses on his soft cheeks. I wanted it to be warm and cozy, anticipating that soon, he would be back in my arms and I would be laying many more butterfly kisses on his cheeks. I truly did not think that my children would sever me completely as they did, so I continued to write after long work days and school nights as though the tears that I shed could erase the anguish that tore me apart.

The thought that I might never see Anwar again made my heart bleed. It brought me to my knees, helpless and hopeless. I wanted to surrender, and to have closure. I wanted to admit defeat and move on. I wanted to make believe that I had no children and to just live my life. I wanted to be heartless, to cover my pain and to pretend that I was a rock unbending in the wind, defiantly thrusting its bare chest against the crashing tide. Sadly I must accept defeat, I wrote. I must carry on to live, and to live, I must abandon my hope. The joy of life had been sucked out of me, and happiness had lost its meaning; for what is it to live and to be happy without your own soul that you breathed into creating two lives conjoined with yours? I had lost my existence and slept every night wishing I might not wake up in the morning.

My heart doesn't belong to me, and I am not who I am. What is life, what is love, and what is humanity? Are you human I ask? I want to believe that you are, but with every passing day, with every passing moment, you remind me that you are robots. You have lost your mercy, and you have got nothing, my children. I don't know you anymore. I really thought I did, but you keep surprising me with your callous hearts and your cruel behavior, and above all, your vengeance and endless worship of punishment, inflicting agony while sitting back and enjoying the thrill and the gratification of your successes. How could a father, for the sake of avenging his own loss deprive his children from the love of their mother, vital to their emotional and psychological well-being? What you have done, Rameh, is wicked. Wicked and evil.

Nour, you changed your telephone number so I could not reach you. Your hatred has become so intense that you could not tolerate hearing the love-you message I left you three weeks ago. Go run, girl, go run till eternity. I am helpless. I cannot stop you. And Anwar, the one I thought had a heart like mine, a heart that did not know hatred, revenge, or wickedness; you really let me down, my lovely boy. You did. Who AM I to you, my beautiful children? You would not do to your enemies what you have done to me. How merciless can you really be? How can you sleep every night without the kisses I once gave you and without the hand that once caressed your cheeks and wiped away your tears? Or the arms that squeezed you, and the heart that beat with joy and pride each time it thought of you? What is betrayal? You say I betrayed you and lied to you, and perhaps you are right.

But my love never left you, and my heart never lied to you. And while I left your father, I never left you. It was your choice to abandon me.

But how can a mother let go? I kept typing away, addressing them as hollow shadows fleeing the storm, fighting to accept that my children were no longer mine. My feelings would sway from anger, to love, to acceptance, to defiance to disappointment, to hope, to defeat, to fear and to every feeling in the universe anyone can be consumed by.

Anwar, you gave me permission to talk to you by phone only, without any visitations as the court ordered; and I respected your wishes and asked you how often. You said once a week, but every time I call, you treat me like a pest, a leper disowned by her own flesh and blood. You say nothing and simply respond passively to the silly questions that I try to ask, just to steal another few seconds from you and to hear a few more of your breaths. You cut me off; say you have to go or come up with an excuse and hang up before I have a chance to say goodbye. And when I call more frequently—the one time I did—you say I am pushing you. What am I to you, my son? Vermin? An insect?...*Yee*, I am but a used rag, riddled with holes from years of overuse, her lifeless body tossed into the abyss, where no one can see her tears, and hear her screeching dying soul.

Today, for the second time, Anwar, you removed my "Keep up the great work Anwar. I am so proud of you" comment that I left on your webpage. I pled with you to call and let me know where to meet you for your birthday, and when you did not call, I tried for five days, only to get your voice mail. I pled that you let me know that you were all right, so you changed your voice mail to say that you had gone swimming with your phone, as though you were trying to send me a response without having to call.

So go ahead, protect your father, and never mind my messages, my love notes, my unanswered requests to see you, my lovely child. You think

I caused your father pain and suffering; and maybe I did, but such is temporary, for a man always forgets his woman and moves on with life, but a mother never moves on, never. My suffering will endure until I am relieved by the shadow of death, for once a mother is stripped from her children, she is stripped from anything that has meaning in life, even love. I have nothing left, nothing. The emptiness and solitude are vicious and are eating me up, injecting venom of the worst kind. Slowly I succumb.

I shall close this chapter now, and with the remaining breaths in me—if God can still give me a few—I shall forget my past and do what I must do: block every memory of my beautiful children. I shall remove pictures and albums, memories and moments and live yet another lie.

This time, the truth will not reveal me because the truth is what I feel and see but what I must shun, and shunning is what I ask God to give me the strength to uphold. Perhaps my new life, devoid of love, will turn me into a robot, just like you are. I have no pain, and I have no sorrow, for I have no children.

CHAPTER 2

Childhood In Lebanon

My life, my disappointments throughout the decades, the loss, the abandonment, the void, the deception, the love, the innocence, the betrayal and the childhood years stolen by a vicious civil war, riddled with danger and uncertainty, came flashing through my head, bringing with it suffocating memories of pain and suffering. I stood anguished, reliving the memories of a five-year-old tender girl ripped from her father's loving embrace.

I was just about a year old when my parents returned to our homeland, Lebanon, to resettle after closing their business in Venezuela where my three siblings and I were born.

Father had large, dark hazel eyes that spoke to you each time you looked at them. They glowed with tender sentiment and compassion. Through them, you read his heart. His round chubby face and bald head were as smooth as silk. I often rubbed them with my palms, feeling his sweetness. He was very hairy. He told us stories of when, as a young man in Venezuela, others looked in astonishment at his bare chest, thick hair crawling up his neck; pounded their chests and called him *Mono, Mono* (monkey). Father did not seem to be offended. Lebanese men unbutton their shirts half way down, displaying their masculinity proudly. Father mimicked monkey moves, laughing each time he told the story. I laughed with him.

Father was twenty-two years old when he first immigrated to the Dominican Republic in order to start a better life. He joined his uncle and for a year and a half sold empty sugar bags before he moved to Venezuela, and joined another relative in opening a clothing and household-materials store in the capital, Bolivar. After that, he moved to El Dorado, a remote village, and he opened his own store. He settled there, making Venezuela his home. A few years later, he returned to Lebanon to find a bride. As the country's customs dictated, his marriage to my mother, Sabira, in 1954, was arranged, though with her consent. He returned with her to El Dorado where they had my brother, Hassan, ten months later. Then the family moved to another village, El Callao, were I, my brother, Sami, and my sister, Jamileh, were born.

During that time, life in the village was very primitive relative to what was considered modern in Lebanon, for what you could call modern during that era. We lived adjacent to my parent's store in a make-shift house that had no shower or hot water. A hose in the back sufficed to wash the sweaty bodies of children running up the streets and playing joyfully in the neighborhood. In 1962, mother decided to visit her family in Lebanon, and she took my siblings with her. She intended to return with them to Venezuela, but two months later, returned without them. My parents were from the same pristine village in Northern Lebanon where rugged, graceful mountains embraced the plains, abundant in vegetation, fruit trees, and charming landscape. Water cascaded from several cliffs, down to flowing rivers that careened through small villages where the air was filled with the scent of sheep being herded in the morning sun, and the soft breeze created an enchanting melody as it joined the songs of farmers plowing the land and the laughter of women as they baked their Tannour (Tandoor) bread in the clay ovens outside their homes. Farmers barreled their donkeys loaded with fresh produce yelled out the fruit and vegetables they had carried to sell to the villagers. Olive trees graced the landscape and chickens roamed freely, chased by children along the village's narrow unpaved alleys, who stopped for nothing but their mothers' calls from far away to come home for meal time. It was the same village where Rameh and I spent our best childhood summer months and also where we met, I at fourteen, and he at fifteen.

My beloved village was my second home, my sanctuary. In the three summer months and holiday breaks we spent there, I grew up embracing its thickets, its ravines, the orchards, the abundant aromatic fruit and pine trees, even the crowing of a farmhouse rooster a mile away that woke me up every morning. There, I was myself; the tomboy within me blossomed. I ran my bicycle up and down its narrow alleys and cliffs, climbed and jumped off of trees and rooftops, quenched my thirst from its cold springs, and savored wild berries and any fruit that dangled low enough for my tiny hands to reach.

I often got up before dawn to join Grandma on her treks to where the fig trees and grapevines crowned the hilltops. We filled a couple of straw baskets with these each time and covered them with fresh grape leaves. By the time we got home, our baskets were half empty. It is a Lebanese custom to offer fellow villagers a treat from the bounty of your land as you walk by their houses along your way.

In the afternoons, as village women sat around a long shallow table, their legs stretched underneath, I squeezed myself anywhere I could find between their voluptuous bodies and the newly harvested heaps of wheat, helping them sift out the fine grains of soil and tiny pebbles. I learned in a few minutes all the stories that were happening in the village and the juicy ones that I was not supposed to. I could not understand their jokes or why they laughed so hard. But I joined them nevertheless.

Sami and I spent many hours in the creek below our house catching tadpoles and water snakes. We chased grasshoppers and dragonflies and swam in its shallow pools listening to the croaking frogs. As I lay my head on my pillow at night, the chirping crickets were the lullabies that put me to sleep. At the start of a new school year, we returned to Beirut. Musty air and covered furniture greeted us as we opened the door. A part of me always stayed in my village. It is still there today.

This is the village that my mother had left and to which she longed to return to in order to raise her children. However, she aspired to a better future for them in the capital, Beirut. My Grandmother was left lonely in the village with only two of her thirteen children, after the older ones emigrated to other parts of the world. Pitying her mother, and convinced that life would be better for her children in the homeland, mother decided to leave my siblings with Grandmother, and returned alone to Venezuela, thinking that after a few years, she and my father would join the family in Lebanon. Sami was six months, Jamileh, three and Hassan, five. My father was in agreement with her plan. Once back in Venezuela, they both worked hard to save money. She took over the store in El Dorado and my father joined ventures with his brother in another town—Tomeremo and started saving for the final return to our homeland. He visited my mom once or twice a week in the evening, and then he returned to his village, 40 kilometers away, in the early morning hours.

With the reopening of a gold mine in El-Callao, business boomed and my parents' profits quadrupled. I was born during that time in 1964. A year later, my dad's father became blind, so he felt he needed to be near him and he decided to return to Lebanon sooner than expected. That year, my parents spent it taking care of my grandparents' medical treatment, having little time for their own children. The following year, they rented a nice apartment along the Mediterranean coast, in an upper Middle-Class district in Beirut. The girls started attending an all-girls British Evangelical School, while the boys went to a Friar French one. They opened a small grocery store in the same building and tried to live as a normal family. My uncle had some money in Lebanon and gave my parents permission to invest it for their profit. Mother was put in charge of that, and Dad gave her power of attorney. She loaned it to businessmen who bought land and built private schools. However, by 1970, the business was not doing well enough to take care of the family's needs and the money, loaned by my mother, was not generating enough interest since some debtors were not paying back the money they had borrowed. Meanwhile, their store in El-Callao was being run by my aunt. My parents decided that my mom's mother would come to Beirut and raise us while they would go back to Venezuela and take over the store in order to provide the life of comfort Mother always wanted for her children.

Why did they not consider taking us with them remained a question that vexed me for the rest of my life. I was never satisfied by the responses I received when I asked Mother that question as we sat in her later years reviewing the past. I tried to understand, without judgment, decisions that my parents made that gravely impacted each one of us in our own way for many decades to come, but was never satisfied with any reason. What she said was that it was always my parent's intention to live together as one family, but that the circumstances did not allow for it. Not surprised by the answer, I decided to let it go, not wishing to open a Pandora's box of feelings which I had never shared with her and the ones that I did not think she would understand. After all, it was customary in that part of the world that children be raised by the grandparents, or by one parent while the other sought work overseas. In her limited mind, and given her own upbringing, as long as the intent was good, (and it sure was in our case), the means justified the end. It was always their plan, she explained, to return together to Lebanon, but sadly, it never happened and the family remained fractured.

For one, she explained, she did not want to disrupt our life, our routine, our schools, or the bonds we had forged with family and friends. What she did not admit (as I strongly speculate) is that she deeply believed that being raised in the only homeland she could belong to, one she so loved and was proud of, she would then provide her family better social norms, value systems, and ironically, familial ties and structure. She sought and worked very hard to raise us with very comfortable means to go to the best private schools, to live in the best neighborhoods, and to be among the best dressed and culturally exposed. Then, I did not realize the privileged life we lived, even though Mother tried to remind us every day that every *Lira* (Dollar) spent was earned through "sweat and blood." We lived in a bubble, impervious to how other countrymen lived around us until we became teenagers and started venturing outside a bit more. We took our lifestyle for granted, although I always was mindful of not wanting my parents to spend anything on me beyond the basic necessities.

Our parents broke the news to us, and Grandmother moved in. I was only five and a half years old and while I did not quite comprehend fully what that meant, I understood that both were leaving. I then asked my parents this question: "The parents leave, so then who will the kids stay with?" Hearing that, mother told me, she decided to stay, reasoning that she could not leave her children behind. My father left a couple of days later.

I was very attached to my father and followed him everywhere he went. I still remember the hunting trips in the wilderness of the unspoiled expanse of Northern Lebanon, beach trips where I would float on his big belly, times hanging out with him in the store and being in his loving arms, or just relishing his infectious laugh. He was the kindest, most forgiving compassionate parent I knew. We were very close, and I appeared to be his favorite, perhaps because I was the youngest. He loved life, people, and the Mariachi music he had grown accustomed to listening to in Venezuela. He was melancholic, spoke of his rough childhood after his father emigrated to Sierra Leon-Africa- for a better living, his impatience with school and studying, walking for hours to get from the village to the nearest town so he could enjoy partying a bit and searching around the village for cigarette butts to smoke as early as six years of age. But the only story he kept repeating to me many years later, after we reconnected, was about the evening before his departure, which to this day, I still remember vividly. As he was preparing, I sat in his lap in the corner of our living room. I had saved 25 *Kroush* (cents) especially for him and gave it to him saying, "Use it in Venezuela if you run out of money." I do not remember his response, but every time he mentioned the story to me, he smiled, yet his eyes hid more sentiments that he never shared with me. Perhaps he did not want to; and I did not ask.

I returned from school the next day, still expecting my father to be home. I do not remember who told me or what exactly, other than it was at that moment that I realized that my father was not coming back, perhaps ever. My heart was crushed. I screamed at the top of my lungs, tears gushing, calling out to him. I ran through every room, searching everywhere in case he was hiding under the bed, in the closets, in the small attic, under sofas or in the kitchen cabinets. Like a beast, I jumped up and down, beating my legs and my head, crying my heart out, but no one heard. I could not be consoled. I knew then that I had lost the father who was the love of my life. The distress from this traumatic moment haunted me well through my teenage years and through my marriage, creating an immense void that no one could fill and that led to many wrong choices I made in my futile attempt to compensate.

In the years that followed, mother continued working hard, and through the court system she recovered her money from the businessmen she had lent her money to. It took her about two years to settle everything and return the money to my uncle's daughters who had returned from Venezuela to Lebanon to settle. Mother was always a very strong and determined woman. If I have any resilience in me, enduring many trials, I owe it to her. I have never met anyone like her who could fall hard but graciously lift herself up. And I mean lift herself up not depending or needing anyone but herself to survive and push forward. She was also a very smart woman and loved learning, absorbing every book she read. Her passion for education was so great that she repeated the fourth grade so she could stay in school because, in those days, that was the highest grade she could attend. I will never forget her telling my sister and me over and over, "Your inheritance is your education." She enrolled us in the best schools and instilled in us the value of a higher education. By that inheritance, she ensured that we would stand on our own feet in times of need. "When life treats you badly," she used to say, "you will have your education to sustain yourselves," fearing that women would otherwise be so dependent on their husbands, rendering them powerless and defeated. She was right, although it would take me a lot more than that to break free from an unfulfilling marriage.

Mother was the disciplinarian. Even in her absence, we felt her presence. She set strict guidelines and rules that we knew better than to break. With her well-defined high cheekbones, thick lips— always provocatively colored with red lipstick—small nose slightly turned up, and a firm curvy body, she turned heads everywhere she went. Yet, we were not fooled by her graceful features. Mother sent us trembling each time she raised her eyebrows or swiftly pulled her hand against her chest, threatening to whack us if we went against her wishes. Rarely did she have to. Her stern look was sufficient warning for us to stay out of trouble. As an adolescent, she was the only one in her family to work. Ironing her customers' shirts for 25 *Krouch* each, she made enough money to buy herself a nice wardrobe with handbags that always matched her elegant shoes.

Close to her as I was, Mother struggled to exhibit love and was hardly affectionate. Craving my father's attention and tenderness which I had learned to live without, I still wanted to get as much of it as I could and would curl up by her feet as she lay on the sofa watching television in the evening. I would feel some warmth that I desperately wanted, but she remained clueless. She would caress my hair every now and then, but she never recognized the extent of emotional deprivation and parental love I was longing for.

Mother was loving in her own way, and expressed it by providing a very comfortable living for us, warm home-cooked meals every day, packed school lunches and treats of every kind, but the one kiss on the forehead and a hand on the shoulder that slightly pulled us towards her, was reserved for our birthdays and for our birthdays only. Never did I doubt her love for each one of us, though. It was the expression of that love that was absent. Still, I loved her deeply, knowing that is how she best knew how to show it, not having experienced it from either of her parents, not because it was lacking, but more because she grew up in a household were affection was somehow akin to being weak or even spoiled.

Business savvy and passionate to succeed, she started a new venture, sharing a licensed ownership in a new private school in 1972. The venture proved profitable, which allowed her in a mere year and a half to sell her shares and to partner with her sister to open a boutique in a popular shopping district in Beirut called Hamra. As a side business, she also made money getting commissions as an independent third-party loan officer.

She managed to accumulate enough capital, and opened a partnership seafood restaurant in the same year right at the beach in Auzaai district. As kids, my siblings and I spent countless hours playing in the anchored and abandoned boat that rested on the white sand across. Mother's plan was for my dad to return from Venezuela and to assume the management of the restaurant which was doing very well, while she and her sister would focus on the boutique. Yet again, as a famous Lebanese saying goes, "The winds blow not as the sails desire."

CHAPTER 3

Danger And Uncertainty — Civil War And Beyond

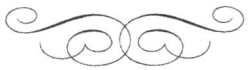

*I*n 1975, Lebanon was devastated by a civil war that ravaged through many towns, reducing them to rubble. It led to the deaths of over 1.2 K inhabitants by a conservative estimate, including many young fighters, women and children. I was eleven years old. It had started as a war against the Palestinian settlers but progressed quickly to engulf the entire country in a vicious sectarian war pitting Christians against Muslims. While the most intense fighting lasted for two years, the civil war officially ended in 1990. The country; however, never ceased to be in turmoil. The restaurant was the first to be bombed as it was close to a Palestinian installation. It closed; never to be reopened. All of my mother's investment was lost. The situation was very precarious in the Hamra district as well, and the boutique would open for a few days and then close for many others, losing a lot of capital. A year later, the boys were sent to France to continue their educations, fearing that they would otherwise be targeted as male

Christians. My sister and I remained with my mother in Lebanon, escaping many close calls.

Vivid in my memory and early in the war is when Egypt signed the Camp David Treaty with Israel. There was intense shelling in our neighborhood. Our building was across from the Egyptian embassy which was targeted by angry protesters. We ran to the shelter below while bombs fell like rain all around us. The Shelter was not equipped for any overnight stays. It was being used only as a storage area at that time. It was cold and damp and was infested with rats and cockroaches. There were no cots or sleeping bags or anything that we could use to sleep on. Babies cried incessantly as mothers tried to console them with sweet baby melodies while shivering in the cold or from the fear of what may come. How we managed I do not know. By the Grace of God, a few days later, we emerged, slowly navigating around the shrapnel that had filled the building entrance and shattered our windows tossing thick glass across the house. Surely, we would have perished under their razor-sharp edges or by their sheer weight since they had blown across the entire apartment, wall to wall. The windows were thick and tall so as to allow for a maximum view of the sea.

Not long after that incident, another miracle escape still makes me tremble by imagining how fragile life can really be. My best friend, Salha, sat in the front seat and I behind her as her father drove us with their cat to the veterinarian for some shots. It was early that day when the Israeli Commandos, disguised as women, broke into the home of a Palestinian Commander and assassinated him. Immediately, the guards started shooting, and we were caught in the fire since our car had made a turn nearby. I do not remember which were louder, our screams or the sound of the twenty-three bullets piercing our car from every direction. The shattered windshield cut through my friend's face injuring her eyes, while I emerged unscathed. But wedged deeply in the cross that I wore was a thick piece of metal that was directly aimed at my heart. I clenched and kissed the cross that my mother had gotten me from the Vatican during one of her business trips, and I thanked God for His second miracle. I wore my cross for many more months as my shield, until one day, our house was broken into, and it was stolen. My friend recovered well, but soon after she left the country with her family making a new home in Paris. Schools closed under the intensity of the fighting, and I was left without my childhood friend whom I had loved very much.

To avoid missing a school year, my cousin, Mary and I took advantage of a public school that had opened with an accelerated program during that summer. It promised to make up for our lost school year and to keep students on track. I had never attended a public school before and did not know what to expect. The classrooms were packed. The playground did not have any benches or tables. Like soldiers, we lined up every morning and after every recess, we marched to our classrooms as ordered by the teachers. Except for a blackboard, the walls were bare, like prison cells. The teachers were stricter than the English Evangelists I had gotten used to. It was the first time that I had been taught by a male teacher whose ego allowed him to punish his students as he saw fit any time they disobeyed him. I was not spared. I do not recall misbehaving, but I had always been a bit of a mischievous student. For my not following what he had commanded, he came up to me while I was seated at my desk and slapped me without warning. I slapped him right back. Life had taught me to defend myself early on. We have a saying in Lebanon, "If you do not become a wolf, the wolves will eat you." I don't remember being disciplined for my defiance. Still, I was lucky to get my certificate and to move up a grade the following year. Perhaps my good grades had saved me.

Getting an education during those times was very challenging. I went to at least a couple of schools in the year that followed, selecting ones that had been the least impacted by the fighting. That meant long walks every morning and afternoon, crossing dangerous combat zones along the way. To make things worse, we lost our electricity and running water. I studied endless nights by candlelight, and I hauled many gallons of water from a nearby cistern up to the first floor where we lived, just to wash dishes, to flush the toilets and to take baths. Winter was harsh. It was very cold and damp. With no heaters, there was nothing I could do to get comfortable in our apartment. Even wearing thick sweatshirts, heavy jackets and double socks did no good. We heated water on the stove, if we had been lucky enough to find a propane tank. This limited our showers to every other day.

These would not be the only incidents that I faced growing up in that environment. What followed were devastating events that stayed etched in my brain and in my psyche forever; those images of many lives, innocent or not, that had perished under the heavy fighting, sectarian killings, torture, and sniper bullets. There were Israeli invasions and bombings of the Marine Barracks and of the U.S. Embassy which were less than a mile away from our house, places I passed by everyday during my daily walk to the American University of Beirut (AUB) campus that I was attending. Newspapers, television and other media outlets showed without any reservations gruesome pictures of dismembered human bodies, flesh ripped apart or in pieces tossed onto the streets where, as unfortunate to be passers-by, their lives were cut short by detonated cars, by random shelling or by militia gunfire that would break without a warning, without a care or for any regard for human souls, young, old, innocent, or guilty.

Life at home was hell. In a very patriarchal society, it was an anomaly that a family of four children be raised by one parent, let alone a mother, in the absence of the father. It was the tradition in Lebanon, as in the rest of Middle Eastern countries, that the head of the household, the father, make all the decisions, ensure propriety in behavior, maintain, through force, if necessary, the family's honor, integrity and the girls' good reputations. In the absence of the father, generally, the uncle stepped in to take his place. In our family, we had neither. Not only was my father thousands of miles away, so were all the brothers from both sides of the family. I don't think it was my mother's intention to relegate that responsibility to my then teenage brother, Hassan, but that is what happened, perhaps being overwhelmed by all the responsibility or by default, by custom, by social pressure or by all of the above. She, too, had been left without a man in her life and was forced to tend to the family, doing the best she could to assume both roles, the mother as well as the father. She succumbed under the pressure and allowed my brother the upper hand, resulting in devastating and everlasting consequences, both for himself and for us, but mostly for me.

The absence of a father in our lives had affected each one of us in its own unique way. What for me was a resulting deep need for love and affection, for my brother, Hassan, there was anger, a premature sense of responsibility, an ill-perceived power and authority over us, and a false sense of superiority and control expressed through physical abuse. With all my vulnerabilities, I was still a very defiant young girl. I exhibited confidence, assertiveness and the might to stand my ground no matter the cost, traits I inherited from my mother. My classmates were not surprised at my reaction when the principal delivered the honor-roll certificates one year. As he called my name, I approached the podium to receive my certificate, and I extended my hand to shake his. Instead, he only gave me his pinky finger because my behavior on campus had not met his expectations. I backed off saying, "You can keep it then." It was the same principal who time and again called me into his office, pulled a jacket from a pile of clothes and forced me to cover my bare arms. I obeyed each time, but took the jacket off as soon as I was out of his sight.

My defiance was never tempered even as an adult. In 2006, when Nour was stuck in Lebanon during a visit, Israeli bombs fell like rain on the cities for thirty days. I sent e-mails to all my co-workers asking them to pray for her. After she was rescued by the U.S. Marines, put on a ship, and brought back to the country, I sent more e-mails thanking them for their prayers, but I added that while she was home safely, many other innocent lives continued to suffer under "Israeli aggression." The statement brought rebukes from a few Jewish employees who had accused me of implicating them. They were not satisfied when I explained that my comment was directed at Israel, not at Jews. My manager insisted that I apologize. My job was on the line. I refused. Nothing I had said was derogatory or demeaning to any group. Somehow, I did not lose my job.

Growing up, I always was the anomaly in a very traditional society. Rather than playing with dolls, I preferred the outdoors, climbing trees, jumping off of rooftops and running my bicycle down the steep hills of my village. I did not care about dressing up, about wearing makeup or about making myself pretty for anyone who believed that my destiny is to prepare myself for marriage, to learn how to cook, to clean, to raise children and to be an obedient compliant wife. I was a person who believed in the power of being an independent thinker, needing a man only to complement me and my needs that I had been stripped of as a young child, but not to control or enslave me as was the fate of many women in that society.

The society, value system, culture and way of life were all phony to me. I distrusted people's displays of affection for one another when they were no more than acquaintances. I despised the shallow expression of love in their greetings, their hugs and kisses professing how much they had missed each other, yet soon afterwards turned around and spoke ill of each other. I could not understand how they did that to others knowing that the others did that to them. Yet, they carried on with these silly obligations and traditions without any complaint. I was not part of that and did not wish to be. I wanted people to be genuine, particularly with their expressions of love. I wanted them to be true to their hearts and to be who they were, but I also knew I could not change them, and so I felt lonely and sad. Somehow, I felt I should escape to a place where I knew no one and no one knew me, a place where I could thrive as myself and be judged for my own character, not by how society expected me to be.

Rebelling against the societal norms, I continued to behave and live my life the way I thought it ought to be: simple, genuine, humble and kind. At that time, I was most comfortable wearing jeans and sneakers instead of dresses and high heels. I would rather play soccer, basketball or track and field instead of sitting around at gossipy tea parties making silly talk. I enjoyed the company of male friends who were direct and pragmatic, less the company of female friends with all their drama. I was very opinionated, but I was honest and straightforward. I cared less to be pretentious, to follow the strictly adhered to social norms or to play the game of cat and mouse when it came to boys. I chose instead to let them know early on when I liked them. I was who I was, and I was not going to let anyone change me. My brother, however, saw it differently.

Because of his own insecurities and failures (as I saw it), he started drinking heavily at a very young age. Memories of him drinking whisky early in the morning, alone, saddened me. Many a night, as he, Sami and I slept in the same room, I would be awaken by his loud vomiting. I would hide my face under the bed covers to escape watching my mother's agonized face as she cleaned him up. What distinguished us early in our childhood was that he had surrendered to his situation in the worst way; whereas in my lowest moments, crying in my silence, I was determined to overcome and to push forward.

I could not understand how anyone could allow himself to be enslaved by any substance or by any addiction that could only perpetuate his misery, his defeats or failures. He thought he could pacify his tormented soul by binge drinking and by beating me, my sister and yes, even my mother. I released it through exercise, playing sports, with walks along the beach, and by writing my life's journal. Even as I felt weak and depressed, I believed in my inner strength, asking God every day to help me. My family was not all that religious, and neither was I. We did go to church during the holidays, but in times of need, I always found myself calling on to God to help me and to have mercy on me. And He did. Every time I fell, He picked me up and He carried me in His loving arms until I got to safe shores. This pattern has been repeated many times in my life, and it is what sustains me every day.

Hassan's rage would spill out every time he did not get his way or if he felt his orders were not being followed. He became increasingly vicious and cruel. While he beat my sister as well and broke her nose one time, I got most of the abuse for my defiance. It was difficult to predict how he would react when I refused to obey him, particularly for petty things such as refusing to go to the market to buy him what he wanted, or sneaking to see my cousin and her family after he had quarreled with them. But every time something trivial like that happened, I was beaten badly. And when it came to boyfriends, he was obviously not going to accept any of it. It did not matter that I had such pride and self-respect, shaped somehow by my strict upbringing and my own value system, that my relationship with any boyfriend was strictly limited to kissing and mild flirtations. His interpretation of any relationship at all was a dishonor to him, to the family and to the society at large. He treated my sister and me as whores. Perhaps he had engaged many himself.

On one occasion, dressed in my thick robe and with no impropriety, I went to the front yard in order to meet Rameh early in our relationship. Hassan saw me and ordered me inside. It did not matter that our flirtations were innocent and did not involve any sex. In his deranged mind, I was promiscuous and deserved punishment. For all my defiance, I suffered helplessly from his beatings with fists, being dragged by my hair across the room, belted, kicked, shoved, pushed, having my head banged against the wall or the furniture. Through my screeching cries, there was no mother to wipe my tears or to shield me against yet another round. I hated him and wanted him to leave and never come back. My relief lasted for a little over a year when he went to France, but later, the abuse continued after his return and it did not stop until he went to the United States to go to college. I felt alone and week, with no one to defend me but myself. I am not sure what else led to my despair, my anxiety and depression (or at least what I thought was depression). Was it the war with all of its induced fear, anger, uncertainty, loss of innocence, helplessness and chaos? Or was it the years of physical abuse? Perhaps both, compounding my internal battle with my own loss of a father that had left me vulnerable, seeking love where I could find it in order to pacify my longing for affection, for security, for tenderness, empathy and stability.

During these tough times, Dad did what he could to support us, but the remittances were insufficient to sustain our lifestyle, pay for private schools and for two young boys in France. As the two-year civil war calmed down a bit, Hassan returned to Lebanon and was admitted to medical school at AUB. Jamileh enrolled in International College (more expensive than any other). Sami also returned to Lebanon and hopped from one school to another trying to pass another year with failing grades. I chose a more local but prestigious school, determined to excel and to be admitted to AUB, dreaming of becoming a journalist. Expenses kept increasing. Mother decided to return to Venezuela, confident she would make more money there. She left the boutique to my aunt in July or August 1977 and started revamping the business that my father was not managing very well. After a short while, Hassan left for the U.S. and Sami returned to France. I became the burden that my sister had no choice but to assume, caring for a fifteen-year- old girl. Jamileh was only nineteen herself.

Mother was confident in Jamileh's ability to care for me, enough to command such a hard sentence on a young girl, particularly under such dangerous war times that had continued to render us fearful, insecure and under threat constantly. Jamileh did her best to take care of me and the house needs. She bought groceries, cooked and oversaw the finances. I loved her dearly, and I looked up to her as my idol. Neither she nor my mother, however, realized my anxiety, my loneliness and the confusion I was reeling under. After all, my mother was a continent away, and my sister could barely keep up with all the responsibility while still going to school or working and trying to live her life.

There were many days I would sit by our large window in the enclosed patio room, look out to the sea and cry and cry till the day's end. I also spoke to my pet cat when I had no one else to talk to, and I swear she was listening, blinking her eyes as though to tell me that she felt my pain. My heart beat so fast and my shortness of breath would make me quiver in fear, yet I saw no doctor or a therapist. Why did I not confide in my sister, I do not know. Perhaps having to fend for myself all those years had toughened me or made me realize that my feelings were only mine to endure and overcome. My only intimate moments were with my pen and journal where I spilled all of these sentiments as much as I could. Left without guidance, I was on my own to make choices and to bear the consequences; and bear the consequence I did, as my future unfolded.

At the end of that year, my father came to Lebanon to visit, rushing to return only six weeks later. It was the first time I had seen my father since his departure. There had been the rare phone calls and some letters he sent which my mother would read to us, and a talking doll he had sent me one year. Other than that, I had had no communication with him for the nine or ten years he was away. I don't know why he could not call us more often, but I assumed in my adult years that back in that day, the access had been limited. I wondered why he could not visit us every year while we were growing up, but I had to make believe that he could not leave the store unattended. I wanted very much to convince myself that he never forgot us, that he dreamed and lived for the day that he would reunite with us. But the truth, I later came to believe, is that having been surrounded in Venezuela by his nieces and a nephew, who were born and raised close to him and who held him in the highest regard, had been enough to satisfy him.

During those six weeks, and my two-month visit to Venezuela at fifteen a couple of years later, I came to know the father whom I had missed and loved so much. In my journal, I described him as a compassionate soul who knew no animosity. He had a very soft and gentle heart, deeply sensitive and caring. In it, I acknowledged his love for us and appreciated the sacrifices he had made, living in Venezuela, so we could have a good life in the homeland. I guessed that for the forty years he had lived there, he too, must have felt the agony of separation from his own parents, family, friends, from his homeland and, of course, from his children and wife years later. But what I truly wanted to know, I did not ask. Perhaps I was too young to have realized the importance of having such a conversation, or perhaps I wanted bygones to be bygones, satisfied with the father I now had.

The business in Venezuela started picking up again, thanks to my mother's entrepreneurial skills. With Hassan in the United States and Sami in France, still, it was her hard work that allowed us to sustain our ever-increasing expenses. The idea of returning permanently to Lebanon was abandoned and never entertained after that. Mother went back and forth to Lebanon from time to time, staying for short periods of time until I left to continue my education in the U.S. at age twenty, four years later. Try as she might to exert her control over us, she failed, for her absence had made us grow up precariously independent, too prematurely for our ages.

During that time, Jamileh and I were left alone making the best we could of a bad situation. We survived many skirmishes that continued to pit the parties against one another, bringing unsettled times and fear for our safety. We witnessed the Israeli invasion unfold as its naval ships dispatched soldiers along the coast in front of our home. We were arrested a couple of times for having violated a curfew. We stayed at the station for hours trembling in fear for what might become our fate until my cousin's husband used his military connections to get us out. We had to abandon our home and run for the safety of Eastern Beirut and live with my aunt for the summer. Escaping to the tranquility of our Northern village was also disrupted many times because of road closures, bombing and checkpoints set up by militias, Syrian soldiers, Palestinian Commandos and other rene-gade groups that claimed different sections of cities along the way. During these turbulent times, I met Rameh in our beloved village where that other journey had begún. And it would be eight years more before I saw my father again, who came with my mother to attend our wedding in California where we lived. The year was 1986. By then, I was twenty-two-years old and had just graduated with a Bachelor of Science in Journalism. Rameh was twenty-three and was in and out of college due to financial hardship.

My parents visited us almost yearly after that, but the conversation about the choices they made in our upbringing and the family break up never came up. By then, I was so caught up in raising my children and working that I left the past dormant, as I did my own troubled marriage. But when the time was ripe, I felt I could not burden his heart and his mind that was slowing succumbing to Alzheimer's disease with a past that he was probably oblivious to. I did not think he would be able to satisfy me with any rational response to my questions. I surmised that he would tell me that as hard as it was for him to be separated from his family, he did what he did for our sake. I supposed he would add that it had been customary in his generation, as his father did before him, for the father to leave the home for the sake of better opportunity. Perhaps I knew all of that was true, or partly true, but it was not going to bring me the closure I sought, for in my heart, I was afraid that my father really did not miss us as we liked to think he did. I really wanted to confront him with the notion that he perhaps loved and received love from my cousins and thus his bond with us slowly faded, but could not muster the courage to do so. Perhaps I did not want to bring him painful reflections, or wanted the truth to remain unspoken, so I could still give him the benefit of the doubt, and myself some assurance that the father I so adored had endured a loss no less profound than mine.

CHAPTER 4

Teenage Years — What You Call Love Then

$$\sim\!\!\mathcal{O}\!\!\sim\!\!\mathcal{O}\!\!\sim$$

During our first encounter, Rameh was sitting angrily in the swing on my friend's patio. I was just leaving the party where we had teased him trying to snatch the bucket of popcorn he had just popped. He was thin but tall by Lebanese standards. He was handsome. His large mouth and thick lips stood out on his skinny face; his blond hair extended below his neck. The darkness of the night disguised his fair complexion and his eyes which, depending on what he was wearing, changed color from green, to blue, to light grey. Years later, I told him how they looked haunted and empty. But during that evening, he was just the popular guy every girl wanted to be with, lured by his charm. He was the center of attention. He had the gift of making people laugh at every party.

He volunteered to walk me home, and I agreed. We chatted along the way; I got home; thanked him and said goodbye. The next day, although

I did not feel anything towards him, I was quick to tell my cousin, Mary, about our encounter the night before. In the coming days, we would meet at several dance parties and I would wait excitedly for him to ask me to the floor. I would wake up in the morning trying to convince myself that I was still in love with my then boyfriend, only to feel shocked that Rameh had stolen my heart and my mind (as I wrote in my journal at that time). The reason why I wrote "shocked" I believe, is because as young as I was, it seemed strange to me that my heart could so quickly switch between boys whom I was convinced I loved very much. And this would repeat itself many times over. Perhaps that is how teenagers' immature minds work, but I did not know that at the time and had no one to guide me through the precarious steps of early adolescence. There were no role models in my life to look up to or follow, no parent to assure me that my feelings were normal or off, and the war had certainly deprived us from exploring relationships in a healthful natural way.

Shortly after, at a dance party, he asked me to be his girlfriend. I looked into his eyes, and with deep love said yes as my heart danced with joy. That was love as I knew it and no more. He was witty, cool, never ran out of something to say, entertaining everyone in his presence with his jokes. He was always the center of attention and appeared to relish it. Naïve as I was, I took him for what I thought he was, not thinking twice that for the remainder of his life, he would seek anything just to inflate his ego, and come out a "winner" as his alienation of my children from their mother would later show. His stubbornness and controlling traits manifested in his disregard and disrespect for me, for our relationship, and for the expectations that followed, I interpreted as strength of character and conviction.

Rameh left to go to school a few days later, and I was stranded in the village due to the increased fighting that had led to a road closure. A mutual friend brought me his news and a letter or two. In one, Rameh stated he was coming up to see me in the village. He signed it, "The one who loves you and will never forget you, Rameh." I jumped for joy and forgave him for all of his neglect. I waited and waited, but he never showed up and he gave no excuse. I was upset and disappointed, but again, I was quick to forgive and forget the next time I saw him. Other times when I called him, excited to hear his voice, his response was dry and disengaged, quick to point out that he had to leave to eat, to study or to run errands. Other times he would come up to the village and not bother to notify me or stop to see me. Once he agreed to meet after I insisted we talk, but he did not show up. And when I called him out on it, he gave a lame excuse: he was with the guys and he did not want to clue them in that we were in a relationship. I felt hurt and abandoned once more by someone I had thought was the only love of my life.

On one New Year, I waited for an invitation that never came. I discovered he was partying with his buddies and when I knocked asking to speak with him, he dashed out yelling at me for interrupting his party. He never remembered my birthday, nor did he take the time to visit me in Beirut, even as he was visiting his friends there. For all his lack, I decided to break up with him while still feeling that I was very much in love. For the years that followed and up to his departure for the U.S., our relationship was characterized by many break ups and getting back together, usually at his request. In between, I would quickly move on and start small innocent relationships with other boys or be enamored with many others. Yet, every time we got back together, I felt the surge of love and never wanted to let him go. Perhaps that is why Rameh was convinced that I truly loved him and would never leave him for another. And while I wrote in my journal about the intensity of the love I had for him, many other times I wrote about the lack of it as well.

There was only one time that I could remember, two years after the breakup, during which Rameh said that he had been wrong and I had been right: that he had not treated me as I deserved, had neglected me, had avoided spending time with me, etc. Perhaps he did it betting that I was lonely and would agree to go back to him. The reality was that I was still hopeful that my then boyfriend, Julio, who had fled to Africa for fear of persecution, would write me and ask me to wait for him. When Rameh had told me that he had always loved me, I did not believe him. I said, "Rameh will never love." We decided to remain just friends.

Julio was short and skinny. He wore thick sunglasses day and night in order to disguise a blind left eye, deformed by a misfired rifle when he was a child. His other eye, framed by a thick eyebrow, was light hazel, and dominated his small face with his tight mouth and thin lips. His hair was light brown, fuzzy, and left uncombed. There was always a pack of cigarettes in his hand, his teeth yellowed from smoking heavily.

I never heard from my Julio again. During a two-month trip to Venezuela, I started thinking about Rameh and Julio, and I realized how much they differed from one another. The only thing they had in common was that they were from the same village. Rameh was educated, had a good future, his family liked me, people liked him, and my parents approved of him. Julio, on the other hand, was struggling in school, did not appear to have a future or any ambition and was a recluse and a dreamer. On the other hand, no other boy had ever made me feel so complete. I felt he was my other half. What bonded us even more was a true sense of loss of a father neither one of us had known. We sat for long hours in the wee hours of the night, crying for no apparent cause, and then consoled each other for what neither one of us could articulate the basis of. We both felt lost, but we had found one another. He was the only boy who made me feel the intensity of his love for me. He would go to hell and back for me, loved me like no other, was affectionate and caring. He was very romantic, tender, kind, and empathetic and had a very gentle soul. I loved all of his traits, but I could not love him more than a very dear and inseparable friend, although I had convinced myself that we were lovers.

Rameh, on the other hand, appeared to be a strong tough man of conviction, funny but very serious when he needed to be, charismatic, confident, determined, and ambitious with a very optimistic outlook on life. He seemed the rational choice. I admired his characteristics at the expense of ignoring how much he had marginalized me and my feelings. He was dry, insensitive, egotistical and unforgiving. Many a story I wrote in my journal that showed his lack of empathy, of love and care that had upset me so much and had made me feel miserable in my relationship with him. With each incident, I tried in vain to tell him why it hurt, but he did not listen or he would argue defending his actions, always blaming me and attacking my character. Numerous times I explained to him that I needed a man who loved me, who was tender, who would hug and kiss me lovingly, wrap his arms around me passionately and pull me closely to his chest. He, on the other hand, never caressed my hair, never looked into my eyes passionately, never touched my face or showed any interest in being in my company. I explained I had always felt like I was his second or third best since he would rather spend time with his friends but never with me, or tell me he wanted to meet with me and then not show up. His response was that five minutes with me once every four months was enough for him. The only place he and I went were to the movies, and only three times, and not by his invitation, always mine. I planned, I offered, I invited. But he could not have cared less, not bothered by a monotonous life.

He was also selfish and vindictive, but I was blinded to all that at the time. My journal brings me back to the time when I had snuck with Julio into my friend's basement while Rameh and the guys were outside. My friend's mother asked her why the door was open, and she lied saying that I needed to use the bathroom. She waited for me to exit and locked the door with Julio inside. Luckily, through a small window that opened to the outside, Julio broke free. Hoping to get him in serious trouble, Rameh immediately yelled out to my friend's mother to come and see what had happened. Luckily, she never came down. And while I got so upset with Rameh for his despicable act and stopped talking to him, as time passed, I forgave him as I did time and time again.

Rameh's true colors would show every now and then, but hardly anyone, including myself, recognized how serious they were. He said hurtful things about me to friends while I was out of town during the time when I was with Julio. "May she go to hell." Another time I personally heard him say about me, "If I see her dead on the street, I won't even care." I mention this because he meant every word he said. He was not one to spout in anger. His gift has always been a brilliant and fast thinking brain. No matter his distress, he chooses his words carefully to inflict the worst pain he can upon whomever he decides has wronged him.

It is very difficult through the lens of a naïve teenager to explain why I continued my relationship with someone whose heart was evil and was intent on harming anyone whom he thought had betrayed him. I could not understand that there were people in this word who seek vengeance even as it hurts them and the closest people to them. I did not grow up like that and did not know how to hate. Even as I felt I hated my brother Hassan for all of his abuse, I used to feel sorry for him when he would cry helplessly afterwards, and I forgave him for everything. Yet, every time Rameh asked me to get back with him, slowly but surely it happened; and with each time I felt elated. Was it true love, desperation, insecurity, immaturity, fear of being without a man in my life, or all of the above? I did not know. All I knew was that he was clever and had a way of pulling me back towards him whenever he decided. As his departure for the U.S. neared, I was crippled with the fear that he might forget about me. For the first time, I realized that perhaps I loved him a lot more intensely than he loved me; that while my love was real (or I thought it was), his was childish and immature and while mine was very, very deep, his was shallow and fleeting. I feared I would remain alone loving him only from afar.

I took a taxi and hurried to meet him at the airport at 6:30 a.m. to say my goodbye. His flight was two hours later. I waited and waited until I saw him hurry to board at the last moment. I rushed to him and hugged him, tears flowing, but felt no warmth from him. He was preoccupied with himself, happy he was leaving. I asked him, "Do you still care for me?" He smiled but gave me no reply, proceeded to the gate and did not look back. After his family left the waiting area, he turned and looked at me for a few seconds. I looked at him with eyes weeping over the eternal separation. I hugged him as my heart cried bitter silent tears that no one else but me would notice, not even Rameh. He ascended the stairs, waived his final goodbye and disappeared into the blue sky. In the few months that followed, I still believed I loved him and hoped that living in the U.S. would change him, would make him a better man, someone who would value relationships and know what it takes to maintain one. I was wrong. The game he played for eight years before our marriage was the same twenty one years after, until my epiphany.

CHAPTER 5

Marriage & Early Life In America

***

*N*ot too long following his departure, I stopped thinking about Rameh, deciding that he, after all, did not love me, and that life must go on. I felt lost about a love that could be forgotten. I questioned if I had really loved him or was lying to myself that I did. I contemplated whether or not I would fall for him if we were to meet again but I was not sure that I could. I felt that we grow up living life in a lie, that we convince ourselves that it is the truth simply to move forward, to leave the past behind or to pretend. From an early age, I was determined to overcome adversity no matter my state of helplessness. I cried, I laughed, I fell to my knees, but somehow I always managed to lift myself up and to keep walking. And walk I did. Shortly after, I developed deep crushes here and there during my two-year enrollment at AUB, still longing for a relationship that would fill the void and quench my thirst for love, for tenderness and for romance.

My feelings for one of the guys, an engineering major, handsome, tall and cool, grew more and more intense even as we hardly communicated. I could not explain at the time how anyone could have such strong feelings, even love, for anyone who would never become more than an acquaintance. I spilled into my journal sentiments buried under the heavy weight of the loss of my father juxtaposed to a perpetual need of companionship and romance that never came to be. I cried in my solitude for someone to help me, to guide me, to reassure me, but no one came to my rescue. I decided I only had myself, but not before questioning if love ever existed. Had I ever loved Rameh, would I ever get back to him should we meet again? Why Rameh was always in the back of my mind, I could not explain. I can only fathom that within that man there was an intangible charm that always drew me to him.

Despite the lack of romance in my life, I was happy surrounded by many friends, new and old. I was active in many university clubs and functions, from photography, to folk dancing to soccer, to competing in track and field. I had as many male friends as I did female ones. They were all very sweet, kind and understanding and we spent many long hours hanging out, going to the beach, to parties, and to outings. I felt that that period was the best in my life, the most enjoyable since we were living in a protective bubble, in and around the campus. We did what young students do, oblivious to the danger that surrounded us and to the insecurity that we faced every day as the war continued to ebb and flow with sniper bullets landing unpredictably on any day or at any time.

Still, I cried during many lonely nights, trying to mask my pain by being very active and involved in all aspects of campus life until I became numb. I used to think that reality dictated my life, but my feelings always conquered. They were true and defined who I was. I was free to dream, to fall in love, to hope, to be disappointed, to suffer, to feel the crush of the waves, but with time, I wrote in my journal, I lost it all because reality finally sank in and ripped my soul. It dictated that I no longer dream, no longer fantasize, no longer love, but instead, be stripped of all emotions and become a rock uncrushed under the storm. But how can a person live without emotions? How can a person be defined as human in the absence of the one thing that defines our humanity—love? Will life have a meaning when it is our emotions that bring us sorrow and joy, love or hate? How will I pull through? I do not know! But what I do know, I wrote, is that I shall overcome all this because I don't want to die. I fear death. I shall stand tall and proud of who I am by being true to my nature and to everybody around me. I refuse to be like the rest of my people, conforming to their silly talks and way of life. I think and live in contrast to them. I shall continue to be myself, unbending and unchanging even as I risk their alienation.

I believe in the liberty to think, to speak and to do freely as I see fit, not as a society dictates. For all these reasons, and to follow my dream of becoming a successful journalist, I shall leave the land I love so much, the serenity of the distant waves across my house reminding me every day that the tides come and go. I shall embrace for one last time my beautiful village where in her bosom I lay and ran freely chasing songs in the wind.

I packed two large suitcases, filled with all of my albums and my journal believing I would never return. I looked down from my airplane onto destroyed cities, flanked by yet a still beautiful beach, and remnants of mountains once green and plush that blanketed the landscape. I thought of our mighty cedar trees that built Solomon's Temple and the ships for the first world sailors, our Phoenician ancestors. Some, too, had settled in other foreign lands, just like me; their roots forever planted deeply high up in the Cedar mountain that embraced the barren and beaten plains below in defiance of history's ravaging imprints since biblical times and for eternity.

I arrived in California in late August of 1984 to spend a week with my sister who was vacationing at the time. But it was not her who met me at the airport. A voice too familiar called to me. Rameh smiled and said Jamileh had asked him to pick me up because her plane was delayed. That evening, Rameh took me to his apartment, and we started talking about the past. Little by little, he pulled me to him as usual. Jamileh arrived a week later and within a couple of days, we all left for Colorado where she was living with her husband. I was admitted to the journalism school at the University of Colorado, Boulder, in the fall of 1984, and I graduated two years later. During my studies, Rameh and I called each other often and spoke for hours. He even once drove all the way from California to see me and drove back the next day. I really believed that he was finally making room in his heart for me, and I fell for him once again. We were married upon my graduation two years later.

It only took me six months after the wedding to reopen my journal that had remained shut since my arrival in the U.S. I relived my distress and needed yet again to spill it on paper. I wrote about my disappointments, about how I thought the marriage was going to bring me happiness but didn't, about my loneliness through all the past years creeping back into my life with more vengeance, about the lack of romance that I had hoped I would find with Rameh. His hugs and kisses were empty. His love making was dry and only to satiate his sexual drive. I felt neglected and unloved. I sadly admitted, though to my journal only, that I was unhappy with him and felt that I had failed. I lost the meaning of life, I wrote; the dreams I had built as a child grew up with me and were shattered; old fears grew older too; failure is all I could see. Dreams of becoming a journalist were forgotten. My insecurities for not having a good command of the English language and the meager wages I was earning made me quit my job at a local paper. I felt defeated with no right to dream any longer; better to live day by day, I thought. The goal is lost.

I settled for a job as a bank teller during the day and stocking shelves at a department store at night. Rameh also worked as a teller during the day and resumed schooling at night. The weeks dragged on and on with every day like the next. Growing up in a culture that put a lot of weight on social status, I felt humiliated for accepting menial jobs that did not fit the stature of a college graduate. I blamed America for humbling and destroying my ambition just to survive. I blamed myself for choosing to marry for what I thought would make me happy and proud, carrying the Haddad last name. I resented the hard life that brought me to my knees with no loving relationship to compensate. I did not blame Rameh for our meager lifestyle, but nonetheless, unlike him, struggled to accept such financial hardship that I was not used to and hadn't anticipated. These and other factors were straining our already fragile relationship. For the first time, I felt we could not continue together on this journey.

I really wanted to give our marriage a chance, but in my heart, I knew that no matter how hard we tried, we would eventually break up. Rameh said that I was disrespectful to him, always negative, had an ugly personality, created problems and frowned upon everything. He was sure to remind me of this daily and would always attack my character and nature telling me I was "rough" and lacking in femininity. He never complemented me on anything and had nothing good to say about me. I labored hard at work and at home, cleaning, cooking, washing dishes, and ironing his cloths without any help. Ironically, the domains relegated to women in my culture I so resented, I found myself carrying out dutifully better than any woman could, yet I swallowed my discontent. All I would discuss with him were my needs for love and affection, and above all, acceptance for who I am, but he turned a deaf ear and never took my needs seriously. I felt he was as cold as ice, and I wondered what prevented me from leaving. I was astounded that I felt I only had my journal instead of confronting him as healthy couples do. I could not, for I knew he would start yelling at me, or worse, blame me for everything, as he always had many times before. I was tired of making more attempts that he would not understand or take seriously, so I decided to let go and to move on until I received the most precious gift in my life three years later.

My precious Nour was born in December, 1989, on the very day she was due. Her face was calm, her skin smooth, her body long and thin. She had shiny light brown hair that curled down her neck. Except for her large shimmering eyes, akin to Middle Eastern beauties, her fair skin and hair color, just like her father's, made her look like a European or an American white child. I loved her with every beat of my heart. She was my joy, my pride, my hope, my life, my only happiness in the world. When few things made me smile in life, she was the only beauty I could see or feel. I adored her as I watched her innocent face, large eyes wide open, beaming with excitement for everything around her. She gave me happiness. Nour was an amazing child; very alert to her surroundings with a photographic memory unparalleled as I discovered years later. She was only three months old, yet would instantly giggle and flutter in her little bassinet upon hearing the garage door open, knowing her father had come home as he did every night from school. She seemed to prefer not to be smothered by my loving arms as I fed her the bottle. Yet, after waking up in the middle of the night crying, she could only be calmed after I lay her on my chest and sang traditional Lebanese lullabies to her until she drifted back to asleep.

Nour filled me up as nothing ever did. I did not grow up among young children, being the youngest myself. At times, I was scared of not knowing how to raise a fragile child like her. As soon as I weaned her in order to prepare to return to work at six weeks, her bouts with vomiting began. It was a struggle to keep food in her stomach for she would throw up upon any triggering, be it food texture or smell she did not like, a visitor she did not know, or simply after crying or laughing. After several trips to the doctor and imaging tests, no science could explain what was wrong with her. I surmised that she did not like change, and she expressed her dislikes through vomiting. She would do this three or four times a day and many nights as well. I was frustrated and upset fearing that she was not getting sufficient nutrition, particularly as she was born full-term, but only five pounds, thirteen ounces. I struggled to nourish and nurture her, wanting to care for her, to raise her myself and to spend time with her and to provide her with all my love and affection that abounds in the world. I wanted to ensure that she receive what I had yearned for growing up and which I still felt was missing years later.

I suffered every working day not being able to spend any more than a few moments with her in the morning and a few hours at night. My Mother-in-law was caring for her during the day; Rameh was also working during the day and attending school at night to get his Bachelor's in Industrial Engineering. He was my salvation and hope for a better life for our family, and I supported him all the way. His dream became my dream, and his joy for the anticipated graduation day became my excitement of a child waiting to open her Christmas present.

Prior to Nour's birth, we had bought a condominium in the worst part of the San Fernando Valley, known for its gang infestation. It was the only place we could afford. Times were tough, but it helped that I had just found a state job before getting pregnant which offered a reasonable salary and benefits. A sense of stability slowly calmed me down. Rameh and I tried to put up with each other knowing that our focus needed to be on our child and keeping up with our growing expenses.

Since I was promoted, we decided to have another child about two years later. My adorable Anwar was born in July of 1992 when I was twenty-eight years old. I was filled with the immeasurable joy and love that only a mother is blessed to experience. He was a very happy baby, with an infectious smile that brought delight to anyone who passed by him. He loved my embraces and kisses and slumbered quietly as I tenderly rocked him back and forth in my arms, running my fingers through his long, soft hair.

Nour was very protective of her little brother. Before she was three, and as Anwar started crawling and picking up things, she was always beside him to stop him from putting anything he should not have into his mouth. How did she know that they were potentially hazardous? I do not know. And if I did not secure the safety barrier, she stood by the stairwell to make sure he did not tumble down. At my first doctor's visit after delivering Anwar, she fed him a bottle while waiting with him in the lobby outside the examination room. She knew what to do and when to do it.

I was fortunate that year to afford to be off of work for eleven months and to experience for once the joy of motherhood, cherishing every precious moment with my children. Rameh continued to work and still had two more years left before graduating.

As I returned to work, I discovered that raising two kids while working full time was very challenging. Even as my mother-in-law lived with us for a while, and I subsequently had hired live-in help, I felt overwhelmed and struggled to care for them as a "single parent," given their father's virtual absence. But I was not one to compromise on anything. I wanted to be the best a mother could be, preparing baby food from scratch, cooking fresh homemade meals every day. I played with them, took them to the park, read to them every night, taught them their first alphabet and made sure Arabic was the only language spoken at home so they would never forget their roots. I sang, I danced and laughed with them and steadied their bicycles as they learned how to ride. And I would not give that up for anything. They were more than the world to me, and I thought I was everything to them. Never did it occur to me that one day, my own flesh and blood would disown me.

During that time, Rameh and I quarreled a lot and would go for days not talking to each other. Then, as usual, we would resume our routine as though nothing had happened without ever discussing what had led to the arguments in the first place. This went on for months distressing me more and more. One day, all of a sudden, I felt what I described in my journal, as though something had vanished, much as when the spirit departs the body of the dead. I felt as though Rameh had become an ordinary man to me. I felt we were done and I cried bitter tears, not of loss, but of fear and of fear alone. The difference this time was that I did not fear for myself or for being left without a man. No, that did not occur to me. It was the fear of disappointing my children and of disrupting their future that terrified me. I felt responsible for their well-being and for providing them with a stable family life.

As I returned to work, I knew I did not earn enough to pay for Nour's school, a baby sitter for Anwar, a mortgage and other expenses. I decided to write Rameh a letter detailing all of my frustrations, the reasons for my disappointments and the state of our failing marriage, but he never read it. I kept the letter for a long time until it vanished one day. Perhaps I tore it up years later giving up on his desire to fix our problems; perhaps it was lost in the chaos.

In time, we did have a serious discussion, and he accused me of having changed and of becoming just like my sister, "a devil, spiteful and hard-headed." He said that I followed her evil ways and that was something he would never tolerate and so, I was the one who had to change. Every time we had an argument, he was hateful. He was trying to strip me from my own self as though I had no personality of my own and was merely a follower, an obedient slave to my master. There were times when I would become so distressed that I became like a mad woman, banging doors and countertops, hysterically crying to the point of almost breaking down and fainting. This went on until he graduated in the summer of 1994, and we decided to see a counselor. For the few sessions that my insurance paid for, nothing proved sustainable. Again, he spouted to the counselor the same mischaracterizations, adding that I only thought of the "me" wanting everything only my way. For all the eight years we were married, he said that I was the decision maker in everything, be it the decision to marry, to have children, to buy a house, to manage the finances, etc. without regard or respect to his opinion. He asserted it was this attitude that would probably lead to separation or a divorce.

What I told the counselor was that the main issue with Rameh and me was the breakdown of communication that always ended up in yelling due to his unbending stance and unwillingness to compromise or even to understand my perspective or why. With him, I said, I became incapable of feeling any joy in life or in a partnership. Rameh always put me down, disregarded my aspirations and blamed me for everything that went wrong without ever attempting to even listen, let alone understand my perspective. Instead, he insisted on interpreting everything in his way as fact, criticizing my character, including my yelling fits, refusing to consider that he may have been the trigger himself. He argued that I did not like to hear "criticism" when it was not true. All I had asked was for him to present his grievances constructively and openly without attacking everything I was or believed in and I would keep an open mind and listen. I truly felt that he did not like anything about me and did not want to remedy our relationship unless it was on his terms. I wanted to run away and be free from this cloak of darkness that was enfolding my soul feeling on the verge of a major depression. The marriage therapy got us nowhere, and we made no change.

Sadly, though, in time and due to his constant character assassination, I started doubting myself; if I were truly a bad person incapable of sustaining any relationship because no one would be able to put up with me or with my behavior.

I became so weak and vulnerable that my heart lured me to begin an affair with a co-worker for about a month. Although it allowed me to compromise myself by joining him naked in bed once, my integrity and self respect pulled me back as it became evident that he was only interested in sex. The affair was never consummated. I admitted to it to Rameh and we agreed for me to leave the house for a period of two months in the hope that a separation would allow us both to reflect upon our relationship and hopefully strengthen our bond forever.

I had a live-in babysitter at that time, but would come home three times a week to check on my children who were two and five. It was during that time that his relationship with Nour was strengthened, though in a very destructive way. As I learned later on, he would take her on long drives in the evening, crying as he listened to some romantic songs. It happened so frequently that she learned the Arabic lyrics, not understanding what they meant, and would faithfully sing along with him. The fallout from using his daughter as a five-year-old confidante would repeat itself twelve years later. However, the bond that he built with her then, would become unbreakable, regardless of the detriments that she was, and still is, clueless about or perhaps refuses to entertain. The seeds of "Parental Alienation Syndrome- PAS" had been planted.

In my solitude, I decided that I was not going to let anyone drive me into a miserable state of mind, that I needed to find happiness within myself and through myself. I started setting small goals that I could accomplish or to engage in simple hobbies, telling myself I was not depressed and refused to be from now on. I wanted to savor some happiness and break the cycle of self-defeat because I could no longer tolerate crying or living in hell, worried that otherwise I would succumb. I decided life was too short to waste in being miserable and that the power lies within me to change that. I returned home and for a couple of months after that, upon mutual understanding, we agreed that I would take some time off for myself once every two weeks to engage in my hobbies and that he would do the same for himself.

It was so liberating to roller-blade for a couple of hours along the beach and to feel the gentle wind caress my face. The joy did not last more than a few months, though, as life took another downturn. Rameh's employer started cutting his hours, and our debt was mounting. Instead of pursuing another engineering job elsewhere, he decided to purchase a gas station, fulfilling his long-awaited dream of self-employment. Having no capital of our own, he borrowed thousands of dollars using our credit cards and started a joined venture with my brother in-law and my best friend's husband. He was designated as the manager, working both jobs and many, many long hours through the night. The business lost money from the outset, but Rameh struggled to keep it afloat holding on as best he could. I think that he could not admit to failure. We simply were sold a bad deal to begin with. In the meantime, we bought another house in a nice and safe neighborhood and filed for bankruptcy shortly afterwards.

Those extremely stressful times brought a lot of tension and animosity among the partners, putting me in the middle. My relationships with my best friend and sister soured, and things at home were not getting better either. I slipped again into a state of despair, not knowing how we could manage financially. It did not help that my sister had accused Rameh of theft and that her husband put a lien on our house in his attempt to recover his investment. Neither was it considerate that the other partner pushed us into withdrawing the bankruptcy which led to the garnishing of my wages which were desperately needed as the only source of income for our family. Under these circumstances, I felt that I should support Rameh and

I did, even at the expense of breaking family and friendship ties for many years. I believed I had to stand for what was right. I knew that much, that Rameh was no thief and had worked very hard to sustain the business. That, however, did not salvage our relationship which continued along the same destructive path.

My journal memorializes a day when I felt a vast emptiness. I did not belong to anybody or anything. It was as though I was not from this world and could no longer understand it, neither its simplicities nor its complexities. What is responsibility? What is motherhood? What is love and sacrifice? What is loneliness? What is life? I did not know. I had nothing left to feel for Rameh; he had no place in my heart for love, real or pretended.

I reflected upon all the years I had tried to salvage the marriage. Disappointed with every attempt, I still carried on in the hope that things would somehow improve. I was fed up with working outside and inside the home, with raising my children alone, with putting my dreams on the back burner so that I could support Rameh's dreams, be they his Bachelor's, business venture, or later on, his Master's degree. Finally I was tired and wanted to give up on everything and to escape this reality. I wanted to separate, but I could not muster the courage to do it. I was tired of my monotonous life, of the routine of everyday living that did not get tempered by anything exciting. Rameh had no desire and would not put any effort into joining me on little outings such as hikes, going to dinner, hanging in cafes or traveling every once in a while. These simple, everyday activities that I witnessed many other families share, I could not even dream of for my own family. All that Rameh wanted to do was stay at home and find house projects to keep himself busy, spending long hours on the internet and sending political commentaries.

I felt trapped in a miserable marriage that I could neither change, nor break. With each thought of doing so, the responsibility of raising my children in a stable environment pulled me back. After all, it was not their fault that Rameh and I could not get along. Rameh began to feel the rejection on my part as I stopped wanting him to touch me. He thought it was a dangerous road that I had taken and threatened that it would lead to disaster. To him, separation meant divorce. I wanted to take this gamble in case this brought us closer, but in my heart I knew that my love for him was gone forever. I reasoned that perhaps I would get used to my new life, to adjust and settle, but did not know if that would resolve anything. All I knew was that it would be futile to stay together without love, but only out of familial obligations. Unfortunately, however, that is precisely what I did in the years that followed, though I did it subconsciously.

Slowly, I stopped thinking about my needs; I found justifications for his neglect and pretended that all was good, if it meant the family would stay together. For the remainder of our twenty-one-year marriage, the lie that I unintentionally fed myself brought us stability. Our family appeared to have a normal life like any other. What was buried under all of this facade, though, was Futoun. My persona, my identity and everything that brought me in touch with my inner self had become a whisper in the wind, carried to a faraway land from which there was no return.

Years passed when I never had time to think about how our relationship was being shaped; perhaps I did not want to. Slowly, I got used to my life and accepted it, or so I thought. Working full time, grocery shopping, cooking, cleaning, ironing, doing laundry, driving the kids to school and back, ensuring homework was done, music and Karate lessons, ballet and youth orchestra rehearsals and performances kept me very busy. It was not the time for me to contemplate my needs, or to examine who I was or had become. I simply pushed day after day, not thinking of the day before it or the one to come.

Where was Rameh during that time? As before, in the home office writing his articles, or changing oil in the cars or doing other mechanical work, not as a hobby, he claimed, but in order to save money. I wanted to believe him, so I remained silent. Time he spent with the children was no more than occasional play. Beyond that, he never attended any of their performances, school functions, or competitions. As for me, he spent no time at all, interested only in social gatherings where he would take me to his friends' houses or would impose on me lavish dinners and parties that I had to throw for them regularly with no help from him whatsoever. Oh, he dried some dishes. During our twenty-one-year marriage, we traveled abroad three times only because I insisted. He acquiesced and seemed to enjoy his time, but soon would forget about a hobby he never had any interest in to begin with. I could not look forward to planning yet another trip knowing that he did not share the joy of exploration with me.

During that time, we re-filed for bankruptcy, and Rameh's old engineering job took him back full-time. Soon after and without consulting me, Rameh enrolled in a Master's program in year 2000, breaking the news to me while on a trip to Lebanon. Once again, I felt marginalized, for he knew how much I wanted to obtain my graduate degree which I had put on hold in order to raise the kids while he was getting his Bachelor's. I had hoped that for once, he would consider taking over in order to allow me to go to school at night. However, as always, he never supported me or took my goals into any consideration. I was sidelined and left without a choice. I had to assume all the responsibility of child-rearing, the household chores and everything that came with it, while, of course, continuing my full-time job. Rameh obtained his Master's in Industrial Engineering two years later. Shortly after that, he started a part-time job teaching in the evening at a California State University while maintaining his full-time job as an engineer during the day. Life continued for me as it always had: single-parenting.

While Rameh worked very hard, we really did not need him to work two jobs since our finances were under control. Rameh's narcissism, however, dictated otherwise. He was elated to be called Professor, once even rebuking a student for not addressing him properly. He commanded respect from his students and often lowered their grades for showing up late to class. I could only interpret that as his means of asserting his control. These and earlier signs of his domineering personality went by me unnoticed. Rameh, of course, was never interested in joining the family in any activity. He cited his full schedule, but managed to find time for his computer. The reality was he never cared to spend quality family time with us and had no interest in any of the activities we engaged in. It was I who took the kids to the beach, to the movies, to parks, and who planned vacations which he joined in reluctantly.

As the children grew older and depended less and less on me, I started having a little more time to myself. Rameh encouraged me to leave the house often, saying, "Go, go" and I did. Alone, I started going to the movies, to coffee shops, to the theater, for bike rides, on hikes, to the beach, etc. Life appeared good, but lonely. Slowly, the family was breaking apart. Barring Sunday dinners when I insisted on having the one weekly family meal, each one of us was living a separate life. And I made believe that is was all understandable. After all, the children were teenagers who surely preferred to spend more time with friends than with family, and Rameh was busy with his two jobs and did not share my interests. It was during this time that I met Patrick.

Patrick was a new hire in 2004. My co-worker took me to his cubicle to show me the "new tall, and handsome man" our department had just hired, and I agreed. At over six-feet-tall, broad-shouldered, and muscular, he was very attractive. Black thick hair and reddish tanned skin defined his ancestry: Irish, Mexican, and American Indian. Patrick often appeared serious, but his highly revealed jawline gave way to a bright smile each time he chuckled. He walked slowly, his greyish-blue eyes shy to engage the other employees around him. Even though I did not know anything about him, Patrick appeared gentle and kind, handsome, not conceited. My eyes followed him each time he passed through the hallway by my desk. He was soft-spoken, and he liked to discuss politics with me now and then.

It was unusual for me to meet someone who was familiar with Lebanese and Palestinian history or current events, so I liked engaging with him. More and more, we shared small conversations and group lunches. Over the next two years, we became closer, and the attraction for each other became apparent. By mid 2006, we started slipping out together during lunch and going to the beach for walks.

One day, sitting on a bench at a nearby beach park, time stood still as we talked freely about anything and everything. I admired this man. We developed a friendship that I could never have established with Rameh, no matter how hard I tried. Patrick was attentive, empathetic, and genuine. We talked as equals. He had no desire to dominate or to control me or to win every argument. Unlike Rameh, who always brought out the worst in me, Patrick made me a better person, allowing me to discover qualities within me that I did not know I had. He was supportive, encouraging, and very accepting of who I am. No one had ever treated me so kindly in my life or had made me feel like a woman. My mother had called me a "Tomboy," Rameh made insensitive comments about my being *fijjeh* and *jifsah* or rough and tough like a man (deficient in feminine qualities). Then, I would respond to my mother, "You gave birth to me that way," loving who I was and still am today, though not lacking in femininity in any way. To Rameh, on the other hand, I would say nothing, although his remarks would cut deeply through my heart, even as I knew the life that I was living with him had pushed me to become the mother and the father as much as it had my mother before me.

It was my birthday that day. As we were leaving, he put his arm around my shoulders and pulled me gently towards him, landing a tender kiss on my cheek. He wished me a happy birthday. I could not escape the tight embrace that I had craved all of my life. I felt the warmth and tenderness which I had not felt in decades, and I did not want to let it go. He looked at me firmly and said, "You do not love your husband." The statement struck me to the core, but without hesitation I responded, "Of course, I do." Then confidently he said, "You would not be with me if you did."

It was a profound moment that brought me back to my inner self, questioning my love or what I thought was love for my husband, reflecting upon my lost youth, on my dreams, on aspirations, on loyalty, on betrayal and on many more emotions that I could not describe. We hurried back to the office pretending that all that was said and done that day would be washed away and forgotten. Not for a second did it occur to me that what happened that day would become my path of no return. My awakening had just begun. In the weeks that followed, I examined myself, my desires, my life and how I had been living it for the last 20 years of marriage and for eight years of courtship prior to that.

PART II

Gained It All.
Lost It All

CHAPTER 6

Intoxicating Love

◊

s I had done many times before, I fought myself the feeling of despair I had bottled up for so many years pretending that life was normal. I struggled to face the reality: the happiness that I had given up on, the vacuum that had penetrated my soul, the forgotten love I had chased since I had been a teenager, and all the sadness that came with it. I did not want to be reminded of any of that, believing that I was happy and settled, that what I needed in life was nothing more than to raise my children and to see them prosper and to be successful and happy. I thought, I really thought, that I didn't need all these childhood illusions, the immature feelings that only utopian fools lamented. I thought I had replaced all of these hopes with a sense of stability, a warm home for my children and a mother's unwavering love that was the basic foundation for my children's emotional strength and mental well-being.

Again, I dismissed the love that I was starting to feel for Patrick, and with it, I pretended, months into our courtship that my relationship with

Rameh was on solid ground. Slowly, however, it crept up on me: the years of disappointment and inner estrangement. Patrick continued to e-mail me regularly with loving quotes and reflective thoughts, and I reciprocated. Our love grew so strong that it was unstoppable until one day in October of the same year, he stopped me by the office stairwell and told me it was over. He said he had gone to church the night before and realized that what we were doing was wrong and unethical. He said I could not have him in my life while I was married. He, too, was struggling to be with me while he had a girlfriend of three years. He left me saying, "You have some soul-searching to do."

I was devastated and could not understand how he could just drop me like that. In retrospect, he was right. I just did not want to think of my betrayal then, blinded by a love so deep, one I had waited for all of my life and had since thought would never be realized until it was. This love that was so intoxicating had possessed me, detaching me from a reality I wanted to escape from so badly. For once in my entire life, I had felt the euphoria of loving and being loved equally and passionately that the thought of breaking up did not even cross my mind. As my children would later judge, I perhaps was selfish. Or was I?

It is hard to make sense of what was happening, particularly since I was indulging in my love affair with Patrick while having no intention of leaving my husband. But being selfish has never been one of my characteristics although I can understand how my affair could be seen. When I remember that period, I only see a despondent wife and mother who had dedicated all of her life caring for her children whom she loved beyond anything, and that the thought of leaving them could never be realized. At the same time, the elation I experienced had transcended my being, taking me to a higher place where dreams cradle the distraught, as a mother would her baby, singing soft gentle lullabies that put them into a deep slumber from which they did not want to wake. Still, I think now of how long I might have been able to carry on this double life had Patrick not broken up with me. Knowing myself, I would have inevitably found the courage to face the truth and to file for divorce. Events, however, unfolded so quickly that the same outcome was reached but with unforgiving consequences.

I did some soul searching afterwards, and even though I did not think that Patrick and I would get back together, I knew enough that I could not carry on living the way I was at home, with or without Patrick. The following month, at a coffee shop nearby, I sat with Rameh and explained everything to him about our dysfunctional marriage and my deteriorating love. I told him that if we continued on this path, divorce would be inevitable. I followed with an untitled e-mail, again, elevating him and blaming myself. He later used the same e-mail against me in court. In it, I wrote:

I don't know how to address this e-mail, so I am just going to send it based on how I feel now. I really, really do not want to hurt you, but I know that I already have time and time again. I also know that you do not deserve this, for you have done nothing to hurt me intentionally. Forgive me. I wish I could help it. I am really trying very hard this time, and it is not easy for me to deal with all of that I am going through.

I know I may have waited too long to address the issues that have been torturing me, but I hope it is not too late. I will not know until I genuinely try, and genuinely I will. I wish I could make promises to you and say that I could be okay tomorrow, the day after, or next month, but I cannot. I cannot predict how I will feel. All I can do is try to direct my energy towards loving you, not just because you are a great man, father, and husband, but also because I really want to. I want to be happy in this marriage, and I want to be fulfilled so I may never go through these grim cycles, ever! I really do not want to feel this way ever again.

Thank you for giving me time to recharge. I hope I will not let you down. I pray that I will make it through.

He took it better than I thought he would, or maybe he did not take me seriously. He said he would change his ways and help with the household chores. In the three months that followed, he made some attempts to engage me a bit, such as going to the movies or for coffee now and then, keen to remind me that "A cup of coffee with you at Starbucks' is good to last for a month." Slowly, he slipped back into his old way of life. I could not understand why he would not make a more sustainable effort to save our marriage. Now, I know that people do not change, though they might change their habits if they chose to, or if they genuinely loved or cared for their partner. The truth is that Rameh was unable to meet me half way because it truly was NOT within him to make any sacrifice for anyone but himself, no matter how he had convinced the children otherwise. That affirmed to me that he really never loved me, but only loved what I provided him and the family with, the financial security and the comfort of having assumed all family responsibilities.

In December of that year, I was scheduled for three-day training in San Francisco. Patrick passed by my desk one day and saw my notification posted outside my office for the impending travel plans. That evening, he sent me an e-mail letting me know he was going to meet me there, and he did, for one night on December 13. For the first time in my life, I felt free from all bondage. I was with the love of my life in a city where no one knew me and I did not have to hide from anyone. For the one night we were together, we were lovers as lovers should be. We walked the streets hand-in-hand, had a beer at a cozy local bar, and delighted in the warmth of the Christmas lights while carols emanated from the shops, the streets, the ice rink and from everywhere we walked. It was magical, yet it was surreal, for we were oblivious to whomever was around us, embracing, kissing, laughing in an enchanted world of lovers. The evening sealed our destiny even though I thought I still wanted to fix my broken marriage.

I learned later on that Rameh had been investigating every move I made, had broken into my e-mail and my phone password and had listened to all of my messages, though he denied it. Patrick called a few days later as I was preparing to go on a trip with Rameh to Las Vegas. He told me that he had broken up with his girlfriend because that was the right thing to do. I agreed, contemplating doing the same. Disgusted with myself, on the way back, I told Rameh I wanted a divorce, but he still wanted to prove to me that he had changed, convincing me to carry on. Besides that conversation, we were silent the entire drive back home. He never admitted that he knew about my affair.

Patrick and I tried very hard to keep our distance. He respected my wishes to give the marriage another try, and I restrained myself. Rameh, on the other hand, and without my knowledge, was involving Nour, then seventeen, at every step of our trials, including sharing with her his distress, his profuse tears and whatever e-mails, voice messages and videos he had of Patrick and me walking in the park. It was no revelation that she knew of my San Francisco rendezvous from a voice message that Patrick had left upon his arrival at the airport. The next morning, after Patrick had left, I called her to wish her a happy birthday, but she hung up ranting, "How dare you have sex on my birthday!" Rameh always turned to Nour as his savior and confidante. I do not know, and probably will never know, to what extent Rameh involved my son as well, who was fifteen then. It is my hope that one day, the truth will come out showing how a father, so self-absorbed, destroyed his children's innocence and deprived them of motherly love and nurturing for his own gratification and pursuit of vengeance. For that day, I live and pray.

A week after our return from Las Vegas, Nour sent me an e-mail at work titled, "Don't Give up." It confirmed what I had suspected; that she had taken his side and was not ever going to give me a chance to explain what happened or why. She threatened that if I were to proceed with the divorce, neither she nor my son would ever speak to me again; and that is precisely what happened, at least on her part. More disturbing, in the body of that e-mail, she referred to my affair with Patrick as being my sixth. Surely, Rameh was feeding her such despicable lies in order to garner sympathy, redeem himself as the greatest forgiver, and seal their loyalty. Once again, the parental alienation had started taking permanent roots. Her letter below illustrates the simplistic thinking process of a young inexperienced teen who was manipulated into taking sides and who now, as of this writing at thirty, remains, or rather, chooses to be completely oblivious to it.

The letters from Nour and Anwar inscribed in this book are identical copies of their e-mails to me, with all their punctuation, bracketed words, and grammatical structure, and layout. She wrote:

Don't Give Up

(Reference letter #1- Jan 9, 2007)

Mother

I am writing this e-mail NOT because my father told me to (as you may probably think), but because of my own will.

First of all, I would like to address what you refer to as my display of "dry" feelings. I'm sure this rings a bell somewhere in your mind. I'd like to ask, does it hurt? Does it incur in you any amount of pain and anguish? Especially because it's coming from a daughter whom you've raised for seventeen years of your life? Now, take the time to think of the husband who has been there for you longer than Anwar and I have been. Has he ever once shown you dry feelings? I recall one time when you two were in the family room and you cried out, "Won't you at least try to meet me halfway? I'm extending my arm out halfway, and isn't it only fair that you try to meet me the other half of the way?" I VISIBLY see him try much harder than you ever have or claim to have tried. When he comes home after work, does he not give you a hug and a kiss? Is this not a proper and heart-felt display of your much needed and requested attention? I've never witnessed you running to him when he gets back from work; it is always he who must come to you. That's definitely an unfair expectation. You probably think that I don't love you and that I hate you because of your harsh and unmerciful actions toward my father. No, mother, that is absolutely not true. I love you, and I certainly do not hate you. Yet when I feel that somebody has done something to wrong me or my family, do you not think that I will react in any manner that I see fit? The answer to that is undoubtedly a resounding "yes". How do you expect me to show you any sort of affection if I feel that you are preparing to make the most brash, unreasonable, illogical, and yes, idiotic decision of your entire life? Do you think that I'm going to run up to you every day and warmly embrace you and give you a kiss when I know how much you are hurting my father? How can I express love and affection to somebody who can show so much malice and lack of understanding toward another human being? Do you think this is fair? just? reasonable? Of course not.

You should be able to relate my dry feelings to your own. Don't expect somebody to show feelings toward you when you yourself are unable to express them and consciously choose not to.

Second of all, I would like to address the emotional turmoil and distress that you have so easily and knowingly inflicted first upon my father and second upon the family as an entire entity. You know that you've hurt him a number of times, this being the sixth. Obviously, I'm not going to go into any detail because I'm sure you know it well enough. I just want to make sure that you haven't forgotten it and that you don't refuse to believe that the past is still there. My father is extremely hurt, and I'm sure you know that. However, he is still trying VERY hard, EXTREMELY hard, to try to help you to get over yourself. You absolutely NEED to get out of your self-made bubble and realize that there ARE people out there who do care for you and want to help you get better. My dad is hurt more than any human being on earth should be hurt in his entire life. And not to mention, this is not the first time this has been done, as you very well know. You need to know and understand how much you are hurting him. He has never stopped loving you in his whole life. How can you so easily say to someone "Oh, I don't love you anymore." Or, "Oh, I don't have any feelings for you anymore." Mother, feelings DON'T just disappear. They don't just STOP. Can you imagine yourself telling me or telling Anwar, "Oh, sorry...I just don't love you anymore, I don't see you as my children...You're just regular people." No, of course you can't do that. And with that same logic, you can't say that you don't love your husband anymore. Sure, if you had some type of logical basis for your reasoning, then maybe you could have an argument. But what is your reasoning? What is this faltering logic? It's not there, mother. It's just not there. I don't see it, and nobody does. None of your friends sees it, none of your family sees it. I'm sure the counselor whom you go to doesn't see it either. Once again, I reiterate that feelings ABSOLUTELY do not just disappear. No matter how you try to phrase it, no matter how hard you try to convince everybody that "nobody understands what you are going through", feelings don't just disappear. You need to understand that. It's a fundamental point in this whole crisis you are entering. FEELINGS DO NOT DISAPPEAR. They do not just leave. I remember one time when we were at a wedding for one of your Indian friends, you informed me that the groom was getting married for the third of fourth time in his life. We laughed at the vows that people swore to when they got married: in sickness and in health, in old age... and most importantly, until DEATH do you part. Until DEATH. When we talked, I asked, "Why do people swear to these vows if most of them get divorced anyway?" And do you know what you said? You said that people divorced for foolish reasons that could ALWAYS be worked out if they put in a sufficient amount of effort. You said people shouldn't divorce no matter what, unless if the husband is beating the wife, or something really bad like that. And you said that when kids were involved, it was especially hard and that extreme measures should be taken to ensure that divorce indeed never did happen: most notably, for the sake of the children. Have you thought over the implications of what terrible decisions like yours could incur? Obviously you haven't. For one, you're permanently damaging and scarring the heart of someone who's loved you his entire life. You're also wrecking the financial stability he has worked SO INCREDIBLY HARD to get, for not just you but for the family as a whole.

How can you stand by idly and watch all this hard work go to waste, never to be salvaged again? Lastly, you're breaking up a family. Did you read that? A FAMILY. Not just husband and wife, but two kids whom you both have worked so hard to raise. It is true that while my father was working, you were busy helping raise us, but that does not mean he did not have a role in our development. If that were true, do you think that either Anwar or I would be so emotionally attached to him? Of course not. Mother, you're breaking up a whole entire family. Doesn't that hurt? Just a little tiny bit? How can you bear the thought of living without somebody who loves and cares about you? And how can you live with the thought of having a broken family? No, think of it this way. If things go the way you seem to want them to, you'll end up living in an apartment by yourself. Neither Anwar nor I will take time out of our day to visit you there. If you choose to see us, you'll have to do it in the home where we were raised. Mother, if you go through with a divorce (that you'll have to fill out and sign ALL BY YOURSELF, by the way), we will not be on speaking terms. I can assure you of that. I will not want to see you. I will not want to have anything to do with somebody who can inflict so much unnecessary pain on another individual. I beg you to think of that before you choose the wrong path. Are you willing to risk losing your children just because you want to satisfy your own happiness and wreck the happiness of three other people? Happiness is where you find it. If you look long enough and hard enough, you're bound to find it. And happiness is right under your nose. It's with your family: your husband and your two children. That's exactly where happiness is and forever will be. A trip to Spain isn't going to let you "find yourself" and "assure yourself" or your negative feelings. DON'T BREAK UP A FAMILY. I implore you not to get a divorce; if you truly love your children as you claim you do, you won't do it. You just won't. Be patient. Once again, your feelings ARE there, no matter how you try to mask them or hide them (even though you say that they aren't there, they are). You need some time to find them, and everybody in this household is supporting you 100% of the way. Don't rush into a decision to divorce, because if you do, you'll have no support from your family or your friends. I don't accept divorce as your solution to this problem. You think it's the easy way out, but it's not. It really isn't. Stick it through, and you'll be much happier in the end. I promise. Marriage isn't supposed to be easy, and divorce is never the solution to the problem. NEVER. And if you're going to stay adamant about your decision despite all the sound and caring advice you have received from people whom you supposedly care about (that you blatantly reject anyway), you're going to have to make it on your own (thinking that you can). And if you think you can make it yourself, then that will just make Anwar, my dad, and I more closely knit and more strongly bound together. In the end, it will be you who loses and lives in constant misery. You will gain absolutely nothing and lose everything.

Finally, I'd like to address your OWN feelings about the matter. You're probably thinking, "Nour has no idea what I'm going through. And I don't expect her to understand my feelings [or lack thereof]." I understand what you're going through. And it's not nearly as difficult as what my dad's going through. Not nearly. Not even close. Imagine me telling you "Mom, I don't love you anymore. I don't want to be your child. I'm going to leave this household and live with my grandparents." How would you feel? Terrible? Would you feel that you were a failure? That you messed up somewhere in your life? Maybe numerous times? I'm sure you'd be willing to blame yourself for how I feel, for wanting to disown myself from you and run away and live somewhere else. But wouldn't that hurt you? A lot? Well, that's EXACTLY 100% what you've done to my dad. One hundred percent. You've told him that you've shut down your feelings, and your attempts at salvaging them haven't been very fruitful (mainly because your attempts are extremely weak and you aren't trying hard enough). Can you see me telling you "Mom, I've shut down my feelings for you." And actually, can you imagine me saying it more than once? Six times, maybe? Over a course of several years? And yet he is STILL willing to forgive you mother, STILL willing. He hasn't given up on you, though you're forcing yourself to give up on him. Are you trying to prove a point to yourself? Are you trying to show that you're better than a relationship and that you don't need somebody else in your life? Because this is a very immature way to show it. It truly is.

You're an adult. So handle things like an adult. Whenever you've given me advice, you've said "stick through it, times are sure to get better ahead." And all I can say is, heed your own advice, and don't make the decision that your family will have to pay the price of and that you will learn to regret. If you fail in this endeavor, I suggest that you never give advice to anybody.

Nour

I was upset at her lack of understanding and at her threat to sever any ties with me. Foolishly, unaware of his role in shaping her thoughts, I sought Rameh's help to reason with our children as any parent would. Instead, he wrote me an e-mail stating,

"These are Nour's feelings and she is entitled to have AND express them. I am proud of her courage and wisdom...This misery will end soon, one way or another. Either, our marriage will be rebuilt on solid grounds as WE BOTH wish to see it, else it will be me, not you, who will not allow it to continue as-is."

My son followed a week after Nour's e-mail with a song by P.O.D. Titled *"Goodbye for Now."* I could not tell if Anwar was describing his sentiments, but as I understood the lyrics, and how I translated them into our conundrum, they describe a soul torn between holding on and letting go; between loyalty to an aggrieved father, or accepting an unredeemable mother. This, sadly, has defined our relationship for all the years to come.

The artist, according to my interpretation, speaks of dark times, of confusion, unable to make the "right decisions" on which way to go, or whose side to take. He sits alone in silence as time is fleeting, contemplating what is happening around him and how to react, but always manages to say, without knowing who is to blame, the "right things" or what his father wants to hear. The artist fights within himself to preserve the endearing past, but struggles as he realizes he has no choice but to let it go; so he does, while, in his heart, only he knows that it will always be there. However, he continues to carry the pain of the loss for the mother who is no longer there, a pain the mother will surely bear as well. The wind flows in all directions and nobody knows to where, but when he thinks he knows the final destination, he is disappointed again. If at some point, it leads to brighter sunny days, or if the family is reunited again, then he shall wait for that day. Hope can still be seen at the end of the tunnel. Perhaps, then, he can sing a "new song."

Reading it broke my heart, but I did not know what to say or do. The children during that rough period were very distant. Beyond responding yes or no to my direct questions, they did not talk to me or engage in any conversation, serious or ordinary. I was not sure at the time if they knew of my affair and did not dare to ask. I worried that if I insisted on having a discussion, they would get more upset and turn their backs on me even more.

CHAPTER 7

Goodbyes — Leaving My Soul Behind

A couple of months after that, in March 2007, Rameh and I agreed that I would separate to rediscover myself and perhaps salvage the marriage. Deep inside, I knew the road was closed, for my heart belonged to someone else, even though we were apart. Still, I pushed to give it a try, and I rented a room from Janice, a colleague. It was an opportune time to do it, with Patrick traveling in Europe, leaving me more alone time to contemplate my fate.

I emailed my first letter to my children attempting to explain what had led me to my indiscretions and seeking their forgiveness. I wanted them to read it carefully and not to delete it, to save it and read it over and over each time they missed love in their lives. But how could I memorialize a journey of 43 years in a page and a half? I wrote:

If I Could Tell You

(Reference letter #2-March 13, 2007)

To my beloved and beautiful children:

If I could tell you how I feel and if only you would understand, then I would. But I choose not to burden you beyond the pain I have caused you. For the anguish, sorrow, betrayal, hatred and antagonism that you are experiencing, I am truly sorry.

I want you to know that my life with your dad was very hard on me. For 20 years, I forgot about myself, my needs, my hopes and dreams...I forgot about my soul and what I longed for because I wanted to be the best wife and mother I could be. I wanted to give you my undivided love, attention, time and caresses.

I did whatever I could to give you a stable home, open heart, teach you good values in life and be there for you at any time and in any place. I was there when you cried, when you were sick, when you walked, when you uttered your first words...I watched you grow, took you by the hand when you went to preschool, comforted you when you were hurt, and embraced you when you needed warmth. I nourished you, loved you, hugged you and kissed you and looked at you with the admiring eyes of a mother who saw her seedlings become mature teens and happy children. I was always fond of your convictions, maturity and young wisdom. I talked endlessly about your achievements, your wonderful characters, your wits, smartness.....and I was filled with joy and pride.

And if I had to do it again, I would.

Then came my awakening and the journey I decided to take. It was too burdensome to share and impossible for anyone to understand. I, myself, for a long time, did not realize the extent of my unhappiness in my relationship with your father, and so did not express to him my desires and give him a chance to remedy my failing love towards him. I struggled with my feelings of neglect, being taken for granted, perceiving a lack of appreciation for me on your father's part, and with every negative thought that caused me to spiral downward until I hit rock bottom. I caved and allowed myself to enjoy the beauty of love once more. I formed a relationship with another man, and I thought I would be fulfilled.

Now, I am not so sure.

Throughout my sufferings, I had no intention of inflicting pain upon anyone, certainly not on the most precious beings in my life, my adorable children. I know I did, and I wish I could change history, but I cannot. Reality is here for all of us to face.

You chose to pluck me out of your young lives and sever all communication with me. You shut your hearts and souls and decided to believe that I do not exist. You built not a wall, but a fortress between us and fortified it with steel, big, heavy boulders and magnificent iron doors…and you locked me out. I knocked and knocked, but you refused to hear.

Perhaps with time, prayer and inner love, we can make amends and you will be able to forgive me for all that I have caused you.

I am still on the road of discovery and want you to know that what I have done has nothing to do with you but everything to do with my relationship with your dad; how I perceived it and how it affected me throughout the years. I don't expect you to understand or to receive me with open hearts, but I can still hope that someday, you will return to me and accept me for who I am and have the heart to love me once again, though faintly, and to receive me back into your lives.

My love for you endures and transcends all of your animosity and hatred towards me, all of the insults, anger, hurtful words that you have said to me; all of your rejections, blame, disrespect and lack of care.......because I am a mother and a mother who will always love you unconditionally......one whom I pray you will understand and respect one day, even if I have to wait until you become a mother/father, or until eternity.

Love you always and forever,
Mom

Less than two weeks later, however, Rameh called me crying that I needed to come home or else he was going to kill himself. Like a fool, I believed him. I, too, was being manipulated. Feeling sorry for him, guilty for my actions, missing my children, worried about how they were coping, I succumbed. I packed my belongings; and Rameh and Nour picked me up that weekend. I felt his decision was premature as all I was doing was retracing the same path, reliving a past that was unbending. I returned home out of obligation and duty, not out of a genuine desire to be with someone I knew I could never love. I thought I could suppress my love and carry on like a robot, mechanically fulfilling my responsibilities. Again, I was wrong.

Shortly after I resettled, Patrick called me from Ireland while Nour was in the car with me. Surely she was clued in on who I was talking to, particularly as I informed him that I had returned home. She said nothing and neither did I. Patrick was sad and disappointed, but he could not let go either. He called again a week later from Paris, inspired by the romance of the City of Love and the grandness of the view from atop the Eiffel Tower. He told me that he wished I were there with him, and I said the same, quietly, so no one could hear. But as I turned back, I saw Rameh by the cracked bedroom door eavesdropping. Neither one of us said anything.

During that time, Rameh lost a considerable amount of weight, cried profusely to Nour, and slept by her bedside as she comforted him. He called my mother in Lebanon every day crying to her as well, pleading that she convince me to change my mind. He also enlisted my very close friend, Celina, letting her in on my affair to get her sympathy and support which she never told me about until after the divorce. His calls to her came every day and lasted close to an hour during which he defamed my character as he also did with all of our common friends, including the ones in Lebanon. I did not know it at the time; neither did I know how much evidence he had collected about my affair which he shared with my children in his effort to alienate them from me. His campaign was to smear my name and to render me childless in order to avenge himself.

It did not matter to him that he had scarred his children for life by all the age-inappropriate material he shared with them. It did not matter that he broke their hearts. It did not matter that, directly or indirectly, he was imposing on them a choice between utter loyalty and bonding together as one "family unit," or siding with the enemy risking being disowned as they had disowned me. It did not matter that my children were still young, particularly Anwar who needed a mother's love, support and guidance. Yes, Rameh thought as an adulterer, I did not have the moral compass to be a mother, never mind the seventeen years during which I cared for them as well as any mother could. In his distorted mind and love of vengeance, he blinded himself to the fact that while I could be devastated for losing my children, I was an adult who could endure. The children, however, would be damaged for eternity although he had convinced them otherwise.

I picked up Patrick from the airport with Rameh's knowledge. Patrick was cold and formal. I reacted accordingly hoping that slowly we would drift apart. He gave me my gift, some perfume from Paris that had two love-birds for a top. As I dropped him off, we hugged and kissed for what I thought would be the last time until we met again shortly before my planned trip to Europe in the following month. I boarded the plane for a three-week vacation thinking that I would recover from all this baggage and come back refreshed and ready to join in my new and improved marital life. I wanted to wean myself from this intoxicating love that I had surrendered to helplessly, allowing it to take complete control of my mind, body and soul. But I could not. The power of such extraordinary love which I had waited 43 years for was right before my eyes, ready to embrace me, satiate my hunger, enrich my soul, and nourish my mind with its inescapable allure.

From Spain to Morocco, any chance I had after retiring in the evening, I sent Patrick e-mails describing my day, places I had explored, and yes, I spilled out my passion for a love that I had missed very much. I looked forward to his loving responses as I lay my head on my pillow every night. I was not disappointed except to find out later that many of the phone messages he had left me had been hacked by Rameh and deleted before I had a chance to listen to them. Clueless at the time, my e-mails were being read by him also, just as he had read those between my children and me for many years after our divorce. What exactly he allowed them to read, or kept, or deleted, or modified, I do not know. Voice messages I had left my son were also routed to his phone first before he forwarded them to Anwar, if he chose to. Not only was Rameh intent on securing my children's allegiance, he wanted to ensure their alienation from their mother for a lifetime should they ever have a change of heart. Sadly, he succeeded again, but at their expense.

The trip woke in me the truth that had been dormant for twenty-one years. It brought me back to my inner self, discovering for the first time that I had been lying to myself all that time, believing that life with Rameh was proper and right, that I was happy raising my kids solely and attending to the household; that he was busy working two jobs and would have made time for us if he could have. The reality is that an undefeated spirit, determined to rise above all adversity, sorrow or pain, steered me slowly over the years to accept, to hang on instead of breaking away. Sadly, though, through the process, it became inevitable that I buried the truth and lived a lie just to cope. The trip stripped me naked. I reconnected with myself and learned that once you discover the truth, you can never, ever relive the lie. The truth, undoubtedly, will set you free. This is how anyone could easily blur the lines between selfishness and doing the right thing, as did my children.

To many, parents should sacrifice anything and everything for their children's well-being, and I agree. I did that and more. However, if that means living a lie about a marriage devoid of a love that never was and never would be, then you will perpetuate the lie and steer your children onto the wrong and ruinous path. If the role of parents is to guide and set a good example for their children, then they must live the truth, even having faltered themselves. Acknowledging our wrongdoing and asking forgiveness for our indiscretions is a virtue and the right thing to do. Who is infallible but God? None of us, as humans, are immune from making mistakes, and sometimes, grave ones indeed, as were mine. But to believe that redemption comes with traveling along the same destructive path is accepting that self betrayal is proper. That is not the way to sacrifice for your children's well-being; rather, it is a dangerous precept that will lead them to moral decay.

As for me, it was high time I did the right thing. I decided that my marriage was over but still could not muster the strength to take that leap. I returned home and resumed my life for a while until a heated phone conversation during my lunch break with Rameh convinced me that our marriage was indeed over. He, for the first time, confronted me asking if I had sex with Patrick. As I paused to answer, I knew that admitting to it would bring my release. Surely, I thought, he would not be able to live with this dishonor that no man could accept, especially one from our traditional and very conservative culture. Betrayal will indeed seal my fate. I admitted to it. He followed up with "How many times?" But I only said that it did not matter. Crying in the locker room at work, I called my mother. She sensed my distress and gave me her blessing. It was at that moment that I gained the confidence to divorce. It was then that I realized how much I needed her approval to proceed.

I returned home that day and told Rameh that I would be filing for divorce; that my decision was final. The couple of months that followed until I bought my condominium and moved out were extremely distressing to all of us. I began to feel that I had lost my children, but still had hope that with time, they would forgive me. Nour became her father's protector, defending him with all of her might against a despicable enemy she once called mother. Anwar didn't want to get involved and would leave any time Rameh and I quarreled. I dared not approach them knowing that anything I said would be misinterpreted, their having judged me a perpetual adulterer, unworthy and unredeemable.

To make believe he was in control, Rameh did not wait for me to serve him with the papers. He drafted the divorce agreement and I signed it, trying to avoid further pain for all of us. In it, he stated that we both had custody but that the children would be living with him as they wished, and I believed that was what they wanted. Nour was almost eighteen by then and Anwar was fifteen. I was trying as best I could to minimize the effects of the instability they were facing, with or without me. That meant keeping them in the house, living in the neighborhood near their friends, in the hope that they would visit me in my new place and that in time, we would rebuild our strong bond.

Nour graduated in the summer of 2007, a month before I moved out. Sitting on the bleachers alone in the distance, I heard the principal announce her name and congratulate her on her valedictorian achievement. I was in awe, so proud of my child who was always an exceptional student; who sought nothing short of perfection and who studied long hours in order to reach the top, who always remained humble and modest. I waited until the ceremony ended, then proceeded to the quadrangle (Quad), where the graduates and their families had gathered, to give her her graduation card and a beautiful bouquet of flowers. Perhaps not wanting to give me the luxury of an embrace or a kiss, she disappeared without a trace. Sadly, I went home, left the bouquet in her room with the card about reaching success though introspection, building bridges and not walls, tempering facts with understanding, looking at the actions of others without judgment, and conquering the fears that limit what one dares. I wrote my own wishes as well:

> Life is a journey. Whatever path you choose to take to get to your destination, may it surprise you with pain and suffering so you may understand the essence of happiness; and with obstacles and hardship so that when you persevere and don't lose sight of your dreams, you get there and feel the euphoria of victory. Life is about making choices. You have chosen to succeed and, you did! I sit and marvel at the beautiful, intelligent and mature

young woman you have become, and I thank the Lord for having you in my life. The road ahead will be full of challenges, and life will try you in many ways. Through it all, remember that when the tide tosses you and the wind scatters your sail, you will always have a mother waiting to help you to reset your anchor and to bring you to shore. And when I am no longer in this beautiful world, may the love I gave you throughout the years be your niche!

Congratulations!

Love always,
Mother

In time, Rameh's helplessness turned into anger; his tears into venom, and his supposed love into poisonous hatred gratified only through vengeance. He became emboldened, aggressive, and violent, but only after cutting off all communication with my close friend, Celina, and my mother, now on the blacklist for not convincing me to stay. During the month I waited to close escrow and after some argument or other, he squeezed my arms and started shaking me and screaming at me. I was left heavily bruised, internally and externally with nowhere to turn and no mercy from my child, Nour, who probably believed I deserved every bit of it.

Rameh's violence escalated as I neared my departure. I am still haunted by the memory of Anwar's birthday. While he and his friends were in the backyard playing, Rameh pushed me into our bedroom and closed the door. In his state of frenzy, he threw me on the floor, pulled the gun we had kept unloaded in the drawer of the nightstand and pointed it at my head screaming, "Say I'm sorry; say I'm sorry." At that moment, I did not know if I would live or die. I was not sure if he had loaded the gun or was using it to intimidate me into submission. Begging for mercy while trembling in fear, I told him what his ego wanted to hear. He let go of me. I ran to the office located in the garage and locked the door. Somehow, he managed to open it and pushed himself onto me, grabbed my arms forcefully and started banging my back against the office table, screaming and squeezing my arms while I cried for help and for him to let go. I do not know how I was able to exit the room, but when I did, he followed me. I do not know what Nour had heard, but trailing behind him, she put her arm around his shoulder saying calmly, "It's enough. You can leave her alone now."

Speechless, I ran outside and saw a couple I call my angels. These were people I had never seen. No one ever walked in the small cul-de-sac where we lived. As I walked aimlessly crying with my hands stretched out, they approached me. I yelled out, "He hit me, he hit me." I do not know how my neighbor next door who was a narcotics investigator showed up. He took me to the bedroom and asked me what happened. I told him about the gun, but refused to file charges when he asked me to. Naïve as I was, I thought I was protecting my children. I knew that they would not want to live with me.

CHAPTER 8

Reaching Out — Phases Of Grief

I am not sure how I lived my last week in the house. I slept every night not knowing if Rameh would hurt me or even kill me. As always, God pulled me through until my date of departure. I packed the few items I needed to start a home, some souvenirs of my travels, some of the children's albums, the baby frames to adorn my living room, and my personal items. I packed what I could in the family van and went inside to say goodbye to the children. Nour had left without a care and Anwar refused to leave the office room. He kept the door shut. I took a final gaze at a place I once called home. A piece of me never left. Like a vagabond who had overstayed her welcome, I knew it was time to charter new territory.

I bought a two-bedroom apartment foolishly thinking that the children would have their own space when they came to visit. It was nine miles away, but as time proved, the distance was the infinity. In the dark, I felt my way around, laid my stuff on the floor and crashed, overwhelmed and exhausted. I woke up the next day alone. The idea of eternal separation did not even cross my mind.

I rushed to furnish my home in time for my impending enrollment in graduate school the following month. As I put up the blinds and set up my finances and bill payments, it dawned on me how simple these tasks were, yet Rameh, purposefully putting himself in charge of all of that, had made me feel incompetent and stripped me of my self confidence. Having a limited knowledge of the computer system beyond what I needed for work, Rameh intended for me to remain ignorant and totally dependent on him. He made doing these tasks sound so complex that I thought I could never accomplish what comforts he was providing the family. His strategy worked for all those years until I moved out and realized that, yes, I could put blinds up, could fix the bathroom sink and the garbage disposal, could clear pipes and yes, set up online bill payments. Still, this realization did not clue me to his controlling personality. I wished we could remain friends. We had known each other for twenty-eight years and we had two beautiful children who needed us both.

I trusted that Rameh was a good person who would still impress upon the children the importance of having a relationship with their mother. I learned, however, that the only interest he had was to win his fight and to get even with me, using the only weapon he had, sadly: my children. I waited and waited, tried and tried, but with each attempt to reach their hearts, they grew farther away, refusing to see me or to communicate with me. I called our mutual friends to help me reconnect with my children, but they, too, had disowned me for all the bile Rameh had spilled over to them.

Slowly, I was experiencing the stages of grief but not always in a known linear way. I switched from denial, to anger, to complacency, or a combination of some or all of these feelings. My anger drove me to become unapologetic as manifest in a few early writings or e-mails to the children. That certainly did not help my case, but I became very defensive as the punishment my children had sentenced me to was disproportionate to my crime. In my despair, I became irrational at times. I also wanted to redeem myself, for I knew I was a person who had integrity and self respect. I refused to allow Rameh or my kids portray me as a whore going off on "sexual escapades," as Nour once wrote me. I was not going to allow anyone to take away my dignity and my pride.

Yet I wanted to try anything and everything to bring my children back to me. Nothing was going to make me give up even though I may have shot myself in the foot a few times. In my desperation, I contacted our divorce attorney who I thought would remain impartial even though he was Rameh's friend. I wrote him an e-mail imploring him to mediate.

Dear Sam:

I really hate to bother you, but I have no one to turn to. I am not trying to play the victim or to gather any sympathy because of my situation. I am simply a mother who misses her children very much and wants and has the right to see them and to be with them. More importantly, I need to be involved in their lives because I do believe that is in their best interest, emotionally, mentally and spiritually. I know this is not a legal matter since I do have 50 percent legal custody and the kids have chosen not to speak to me or to see me, but I am appealing to you as a father, as a parent and as a friend to talk to Rameh and to convince him that he needs to pressure the kids to see their mother, the only mother they will ever have. You may not be convinced that Rameh played a terrible role in involving the kids in every step of our marital problems, including very intimate details about my relationship with another man. You may feel he was totally justified in doing so because after all he was a "helpless victim" who lost his life-long partner to another man, or so he, the kids, and everybody else believe. You may even think, as I believe Rameh and the kids think, that I even deserve to be punished by being cast out of the community, treated like a whore, and deprived of my own flesh and blood, my children for whom I had sacrificed everything I ever wanted in my life so that I could see them grow and prosper. You may disagree in how I went about pursuing my own happiness, thinking I was selfish, careless and an unloving parent. I am not here to play the victim like Rameh has been doing with my kids and everybody we knew. I am not here to ask forgiveness or profess my remorse. I am simply trying to seek your help in reasoning with him; that the children should have a meaningful relationship with their mother; that by allowing them to choose not to communicate with me or to see me, that he is depriving them the irreplaceable love of a parent that no child should ever have to do without. Instead of lavishing in the support and sympathy he is getting from everybody around him, including the kids, Rameh needs to set his ego aside and recognize that I am a mother and have every right to be with my children, that he is indeed harming them irreparably, in the long run, by giving them a choice of severing me from their lives. Children need both parents. I do not have to convince you of that. They need to realize that regardless of who they perceive is right or wrong, my relationship with them is totally different and separate from the one I had with their father, and no matter what he and I went through, they need to understand and recognize that I never abandoned them or neglected my responsibilities towards them. If I elected to regain my life, I did not do so at anyone's expense. Unfortunately, the kids perceive it in this way, and Rameh is doing utterly nothing to remedy that. In fact, their behavior and attitude towards me is witness to the severe mental and emotional damage Rameh inflicted upon them prior to our separation. However, if Rameh truly loves his children and wants only what is in their best interest, the same way he succeeded in manipulating their young, uncorrupted, immature and innocent minds, directly or indirectly, enough to make them decide to exclude me from their lives, he can also mold them again, insisting they bring me back aboard. He needs to do that NOT for my sake but for their sake knowing this will improve their well-being. After all, I am a good person, a hard working and loving mother who gave all and got nothing. Children should never be deprived of the only true love they will have in their lives, the love of both parents, even though they themselves may have chosen to reject it. We all know children do not always make the best choices, which is why as parents we need to be their guides. Sadly, Rameh is not seeing beyond his pain enough to take his parental responsibility seriously. I am hoping that you will be his guide and his mentor. I know I am asking you to extend your assistance beyond your calling, but I have always respected you and have believed you are a very decent man of nature and of God. If you don't wish to be involved, I will certainly understand and respect your decision. However, if you do, I will forever be indebted to you for your kindness and your open heart. I wish you well with all the happiness and success that you deserve.

Best Regards,
Futoun Haddad

The response I got was insensitive. It proved how tough my battle was going to be. Sam wrote:

Hello Futoun:

I am in a very difficult position. I am sorry if the things I will say below may sound harsh, but they reflect my honest thinking. I think that your children feel that you have abandoned them and their father in pursuit of a more favorable romantic relationship with a man other than their dedicated and loving father. You made the conscious choice to break the family apart and to put your romantic and other interests above your devotion to your children and your husband. If I am faced with a similar situation, I would use the kids as leverage (or as a tool) to try to stop a divorce and keep my family together. Divorce is indescribably devastating, and irreparably harmful to children. The unconditional and immeasurable love for children should prevent parents from taking things in the divorce direction. They should sacrifice everything for the children. This is especially true if the kids are grown up like yours. Your relationship with your children is not totally separate from your relationship with Rameh. It is greatly affected by your relationship with Rameh. Your decision to divorce is psychological, causing the physical abandonment of your children. Your decision to leave their father for another man was at their expense. It is you and not Rameh who inflicted severe mental and emotional damage on them. The best way to bring you back aboard is if you come back to the family and terminate your relationship with your new man, and allow time to heal all the wounds that have resulted from your insistence on the divorce. Adults too (and not only children) don't always make the right choices. I think you made the wrong choice in seeking a divorce. In the eyes of the children, and in the absence of violence, cruelty, and other extreme behavior, it is the parent who initiates and insists on the divorce who is the one who is to blame for the divorce and for the breaking up of the family.

I am sorry for telling exactly what I think. Divorce is the most horrible thing for children and must be avoided except in extreme circumstances. I think it is selfish to divorce in the absence of violence and other extreme circumstances.

Having said that, I will call Rameh and convey your request to him.

Best,
Sam

Of course, I never received any response from Rameh and did not expect any. Three months had passed since my departure. I kept myself very busy working full-time and attending school at night, studying in the evening and on weekends. I had little or no time to do anything. Patrick and I met once a week, and occasionally I would enjoy a cup of coffee with my closest friends. I would get myself up every morning, dress up nicely, wear my lipstick and blush and head to work without missing a beat. I kept up my exercise routine and my healthful eating habits. I still had hope that the children would turn around and be back into my life once again.

I made many attempts to contact my children to no avail. I sent e-mails, left voice messages and sent letters, but all went unanswered. Unless it benefited them somehow, such as when they requested that I pay their tuition, they were resolute on wiping me completely from their lives. In one such response to Nour's request to pay school fees and tuition, my anger, mixed with desperation and disbelief to what started to feel as my new reality, spilled harshly in an e-mail to her. I had run out of ways to make her see and remember that she and her brother were the ones who left me; that I did not leave them simply by leaving their father; that I had raised her for seventeen years giving the utmost care and love any mother could provide. I could not control my pen when I wrote:

I will Not Give Up On You

Hi again, my sweetheart:

Please see the attached for the best that I could have done under the circumstances. They will not accept a faxed authorization to release the money, so I sent them this letter this morning. They will process the check as soon as they receive it, so hopefully the school will get it by Oct. 5th.

No matter how you try to dehumanize me by your insensitive e-mail, your lack of care and your rude communication with your Mother— yes, don't you ever forget that I am your mother and will always be whether you like it or not and no matter how much hate your heart can harbor— as a transaction, you will someday realize that you purposely stripped your heart of love and.... were left with nothing.

Your spitefulness, vengefulness, and attempts to punish me have worked, so great...more power to you. You have succeeded in inflicting the worst pain any mother has to endure and I hope you are a happy "winner." If this is what you wanted, you got it. So get over it now, and move on with your life.

As for me, I do not look at my relationship with you as a game, and neither will I reject you for you are my flesh and blood. You are my love, my joy and yes, my excruciating pain that I will endure for as long as I have to until you wake up one day, cleanse your poisoned mind and open your heart to receive me back in your life.

I hope you still have God in your heart to guide you because only God can lead you back to me. Only He knows how much I love you and only He will make you see that for twenty-one years I have sacrificed everything dear to me, including my spirit, to see you grow and become the intelligent beautiful woman you have become. Sadly, I never suspected that I could raise a daughter who is capable of so much hatred toward her own mother. I am very disappointed to say the least!

Life will shake you and will make you see that you were unjust in judging me and my actions; that you decided to remain disrespectful and so stubborn as to not seek the truth, but only to see what your father has fed you about me regardless of the seventeen years I spent nurturing you better than any mother could have. I gave you everything I had and you kicked it far trampling upon every beautiful moment we shared.

If God is still in your heart, He will make you understand that my relationship with you and your brother is totally independent and separate from my relationship with your father, and soon you will see and believe that I divorced your father, but I did not divorce you. He will make you admit that it was YOUR choice, not mine to sever me from your life. You have abandoned me, not the other way around. You have decided to reject me. You have made the choice to ostracize me pretending that I do not exist. You forget that a lot of where you are and who you are today is because of me, because of my selfless dedication to you and to your brother, because of years of relentless struggle to work hard and give you the best I could even if it meant living in misery, silent tears running down my heart and bright smiles to mask the pain.

God will make you see that you are only thinking about your own comfort, about your own happiness, your self-greed, without regard to the human who raised you, who tucked you in bed, who spent nights watching over you, who taught you your first steps and your first words, who covered you and gave you a kiss as you lay asleep sick at night, who made you a healthful hot meal every day and who packed your lunch and readied your breakfast every morning, who spent hours educating you, going through your homework, practicing your speeches in front of the stuffed animals in your room, who practiced piano and violin with you until you kick started and took you to every lesson, to every party and every friend you saw, the human who shed tears as you vomited three times a day and who took you to doctor after doctor to find you a cure, the human who soothed you when your first best friend abandoned you for another and when you got your first B, the human who taught you that life is not about perfection, but all about living it with love and in pursuit of mindful happiness, cherishing the limited time we have and making the best out of a bad situation because life is indeed beautiful, and we are lucky to be given this gift, the human, the human, the human, the human being you have ostracized, cast out and demonized, the human being you once called mother.

Life will give you a rude awakening one day, and when that happens, I want you to know that I will always receive you in my arms and keep your heart warm. No, I will not give up on you or your brother, ever. Yes, I gave it all and received nothing, but

I am a mother whose love is unconditional and limitless...so go ahead and show me all the disrespect, hate and ungratefulness. I will still leave it up to God to make you see the light and give you the maturity that can only come through experiencing your own sorrow and by walking the many paths of life.

I still remember the great speech your friend gave (mentioning the poem below) during your graduation ceremony, and I remember Robert Frost's "The Road Less Traveled." If you read it, you will know what I mean when I say that the path in life is not always one way and not always a straight line.

Love always,
Mother

Two roads diverged in a yellow wood,
And sorry I could not travel both
And be one traveler, long I stood
And looked down one as far as I could
To where it bent in the undergrowth;

Then took the other, as just as fair,
And having perhaps the better claim,
Because it was grassy and wanted wear;
Though as for that the passing there
Had worn them really about the same,

And both that morning equally lay
In leaves no step had trodden black.
Oh, I kept the first for another day!
Yet knowing how way leads on to way,
I doubted if I should ever come back.

I shall be telling this with a sigh

Somewhere ages and ages hence:
Two roads diverged in a wood, and I—
I took the one less traveled by,
And that has made all the difference

Robert Frost

At other times, frustration and grieving would mix in with hope and faith. I sent the children inspirational quotes and passages in the hope that they would bring about some introspection. Nothing ever touched their hearts, from what I could gather, no matter how genuine my feelings were expressed verbally, or in poetry, such as when I sent in quotations, the *"Quilt of Holes"* from an unknown author. It was submitted by "twoangels" on Scrapbook.com:

As I faced my Maker at the last judgment, I knelt
before the Lord along with all the other souls.

Before each of us laid our lives like the squares
of a quilt in many
piles; an angel sat before each of us sewing our
quilt squares together into a tapestry that is our life.

But as my angel took each piece of cloth off the
pile, I noticed how ragged
and empty each of my squares was. They were filled with giant holes. Each
square was labeled with a part of my life that had
been difficult, the
challenges and temptations I was faced with in
every day life. I saw hardships that I endured,
which were the largest holes of all.

I glanced around me. Nobody else had such
squares. Other than a tiny hole here and there,
the other tapestries were filled

with rich color and the bright hues of worldly
fortune. I gazed upon my own
life and was disheartened.

My angel was sewing the ragged pieces of cloth together,
threadbare and empty, like binding air.

Finally the time came when each life was to be
displayed, held up to the scrutiny of truth. The others rose; each
in turn, holding up their tapestries. So filled their lives had been.
My angel looked upon me, and nodded for me to rise.

My gaze dropped to the ground in shame. I hadn't
had all the earthly fortunes. I had love in my life, and laughter. But
there had also been trials of illness, and wealth, and false
accusations that took from me my
world, as I knew it. I had to start over many
times. I often struggled with
the temptation to quit, only to somehow muster the strength to pick up and
begin again. I spent many nights on my knees in
prayer, asking for help and
guidance in my life. I had often been held up to
ridicule, which I endured
painfully, each time offering it up to the Father
in hopes that I would not
melt within my skin beneath the judgmental gaze of
those who unfairly judged me.

And now, I had to face the truth. My life was
what it was, and I had to accept it for what it was.
I rose and slowly lifted the combined squares of
my life to the light.

An awe-filled gasp filled the air. I gazed around
at the others who stared at me with wide eyes.

Then, I looked upon the tapestry before me. Light
flooded the many holes,
creating an image, the face of Christ. Then our
Lord stood before me, with
warmth and love in His eyes. He said, "Every time
you gave over your life
to Me, it became My life, My hardships, and My
struggles.

Each point of light in your life is when you
stepped aside and let Me shine
through, until there was more of Me than there was
of you."

May all our quilts be threadbare and worn, allowing
Christ to shine through!

Author: Unknown

CHAPTER 9

No Redemption —
Sorry Cannot Say Enough

As if it hadn't been painful enough to be deprived of my children, soon, I learned that my father had lung cancer and did not have much time to live. One week is all I could spare from work and school to comfort him in his last moments. Father was still able to walk slowly when I got home, but he deteriorated rapidly. In my short, last days with him, I sat next to him, caressing his bald head; I lay in bed next to him, my arm around his now thin belly, hugging him as he rambled on and on throughout the nights not making any sense. I spoon-fed him gently as he struggled to chew, and I got him the urinal when he needed it. He still had his funny sense of humor and retold me stories that I had heard many times over, clueless of his impending death.

Every time I kissed him, I said, "I love you Pappy…." He always responded in English…"I love you more." I would hold his hand and kiss it and he would then wrap his arm around my shoulder and tell me, "No, I should be the one kissing your hand, *"ya Futoun, ya imm ilhanoun"* (oh Futoun, oh tender mother).

I bid him farewell and carried on with my life. He passed on quietly on October 4, 2007, two days after I had arrived in the U.S. and two hours after my brothers and sister had arrived in Lebanon. I was driving to school that evening when my sister called to give me the news. I became numb but continued to class. I sat there stoically as the professor lectured, staring into emptiness, at the bare walls that reminded me of how reality strips you from the luster of life just so you can persevere. Half an hour later, I wept silently, but my professor noticed and looked at me compassionately. I told him that I had just received the news and excused myself.

That night, between the tears of loss and the thoughts of his infectious laugh that truly came from the heart, I tried to remember the good times he and I had shared during his last days. I knew in my heart that he passed on in peace, knowing he had seen all of his children and that he had lived a good long life full of compassion and kindness. I reflected upon his legacy as a humble tender father who choked every time he talked to me while away in Venezuela, who caressed my hair as I sat next to him in his last hours and who told me how sweet my kisses were. During the last moments I had with him he continued to joke and recall great times in his life. As I gathered my tears and held back the pain of eternal separation, he gazed into my eyes and said, "We all are passing through life's journey, we are nothing but a journey…" and he sang me this melancholic old song by Abdul Wahab, ***"Ya Dunia Ya Gharami (Oh Life, My Beloved)"*** that he loved so much and sang often……

Oh life, my passions, my tears and my smiles,
No matter the sorrows and pains you aggrieved me,

My heart will always love you...

Mother told me that days later, Rameh called to give her his condolences. Yet she received none from my children, and neither did I. I wondered how they could not be moved by death, by sorrow or loss. I was not sure if they had been stripped of their humanity or if they even had any at all. I wanted to know; I really wanted to know if they had any compassion left in their hearts, so I wrote them this e-mail for which I never got a response. Months later, Rameh tried to justify their lack of sympathy in one of his court documents stating, it was not a tradition they were accustomed to. *Yee*, empathy is a trait that must be taught, I suppose. I must have failed at that.

> *What has become of you, my lovely children, that I have received*
> *the support of so many, yet not a word of condolences from you,*
> *Nour and Anwar? What crime have I committed that you had*
> *to punish my father, on his death bed, without a kind word to*
> *show your affection and care and to comfort him in his last*
> *moments, or to deprive your grandmother of some words of love*
> *to help her mourn his loss? What has become of you that you*
> *have lost your souls so that even in death, you could not gather*
> *some basic sense of common human decency to express your*
> *sorrow, that is if you have any left in your hearts. Why would*
> *you not? Has he not hugged you, loved you, kissed you, held you*
> *and laughed with you? Has he been a total stranger in your lives?*
> *An animal would have received more compassion. But perhaps*
> *you forgot that he was your grandfather, that he too, like me,*
> *was a human, a tender, kind and loving father who I wish you*
> *really cared to know...or at least, had a spark left in your hearts*
> *to bring a smile to his dying spirit and his heart that until his*

death, (on his deathbed) mentioned your names, "Anwarito, Nourita, bonita muy linda....":

For a few months after I moved out, Rameh kept in marginal contact with my brother, Sami, in as effort to show that he was civil or to pass the message on to me that he was strong and recovered from his loss. During a visit from Sami in late October of 2007, I asked that he slip a letter to Anwar explaining how much I had missed him and his sister and again, asking for their forgiveness. It was my second sincere apology, summary of my awakening and of all the issues in my life that had led to the choices I had made. I had sent the same letter to Nour's last known Address at the University of California, San Diego where she was attending school. I wrote:

Sorry Cannot Say Enough

(Reference letter #3-October 27, 2007)

My beloved children, Nour & Anwar:

It has been three and a half months since I last heard your voice or touched your skin. I don't know for how long this suffering on both sides will continue, and I am not sure how to reach your hearts or to appeal to your spirits. I stand helpless, hopeless and in despair.

You really do not need to strike me out of your lives for you to show me how angry, hurt and disappointed you are in me. I do know that and more; I too acknowledge your pain and feel it in my bones and under my skin. Believe me, I know what it means to lose a loved one. I really want you to know that there is nothing in what I have done that was meant to cause you sorrow or pain. There was nothing I intended in my actions to rob your hearts from precious youth or your souls from spirit.

I am so sorry to be the cause of so much agony in your lives. I am so sorry I broke up the family, shattered your serene lives and caused you the loss of the stability that comes with a family unit. I am so sorry that your anger has caused you to reject love and to shun human affection. I am so sorry that your suffering is preventing you from embracing the mother you once loved, from breaking this cocoon that you have built around yourselves, this shell that you cannot break. I am sorry that in your despair, you have lost the joy of the motherly nourishment that you so desperately need. I am so sorry that you may grow up not feeling the unwavering love and affection a mother can give her child especially in times of crisis. I am sorry that your lives will be devoid of something so precious to you and to your emotional well-being and maturity. A mother would never want that for her children, and neither would she intentionally inflict it upon them.

Not by choice I grew up without a father, and I know how devastating this has been in my life, and I wish NOT for you to suffer this emptiness that no one could ever fill...and I wish I could turn back time. I wish I could have approached my failing relationship with your father differently. I wish I had realized how miserable I was and had simply faced it, rather than masking my pain to avoid more of it and to escape dealing with the fear of the unknown and the destruction of everything beautiful I had built over twenty-one years and risking the abandonment of my own flesh and blood, my source of joy in this world, you, my precious children.

I wish, I really wish that I could have recognized that I was unhappy and needed to end my marriage, and had the courage to act upon it before I started a relationship with another man. Unfortunately, I was in so much denial about my plight, driven to raise you at all cost, trying to make up to you what my parents did not give me—love. Then came the catalyst to wake up my dormant desires for self fulfillment; I let myself indulge in the beauty of loving and of being loved equally for the first time in my life. I am sorry I lied to you. I betrayed your trust and perhaps made you feel that I did not care about you or about anybody but myself. I could never love anybody more than you, not even my own self, whether you believe me or not. But never did I imagine that you would treat me the way you did, cast me as a demon and sentence me to hell for eternity.

I wish I had not lived my life for twenty-one years lying to myself and to you making believe that my marriage was all right; that life was normal; that I could keep going living it the way I was into eternity. The time came, as it always does, when people must face reality and shed the cloak of deception. I faced my life and decided I could no longer live a lie, that the truth would set me free. I sought a divorce because that was the right thing to do and the fairest thing for you, for your father and for me.

I am so sorry for the words, the actions, or for anything I have done that caused you heartache. I wish I could turn back the clock, retrace my steps and do things in the proper order, but I cannot. Time stops for no one. Life does not prompt you to follow a direct path, so you twist and turn and bend with its curves, overcome the challenges, and with perseverance, finally reach your destination. I will never ever give up on you and my love will always shine through you. My hope, my dream, my passion is that the day comes when you will forgive me, like God forgives

*his creatures and that once more, I will have you back in my
arms. For that joyful reunion, I shall live.*

Love forever,
Mom

Sami precariously entered Anwar's room and slipped my letter under
his pillow. Somehow, Rameh sensed what my brother was doing but waited
until he left. On his way back home, my brother got a call from Rameh
rebuking him for what he had done. He never heard from him again.
Suspecting that Rameh did not give the letter to my son, I sent Anwar an
e-mail with a copy and another to his sister asking her to pass the information along. In it, I stated that I was worried that Anwar was not getting my
phone messages; that my e-mails to both of them were being intercepted
and read.

Until that moment, I could not comprehend clearly how a father would
deprive his children of the love and care of their mother; I could not fathom
the thought that he would not know how detrimental it could be for the
children's emotional and mental well-being to be injected with hate, or to
be told insidious lies about their mother. He had to have known; he had to
have known. He is no fool, I thought. I could only conclude that his love of
vengeance overrode his love for his children. This pained me immensely
and I didn't want my children to know this truth. I wanted to spare them
the agony of realizing that their father cared less about them than about
destroying their mother. I thought that they had suffered enough, endured
enough. I had to protect them against such devastating heartbreak.

I grew up never questioning the love of my parents, assured that they
did what they did to provide us with a good life, regardless of their bad
choices. Yet, the deprivation of not having experienced that tangible love
led me to my own demise and to many poor choices years later. I could not

imagine how adversely my children's future would be impacted when they discovered that their father's narcissistic tendencies outweighed his love for them. It was this fear I was referring to when I asked to meet Nour in my e-mail after this last incident stating "I fear for you in ways I dare not say, but I don't want to lose you ever...," NOT suggesting any incest between her and her father as she later accused me of suggesting.

When Nour did not respond, I called her soon after. I believe she said, "You lied" before hanging up. I am not sure what she meant by that, but I felt compelled to respond to her. To reassure her of my love, I wrote:

The Heart Does Not Lie

My love, Nour:

I am not sure of what you said when you picked up the phone for the first time in four months and muttered a word or two. I did not hear you well, but I may have heard you say, "You lie!"

I don't know why you continue to think that I lie. The heart does not lie. What is there left to lie about? There is nothing that I have not told you, and my life has been made by your father a mockery, an open chapter.

My heart does not lie, Nour. When I say I love you, you know that I do. When I say I need you, you know that I do. When I say you are the beauty in my life, you know that you are. When I say I miss you, you know that I do....a mother's love is always true... and when I say I am sorry for all the pain I caused you, you know that it is coming from the heart, and you know that this letter that I have sent and that I am attaching (Sorry Cannot Say Enough) is testimony to what I have just said. I wish you to read it and to read it again and again and again and again until you drop your first tear because then you will know that every word, every thought I put into it is true. I want you to know that you are always in my mind, and in my heart, and in my soul.

I need to talk to you and to see you. I plan to drive to San Diego next week so that we can sit as adults and just talk, just talk. Please, just hear me out. That is all I ask. You are soon to be eighteen and "fully emancipated." You are soon to become a woman, a beautiful one, I am sure; a woman who will have her own mind; who will decide on her own future....I wish it to be a bright one as I have always envisioned it for you, my child. And I wish for you to really be emancipated....

Love you always,
Mom

PART III

The Fight

CHAPTER 10

Court Battles — Visitation Petitions & Manifesto

As usual, she did not respond, at least not then. Later, her father convinced her that I was alluding to incest as her subsequent e-mail revealed. The weeks turned into months, and I started realizing that my children were forever lost. The hope that Rameh would be a responsible parent, ensuring a healthy mother-child relationship became wishful thinking. I had to do something that would change this terrible situation, so on November 11, 2007, I filed a petition to reopen the divorce proceedings and to amend them with respect to child visitation. My daughter was just turning eighteen by that time, so my focus was on my son. The details of the petitions/transcripts and decisions are copied verbatim to illustrate the battle that was won and lost and as undeniable proof of my resolution to turn the tide in my son's favor. I chose to provide as many details as I could so that one day, if my children ever become interested in learning the truth and what their mother did in order to protect them, they would have this book as testimony of my relentless pursuit. My motion to the judge followed ten days later, whereby I asked the court for the following:

Your Honor:

I write pleading with you to allow me a chance to affirm and grant me my right to see and speak to my children whom I have been deprived of ever since I moved out of the house after the filing of my divorce four months ago. I understand that by the time this motion is filed, my daughter, Nour Haddad, will be eighteen and out of the jurisdiction of the court. My son, Anwar Haddad, however, is still only fifteen years of age. He ostracized his mother having been manipulated by his father. His father has made him believe that he is motherless; that I disgraced and shamed the family for having been involved with another man; that he would be better off with his father only, without any contact with his mother who raised him with love, affection and care virtually as a single parent for all of his life. I feel that I should be granted the following by the court:

1. *Visitation order-therapeutic and general*

2. *Conjoined or one-on-one therapy sessions with a family counselor (MFCC).*

3. *Assignment of a social worker to his case in order to monitor his progress*

4. *Assignment of a mediator to facilitate the execution of the above and suggest other alternatives for a resolution should the order is objected to by my ex-husband or by my son.*

5. *Any other program/plan the mediator or the law deems necessary to foster a meaningful relationship between my son and me to preserve this precious maternal link.*

6. *Your Honor, my children's judgment has been seriously impaired because their father, playing the victim to win their support, involved them in every aspect of our failing twenty-one-year marriage, sharing everything with them, as if they were his confidantes. He shared age-inappropriate material with them such as all surveillance pictures, phone messages, and intimate e-mails between my partner and me. They became so upset, angry and hurt that they did what all children would do to protect themselves; they sided with him, defended him with all their might, refused to hear my reasons and decided to sever ties with me. They felt that by doing so, they would punish me for my actions and prove their unequivocal support for their victimized father whom they believed would be betrayed should they have spoken to me.*

Your Honor, my children have become so callous towards me that ever since I moved out, they do not answer their phones and they ignore the e-mails I send them. They delete my "love you" messages from their cell phones without hearing them. They have also blocked my e-mail address so I cannot communicate with them. They have returned all the gifts I had bought them in the last year and told my brother to tell me never to call them or to try to see them again. Their father filled them with so much hatred that even when my father was on his deathbed, they did not call to console him and neither did they call my mother after his passing to give their condolences.

It does not take a psychologist to realize that they are being tormented, yet they lack the experience to realize what an immense loss they will suffer by choosing not to have me in their lives. A time may come when they are older that they have a change of heart. However, your honor, I do not want to wait until it is too late, the damage irreversible.

With enforced therapy and some kind of a relationship with his mother, my son will greatly benefit, and I hope he will recover from this terrible tragedy. He should not be permitted to choose NOT to speak to me or to see me since he is just a child who doesn't know what is best for him, certainly not while he is living in his father's shadow.

I daresay that I raised my children better than any mother could have, and I challenge them to say otherwise. A line of witnesses who have known me for longer than nineteen years would be glad to testify to the unconditional love and dedication I gave to my family. I have been trying for the last four months to communicate with my children through any means, but all my efforts have been intercepted or rejected. I wrote to my ex-husband's lawyer in the hope that he could convince him to encourage the children to talk to me. I called our old friends, but all of them have ostracized me too, having read all my personal e-mails and seen the pictures that my ex-husband sent them and posted on the internet. I am enclosing copies of my correspondence in chronological order for your review.

Your honor, I urge the court to enforce my rights and protect my child.

Futoun Haddad

With the letter, I also enclosed my hand-written original filing requesting an order to require Rameh to cease and desist discussing any aspect of our marriage with my children or from making any derogatory remarks about me.

Nour's birthday was coming up shortly before Christmas. My mother had arrived to visit from Lebanon, so I thought I would give her some presents to take to the children. On December 17, 2007, she dropped by the house. Sadly, my children would not engage in any discussion with her. Rameh told Mother to tell me to back off from causing the children and himself harm. He said that he would "Respond forcefully to the case."

He blatantly threatened to my mom to "drag" me to court and to open hell's gates unless I dropped my case for visitation. He returned the gifts, along with the souvenirs I had bought my children while on my trip to Spain and Morocco: slippers, a handbag, and a wallet. The ceramic small figurine of a mother and daughter I had left in Nour's closet was also returned unopened in its original wrapping paper, bow and all. He gave her the letter I had mailed to Nour and the same one in its unopened envelope that my brother had snuck into Anwar's room as well. It was the last time Rameh or my children communicated with my mother. Later, however, as the court documents revealed, this and much of my other correspondence was shared with him, either by Nour directly forwarding her e-mails to her father, or by his hacking into her account. Needless to say, to Rameh's delight, the children were now completely cut off from anyone related to me who could talk any sense to them or remind them of their mother. He had reached the pinnacle of his success. His plan to alienate me from my children had succeeded.

When my mother told me about the encounter, I sent Nour a copy of my petition inquiring as to why her father, claiming to give them the choice to see me or not, would threaten to take all my family to court unless I dropped my request for a child visitation hearing. In the exchange below, she brought up the e-mail I had mistakenly forwarded to her, after sending it to Patrick, when I was asking her to pass on my visitation petition to Anwar. She also brought up the time when my sister had not exercised good judgment and insinuated that there was incest when Rameh would crawl in Nour's bed sobbing until she consoled him to sleep. Sadly, she accused me of making the same allegation which was baseless. She also affirmed that it was their choice, not through any coercion from their father, to sever their relationships with me. Perhaps the "lie" that she was referring to in the e-mail below is the same as the one she stated to me on the phone the other day before hanging up. She wrote:

We Don't Want To See You

(Reference letter #4-December 17, 2007)

just a quick comment about that e-mail. i think it's REALLY FUNNY how you send that Anwar and then to "another person" and finally to me. and you really expected me to forward that to Anwar, ESPECIALLY after seeing to whom it was forwarded after it was sent to Anwar? that's hilarious. you have such a great sense of humor.

leave my dad out of this. the divorce papers say that there is 50-50 custody, and HE always tells us that it's OUR choice to see whomever we want to see. he has no problem with us going to see you, ok? just because WE DON'T WANT TO SEE YOU or HAVE ANYTHING TO DO WITH YOU doesn't mean he is the one who's forcing us to live with him. and i'm sick and tired of your mindset, and your claiming that you are so scared for me in ways that nobody can imagine because i live with my dad. what is that supposed to mean? are you disgusting?

yes, of course you are. i don't even WANT to know what you're thinking or what you're trying to imply by that statement, but your judgments lack merit and are completely unfounded and illogical. absolutely despicable and disgusting.

and your court motion. since when has anybody been able to force anybody else against their will to see someone? are you serious? you HONESTLY think that Anwar is going to go to court and exclaim "yes i would LOVE to see my mother because i miss her SO much." again, are you really serious or are you dreaming? HE is the one who SAYS doesn't want to see you or have anything to do with you. you try to argue that what happened was between you and my dad, but that's obviously a straight-out lie that completely attempts to evade the truth. it wasn't just between you and him, it involved all of us, don't even try to lie about it. you didn't just lie to him, you lied to every single one of us. do you think that's a good mother? especially after you tell us that lying is one of the worst things anybody could ever do, and then you go and do it yourself? what gives you that privilege? you think you can just go and do whatever you want without facing any consequences?? you think you just have some kind of power that will allow ONLY you to go back on your word and pathologically lie?? if THAT'S what the meaning of a role model is, then you surely fit it 100%.

look, you made your decision and you're free to do what you want now. and Anwar and i made ours, and we're free to do what WE want now. you can't impose yourself on us. you can't force him to see you because that's going to make him rebel even MORE. if he tells the judge "i don't want to see her", do you think the judge is going to force him to? of course not. the

decision rests with ANWAR, not with you and not with some
court order in which you demand that you see him. custody is
50-50, keep that in mind, even though both Anwar and i urged
our dad to take full custody.

and about coming to MY house and DEFILING my property
with your presence? I can't believe you'd do that, that you'd
even have the AUDACITY to come NEAR where i live happily.
do you really expect me to open my front door with arms wide
open and embrace you and tell you that i need you and i miss
you immensely? you must be dreaming one heck of a dream
if you expect that. i am doing perfectly fine; i don't need you,
just in case you couldn't tell. it's not you who lets me succeed. i
succeed on my own, and if you think that i sit every single day
and contemplate how you're not in my life, then you're mistaken.

I was delighted to have gotten a response from her, as hurtful as it
was. I really wanted my children to express themselves, get angry, yell at
me or do anything to let what they had been bottling up explode. Sadly,
though, beyond a few e-mails, they made the choice to bury all their pain
pretending that they were happy and content with their "GREAT" father,
as Nour described.

My response would be one of my last few correspondences with my
daughter that she probably read. I cannot know what has been intercepted
by her father. I wrote:

My Mistake

(Reference letter #5- December 18, 2007)

My Love, Nour:

First, I want to thank you for your reply. I am delighted to have a response from you, my darling. I will always accept any communication from you, no matter what.

Secondly, let me acknowledge the pain you must have felt when you noticed the message was forwarded to Patrick. I was so distraught that evening and literally at the end of my rope, having even lost the desire to live, that I was not aware I forwarded to you the message from my sent folder. I had no intention to hurt you further and rub it in your face. I truly would never want to hurt you any more than I already have. I am so sorry. Please accept my sincere apology. Again, I wish I could undo this, but I cannot, and, will not lie to you anymore and will not deny that Patrick remains in my life.

I just pray that one day you become experienced in life enough to realize that my divorce, my decisions, and my actions are mine and should not ever come between this special bond that we have built for seventeen years.

I wish I could hug you now and look into your beautiful eyes. My heart is aching for you, my sweetheart. I often dream that you are hugging me and that we are mother and daughter as we once were. Then suddenly I wake up as if God wants to deprive me of even enjoying you in my dreams. My smiles turn into tears. I fear I may never see you again. I don't want to lose my faith, and I feel I am betraying God for feeling I am losing faith in

His wisdom....but as time passes, I cannot but feel that you and Anwar are drifting farther away from me, and I lose hope......

My dear child, I have already lost the most precious beings in my life. Nothing could hurt more. I will still attempt to get a court order as outlined in my letter in the hope I can get a glimpse of Anwar.

I shall not bother you again. I have tried everything I possibly could to get you to talk to me, but sadly, you have made it clear you do not want to see me or hear from me. I will never give up on you, but I will stay away from you if it makes you happy. I really want you to be happy and to live in peace......but should you ever feel the need to talk to someone who will always listen, someone who will always love you unconditionally, I want you to know I will always be there for you.

Goodbye, my love, goodbye

Love always,
Mother

To my surprise, Nour responded the next day with yet another scathing e-mail. She wrote:

It Involves All Of Us: Don't Deny It

(Reference letter #6- December 18, 2007)

I think one day YOU should become experienced enough in life to realize that your actions are yours to bear, because right now you're just saying that and you don't really mean it. otherwise, why else would my grandmother come over and try to play the blame game, accusing me and Anwar of wrongdoing? obviously you don't see yourself as having done wrong, you see yourself as some sort of oppressed angelic figure who has broken free from the chains of domesticity. i'm not the one who needs to understand what you did, because i understand it clearly. don't you remember when you were so proud and arrogant that you claimed that Anwar and i were going to be the ones running back to you, crawling on our hands and knees? well, look how the tables have turned! look who comes to my home, uninvited, trying to get my attention! as you are aware, it didn't work. and your apologies are completely meaningless, by the way. don't you remember how you "came back" in april or may or whatever month it was, and you said you were sorry and you would fix things and make everything right and would stop lying? yeah, that was a lie. that apology was meaningless, as you know very well where it got you. do you think that either Anwar or i have anything to look up to if we think of you? can you answer that question with a "yes"??? of course you can't. because we DON'T have anything to look up to. all we can see is someone who lies, cheats, and violates the commandments of the Bible.

and what's this nonsense about Anwar needing psychological treatment? that's absolutely ridiculous, because he's doing just fine. he couldn't be any better. it's degrading to him to even think that someone doesn't think he's mentally stable, because he is. and when the court does see him, as you insist is necessary, they're not going to find a thing wrong with him. and he won't have to go to any psychological treatments, because THERE'S NOTHING WRONG WITH HIM. and you know why you fail to see that? because you're wrapped up in your own world. you think the whole entire world revolves around you and that there must be something wrong with someone who doesn't want to talk to you. and it's not even that he doesn't have a logical reason to avoid you, because he does. and even though you might think it's illogical, nobody else does. so let's say, hypothetically speaking, that the judge decides to go against Anwar's will and force him to see you. what is Anwar supposed to expect? to go to your house and you introduce him to your "significant other"?? and tell Anwar how happy you are now that you're not some sort of oppressed "slave" and that you can go on sexual escapades whenever you please? i can't even believe that you have the audacity and arrogance to try to force yourself on him. you think that all the slander and libel you have showered my dad with is going to go well in the courts? and you sincerely think that when you attack someone, other people are just supposed to stand by and do nothing about it? are you serious?! because i know that that's what you wanted. you wanted your actions to stay between you and my dad, but how can you reasonably expect that if both Anwar and i were affected by you coming home late at night with really strong perfume on? or LEAVING home with really strong perfume on, claiming that you were just going out? that's ridiculous. don't you DARE say that we should've stayed out of it if you were the one to put us in it in the first place through your incessant lying. i'm not sure what you're expecting the judge to rule, but i can predict that it won't be in your favor. and if you think that Anwar's not living well, think again. my dad cooks food for us, the house is always clean, and my dad is stronger than ever before. he's a GREAT father. actually, more than great. and i don't care what you think about him, honestly, because you're not living here and you don't know how enjoyable it is. we're living a fantastic life. despite however much you want to prove that my dad is a failure at being a father, just know that you'll never be able to do it.

and one last point. about the threatening phone call your witch of a sister left us. you know just as well as i do that you spent a good amount of your life not talking to her, and suddenly for you two to be the best of friends now is absolutely ridiculous. so it would be naive for me to think that you don't know about the phone call. and of course you know the contents of the call and the implication that there is incest going on in this house. that is such a disgusting and filthy thing of her to think, and i'm sure that your mind is just as despicable especially because you "fear for me in ways you can't describe". i am SO unbelievably offended that your family will sink so LOW as to accuse my dad of such an act. and don't even try to convince me that you had no idea, because the odds are in your favor that you TOLD her to say that or at the VERY least implied it. it's the same thing with — (my sister's daughter who had sent similar accusations of incest to Nour) email, where it was quite apparent that you were content that she had sent me such a blasphemous, vile e-mail. i don't expect an apology from you, because even if you gave one it would be meaningless and fake, but just know that it's even MORE proof that this isn't just between you and my dad. it involves all of us. don't try denying it.

This was a very hard e-mail to swallow. I was left speechless and defeated. I knew there was nothing I could do or say that would open up her mind and allow her to listen. Perhaps that is how angry teenagers think, but I was not used to it. After all, Nour was an exceptionally smart young lady, a valedictorian, and on her way to medical school. I could not understand why she refused to even give me a chance to explain my side of the story. I did not expect her to forgive, but at least to understand. I just realized years later, that for all of her logical, intellectual brain that I always bragged about, she lacked the emotional intelligence to reason. I had hoped that with time and age, it would be revealed to her. Sadly, at thirty, she still has not budged whatsoever, remaining just as steadfast as she was as a teenager. Perhaps years of alienation have taken up permanent residence in her mind. So I responded:

Short & Sweet

(Reference letter #7-December 18, 2007)

My love, Nour:

As I stated before, I will accept your communication whatever it is, but I refuse to respond to this one. I think you need a lot of time to heal, and I will give that to you and stay out of your life. That is all I will say. One day, you will see the truth.

I am happy to know that you and Anwar are doing well, though without me. That is good enough for me. And whether or not you will decide never to correspond with or see me again, I still wish you happiness and peace in your future and the best of luck. May the New Year grant you your wishes, and may God always protect you.

Love always,
Mother

In response for my motion to have visitations with my son and therapy, Rameh sent the court his 31-page Manifesto dated January 11, 2008. He enclosed a letter from Anwar arguing why he should not be forced against his will to visit with me; and another letter from Nour supporting her brother's decision. He included several of my e-mail exchanges with the children stating that they "willingly and freely shared" them with him, alleging that through my "conniving tactics" I otherwise was attempting to prevent him from making a good case. The letters/emails are referenced by # 1 through 7 in this and in Part I and II of this book.

The Manifesto was less about arguing his case against visitation than about presenting me in the worst light possible, trashing me and my character, marginalizing my efforts at raising my children and portraying me as a pathological liar and adulterer. To the contrary, in it, he elevated himself and his morality to the highest degree, commanding the loyalty and the utter respect and love of our children. Rameh described the intense pain I caused him from which he emerged happy, strong and victorious. Below, I have extracted excerpts of his transcript to illustrate the extent he went to in order to prevent me from connecting with our children and to shed a glimpse of the psychological construct-Parental Alienation Syndrome (PAS) I alluded to earlier and which I will delve into in more detail in the chapters that follow. I have underlined some statements that demonstrate elements of PAS within my children's writings. The statements below are direct quotations from Rameh's Manifesto, with all the punctuation, bracketed words, and grammatical structure.

His initial attempt to disqualify me as a parent started by his referring to me as the "ex-former-wife" against the recommendation of the mediator that a spouse be referred to as a parent or a mother. Following in his footsteps, my children started referring to me as "mother" in quotes or by my first name or, simply, as "this woman" in the letters that Rameh enclosed. His first request of the court was not to consider the mediator's recommendation for regular mediation therapy stating, "Under no condition whatsoever I am placed in the same room with my ex-wife. It was and is my personal wish that I never see, or hear from this intrinsically hurtful woman." He then enclosed the letters my children wrote as an initiation of his visitation rebuttal:

It was hard for me to conceive that my son had actually written the letter below without indirect coercion from his father. Yet, Rameh described him as an "independent thinker and a very mature teenager." Anwar wrote on January 6, 2008:

> Your Honor, first and foremost, it is my wish not to see, hear or speak to my "mother" in any way, shape or form in the court. I do not believe that anybody has the right to force me, against my will, to see her. All of her accusations are lies; I do not need psychiatric help because I am more mentally stable than she is. I am doing well in school, my sports and my hobbies, and have had more time to do so. I have all honors classes, and one AP class and I have good grades in all.
>
> My father and I are having great time together, and more fun when Nour joins us from her breaks at UCSD. My dad and I go together to my downhill bike races, and I'm tended for in the most caring way and that is all the parental attention I need. I feel insulted to be called a "tender 15 years of age" because my maturity level far exceeds that of Futoun's; and I became even more insulted to be accused to needing a social worker, mediator, or family counselor. She wrongly accused my father of sharing "age inappropriate material, such as surveillance picture, phone messages and intimate e-mails."....may I ask how on EARTH he would be able to do that? She is dragging me to court, for which I will have to miss a school day, so that she can try to earn my respect by manipulating the court system. What she doesn't know, is that she has lost my respect forever for her lying and dishonesty, and the disgusting accusations made by

her and her evil sister. They will NEVER be forgiven not only by me, but by God for the things that they have done. All of their false accusations are from an act of desperation, going low as the disgusting area of incest in the house.

She will continue her acts of desperation until she can acquire some control over me through you, Judge, which I hope will not happen. She will, with no doubt, make a scene at the court, including crying and pleading in order to gain your sympathy. I cannot stress enough that she has no right to force me to see her._ She is an untrustworthy person, who also cheated on my dad back in 1994 when I was only 2; but our father still took very good care of my sister and me, while she was away. My father still had the heart to take her back in for the sake of the integrity of the family. My "tender 15 years" are already in the process of achieving a Driver's License and I am but a few years short of becoming an adult.

We all agreed that when the divorce became final, that my sister and I would be allowed to choose whoever we wanted to live with, without intervention from either parent. My father has not been influencing me at all in my decision, as she accused him of. He has played a major role in my life, far bigger than anything she has ever done for me. He does not manipulate me in any way, because my views are absolutely rock-hard and even he was to suggest for me to go see her, I would strongly disagree. My views are not influenced by anyone and I follow my own morals and ethics, which included honesty, a trait Futoun does not have. I would definitely not benefit whatsoever by seeing this woman, who I no longer refer to as my mother. The relation is only genetic, and any physical attraction has been severed.

My father takes care of me well; he works long hours in order to pay for the house and for my sister's college tuition; but he is now a free, happy man. We are making modifications to our house here and there, little by little, and improving its homeliness and I am very comfortable with who I am living with. He cooks healthy, traditional Lebanese dishes for me and I am very grateful and happy to be in his care.

Your Honor, I reject all five suggestions that she is asking the court to grant her. My emotional and mental well-being will be seriously jeopardized if I am forced to do anything against my will.

Respectfully,
Anwar Haddad.

Rameh also enclosed another letter of support from Nour dated January 6, 2008. She wrote:

Your Honor:

I am writing in support of my brother Anwar's desire to remain living with my dad as well as his wish to keep away from <u>our "mother" (Mother will be enclosed by quotation marks to signify That I do not really think of her as my mother).</u>

I would like to stress that despite what <u>our "mother"</u> might say, our dad has been an extremely influential part in our lives from the very beginning; otherwise why is it that we were so attached to him that we decided to live under his roof? I would like to note that at the time the divorce was being filed, <u>my brother and I implored our dad to request full custody</u> (my brother even more so than I). And honestly speaking, I sincerely wish that *my dad was able to do so. I do not think my brother would be in this quagmire had that been the course of action. The living arrangement has been a problem for neither me nor my brother. Yet it seems that now <u>our "mother"</u> wants to "reclaim custody." I recall that both our "mother" and dad agreed that the decision would rest with us,, the children. We were supposed to be able to decide with whom we would stay. Now, though, <u>our "mother"</u> wants to force Anwar to see her. I entreat you Your Honor. to keep in mind that my brother chose to stay with our dad due to the <u>emotional havoc that our "mother" wreaked upon us during the ordeal.</u> Anwar has, and was never prevented from the ability to choose if he wants to see her or not.*

The decision clearly rests in your judgment, the rationale of which I am in no position to dispute. I simply make one request of you, which is to seriously analyze my brother's stance as well as the idea that nobody should be forced unwillingly to be in the company of another.

Sincerely;
Nour Haddad

Rameh then continued with his insidious accusations and character assassination in the hope the judge would rule in his favor. Below are some excerpts.

Clearly, no one but their mother caused the children undue pain and suffering; however, both of them proved to be very resilient in overcoming her burdens. "Manipulating or injecting hatred in them" as my ex-wife baselessly claims, so that both children feel and act the way they do in rejecting her behavior, was neither sought after nor needed on my part.

Rameh then enclosed letter # 1 and # 2 mentioned in earlier chapters. Describing how despite being "selfless" in absorbing the pain I had caused him, he continued:

I will never wish her harm and I certainly would not wish the pain I have personally endured onto anyone, not even to an enemy as it constitutes a form of cruel and unusual punishment...resulting from the betrayal and infidelity of my ex-wife imprinted on each and every cell in my body and I doubt that it will ever disappear but until the day I meet our Creator. Although I truly forgave her (again) and offered her so many chances which no husband will ever do, she unfortunately considered my goodness to be a sign of weakness and helplessness....

She proceeded with her pathological lies, systemic cheating and emotional abuse despite all of her promises and pledges otherwise to her children myself and others. Indeed the shock of her infidelity was a harsh blow that brought me down to my knees at the peak of success and stability on many professional and familial fronts. Although I became physically ill having lost 68 pounds and been tormented from inside out by my so-called life partner, I am blessed to be able to be a unique person. I was not shattered and helpless...But as usual, selfish and vindictive beings do not understand it; on the contrary, they take advantage of it. Petty souls cannot look at the greatness of forgiveness; It is too difficult for their comprehension.

My ex-wife lacks tangible credibility in each and every way. She suffers severely from the "I" complex, the epitome of selfishness by which she neither clearly understood the sanctity of the institution of marriage nor the continuous sacrifice required for nourishing a family. It is all about her, no one else, as it has been all along. As for being a fit or an unfit mother, it is only our children who can offer the true, best and equitable judgment of such.

I am not surprised any longer buy anything that my ex-wife does or attempts to do. It is unrealistic to expect of her as an adulterer that she says anything contrary to having been miserable in the marriage, unhappy, unfulfilled, unsatisfied, unappreciated, or even blaming her own parents for not giving her the needed parental love during her childhood, or the immense physical abuse that she suffered on the hands of her then alcoholic and brutally vicious oldest brother, etc. That is the natural and trivial reaction adulterers display all in order to justify their actions. The easiest way out is to blame others, but it is her very own writings that will clearly show the flip-flop stances she has taken even when offering scaled apologies to her children, and naturally none to me.

It is my wish though that in much as my ex-wife had the audacity to indulge in another extra marital affair while clinging to her husband, and her arrogance of not showing genuine remorse upon exposing the affair, that she instead had possessed the integrity and courage to end this marriage prior to her getting involved with other men and gambling with my feelings and my life as well. Her offering of contradicting excuses to seek validation of the deviant path she has endeavored in has yet to reap her everlasting rewards. Here I was living with the woman "making love" to another man over a long period of time while "having sex" concurrently with the father of her children in a typical cover-up tactic, placing him at the risk of acquiring sexually transmitted diseases. Only God knows who her current lover was or has been conjugating with.....Luckily my AIDS and SDT test results with Kaiser turned out to be negative to my relief and that of my children as well.

Had it not been for her derogatory, utterly fallacious and slanderous statements made by the petitioner; My former wife Futoun Haddad, toward me and our children, and for myself being morally and legally obligated to refute her systemic lies; facts-twisting and manipulative venues, I would not even waste a second of my scarce and precious time to respond to her silly claims and baseless allegations. I remained silent for so long, but enough is enough. "In a war act like a warrior."

In a nutshell, she built her case seeking sympathy from the court on the futile basis that she is a victimized mother who is being deprived to see her children by her ex-husband. Her selfishness is transparent in this statement which she made to our daughter, Nour, on December 17, 2007: "I still would attempt to get a court order as outlined in my letter in the hopes I can get though a glimpse of an Anwar." ....By exerting common behavioral decency and self-respect on her part, I would have inherently concurred to her wishes that she mends fences with our son Anwar and our daughter Nour too in the healthiest and most fruitful way, as it would be agreed upon by them solely and without my intervention whatsoever; a stance that I have taken all along and one that will not change.

Had my ex-wife allowed ample time to play its positive role as an emotional buffer, and kept a low profile while enjoying her newly-found love and adopted lifestyle, without being coerced by others to exert undue pressure on both children so that they accept "by force" her ill manners and sickening behaviors, and had she refrained from badmouthing her children's father in order to justify her immoral and deviant actions; slandering a decent man whom despite her meager wishes both the children look up to and aspire to be like their father; she would have probably secured slightly better chances that at some juncture in the future, both children may possibly get to be on talking terms with her....

After investing21 years of my life and being loyal to this marriage working relentlessly to steer my front familial ship towards safe shores and securing a comfortable retirement, it was very difficult for me to let go of my family's unity.

How easily the above conviction has changed on her part! It is a real pity that my ex-wife's true and ugly colors had finally surfaced in a wide spectrum of filth and disgust. In an amateurish attempt to cover her shame, my ex-wife and her severely insecure family had stooped so low by attempting to attack my integrity (But all was in vain and to no avail) while amongst many other baseless accusations, they had insinuated that I am involved in a sickening incestuous relationship with my gem and gifted daughter Nour.

Let it be known that I hereby hold my ex-wife eternally responsible for sponsoring this ludicrous charge which was made by her infamous vengeful deranged and most wicked sister Jamileh, who left two threatening messages late in the evening of October 30, 2007 on both my mobile and home voicemails. Interestingly and deservedly so, my children referred to this woman as "Cruella De Vil." For the record my ex-wife was not on talking terms with her own sister for a solid 7 years due to her

arrogance and belligerence and it was only during my divorce
that they were reunited in misery.

Rameh then reminded the court of the divorce and custody agreement
that stated that the parents had joint custody and that the children had the
right to choose to live with either parent, though they had chosen to live
with him. He enclosed my motion rejecting all of the five requests including ceasing to discuss our affairs with my children. He stated that it was
his "basic and unalienable right" to "speak about his life experiences and
credible issues with anyone." He then argued why my son should not have
to visit with me stating:

> *Your Honor, based on the above stipulation there exists no issues*
> *open for mediation with my ex-wife. Under no circumstances*
> *whatsoever would I accept the five requests that she is seeking*
> *the court to grant her....especially ones that are clearly against*
> *the will of our almost sixteen-year-old son Anwar.... My ex-wife*
> *cannot manipulate the facts and expects the judicial system to*
> *force her son against his will to accept her sickening behavior*
> *as if nothing painful occurred in the last 20 months. Rather,*
> *had she given both children adequate time to rest and overcome*
> *her betrayal and abandonment, she would surely have better*
> *chances of mending fences with them.*
>
> *You're Honor, both children have been living with me 100% of*
> *the time since my ex-wife's departure. With the sole exception of*
> *the children's health insurance coverage offered by my ex-wife's*
> *employer, I take care of all their daily needs....In as much as the*
> *financial obligations have surmounted just to keep the same*
> *roof over my children so that they avoid the sufferings and*
> *assumptions associated with family break-ups and relocation,*
> *and in order to offer them a consistently loving, warm and*

nourishing home while being fed healthily and clothed properly, their well-being remains as my primary objective in life. I am certainly enjoying the manageable challenge to overcome such a natural paternal responsibility.

My world revolves around Nour and Anwar. They are my prince and princess. I am their subject and protector too, unconditionally so. I expect from them nothing in return but be given the opportunity to ensure their independence success and happiness. As envisioned, both children are doing very well overall after the transition—they remain healthy, vibrant, outgoing, content and ambitious.

Since that BIG day (Coincidentally) one day past our 21st wedding anniversary, my home has since become cleaner, more organized, classier and way more appealing than during my ex-wife's entire tenure. Tasteless impositions where uprooted and the house is now clutter- free, warmer, filled with serenity and is much more welcoming than ever to the three of us as well as to our beloved friends and guests. It was long overdue and about time that I got liberated from my ex-wife's bigotry, abuse, manipulation, drudgery, fakeness, lies, selfishness, individualism, and materialism. ...I cannot fathom the idea that for much longer than any human being can withstand, I remained tolerant of such a disloyal wife, accepting her immorality and foolishly continuing to have faith in her redemption against all certain odds. I guess it is true that love is blind—but it is no more for me.

Rameh then enclosed letter # 3 and told the story of how I accidentally had shared it with Patrick and later forwarded it to Nour. He used it to defend his claim that I should take *"full responsibility for the havoc she* caused her children and ultimately the family, while also asking both children not to ever share its contents with their father." Again, he claimed that Nour had shared my letter with him. He then moved to tell the story of the day I went to my son's high school to deliver a care-package just to show the court that my son had refused to see me; and also how his sister refused to hear my knocks on her bedroom window as I left that care-package at the house's front door. In that Manifesto he stated that he allowed the children to handle it as they saw fit but threatened to "press trespassing charges" if it were to happen again and to "seek a restraining order" against me. Herein again lies his manipulative tactic to alienate the children from me.

Rameh then enclosed letters # 7, 6, 5 and 4 in that order. He sought for the court to address my sister's accusations of incest although that was never brought up in any of the court proceedings. He added and I, too, had an "obligation; to explain what I meant when I wrote Nour, *"I fear for you in many ways that I dare not say, but I don't want to lose you, ever"* alleging that I inferred the same thing as did my sister. He ended his lengthy and irrelevant Manifesto with another long summary of the same but worth mentioning for the sake of gaining an understanding of the personality of an alienating father.

> *Your Honor, volumes can easily be written about this approximately 2 year long agonizing dilemma. From one side, it involves an illicit extramarital affair by then my wife who willingly and knowingly lead herself "once again" into the temptation of adultery based on her own misperceptions, sexual lust and eagerness all along to seek and try other men while attempting in the most ludicrous and conniving ways to retain me as the backup security blanket, in order to enjoy the cake and it's icing. During his latest affair, she was clearly direction-less for a while as she kept in her mind some assurance*

that at the end of the day she expected that I remain as "the" reliable husband and companion whom she had grown very accustomed to, one who would take her back and forgive her just in case her deviatory endeavors would not ripen. Naturally, my ex-wife enjoyed the promised perks of having an affair this time more so than her first attempt back in 1994 when our children were only five and two years old. It is a lot of fun to feel and live the euphoria, flair, thrill, heat, outings, concert-going, drinking, motel hopping, sexual adventures, newness, but certainly NOT the inherently-expected consequences of such an immoral act of course, only while married. From the children's side and mine, we all had to endure the intentionally-severe and inhumane infliction of hurt- with-malice that an ex-wife and supposedly a mother had blatantly caused upon a solidly-knit family. Amongst the countless people that she had lied to doing her affair, I concentrated only on the two children and myself. It is prudent that my rebuttal addresses all that needs to be addressed for now, and that enough light is shed on most of the relevant topics pertaining to the subject on hand for the time being.

Personally, I do not believe in a patriarchal (man-governed) society. Rather; I am an open-minded man who while holding high moral and ethical values, I do not simply stop short at behavioral mishaps of those closest to me, most importantly my ex-wife during a 21-year unison and seven years of courtship prior to that. I strongly believe that marriage is a sacred institution whereby both husband and wife shall remain loyal, loving and caring towards each other, and as pledged in church, should bond stronger in both health and sickness. Well, my marriage did not fit the above premise. I accepted and truly loved then my ex-wife "as is" with her goodness and frails, however she "supposedly and intermittently" loved me at some point in her life for what she expected me to be, not who I actually am. Ultimately this marital facade had to be dissolved after a long overdue unplugging process of its futile life support mechanism. I filed for divorce in July 2007, after living in hell for almost 2 years (Starting from the summer of 2005) in light of her latest disloyalty and long-held love affair with another man, Patrick, her coworker.... Hindsight is 20/20 and I now wish that I divorced this woman back in 1994 after her first extramarital affair with another coworker. In between those two notable affairs, my ex-wife also had other minor skirmishes excluding side flirtations with other fellow male coworkers. A rich resume by all means and a habitual trait of infidelity[1]!

A few final comments, Your Honor: in her reasoning for making this case, my ex-wife asserted that I injected hatred and bias in my children, stripped them from their emotions and independence and that I made our son to believe that she disgraced and shamed the family for having been involved with another man while married. There is nothing more evident that can prove otherwise than her own actions and writings; not to forget the children's own and true stances.

Also, it is direly important to note that my family was neither ashamed nor disgraced; rather, we stand tall and are very proud of ourselves. The shame and disgrace belong solely to her because wherever we go, the three of us are warmly received and get

---

1 Rameh's fallacious accusations of multiple affairs or flirtations never occurred. The 1994 "fling" was never consummated

acknowledged in the most loving and caring ways. She also stated that my son lives under my shadow which is perfectly true. However, it is a shadow of unmatched paternal love conjoined with absolute loyalty and dedication, along with the senses of offering both children the security and continuity that they need so much, while their independence and unique personalities remain solidly intact.

I now realize how unhappy I was with that women and how we did not share common attributes. I couldn't possibly be happier that another man came along to extract the worst moral liability off my life-ledger. She is his to keep, and I cannot be more content with my life at 44, ongoing. More importantly, both wonderful children, Nour and Anwar are writing their own stories-in- life, where all of the chapters in their books will be filled with nothing less than dignity, honor and pride.

"Reputation is valuable but character is priceless." This is my motto in life.

Your Honor I trust that you will only make the right decision to further protect my son from undue harm pursuant to the State of California family code 3020b.

It was an interesting coincidence that on the day Rameh filed his Manifesto, I had sent Anwar an e-mail including the phrases from the book: **Runaway Bunny** by Margaret Wise Brown.

I really loved this beautiful story because it shows how a mother will never let go of her child. However the bunny may attempt to run, mother bunny will be around the corner to catch him. If he becomes a fish in the deep ocean, he will soon be caught in her net; if he becomes an obscure rock high on a mountain, she will become the climber who will find him;

if he sails far away, she will be the wind that brings him to safe shores; and if, like a bird, he flies away from her, she will become the tree where he returns to nest.

What I wanted Anwar to conclude reading the book is that however he may try to escape my love, my love will always surround him. However he may pretend I do not exist and insist on living alone, my shadow will always follow him. However hard he may try to pluck me out of his heart, out of his mind and forget about our special moments, days, weeks, years... one day, he will realize how much he is loved and will find his way back into my arms.

And as all good stories finish with a happy ending, so does this one... Just as the bunny returns to the delight of his loving mother, so will my beautiful children, I thought, so will they. And for that day, I knew I would patiently wait, across time, distance, and through eternity. The petitions, rebuttals and court hearings proved that that is the best I could hope for. My victory was limited to only two visits with Anwar, for that was all that he would permit me during the eight months of proceedings.

The year that followed was marked by a heightened sense of loss. The palpable silence of the nights, interrupted only by my crying spells, was haunting me. I could not process the intensity of the pain or the likely eternal estrangement to come. Like an imposing old tree that had spread its roots so deeply into the soil, so grounded for so many years, I, in an instant was uprooted, chopped up and abandoned on the desolate earth to rot. Overnight, I went from being the loving dedicated mother of two amazing children, to a barren forgotten phantom who belonged to no one and from whom the seedlings had been blown in the wind settling in a very, very distant land. Many a night I suddenly woke up in sweats, feeling a heavy weight on my chest. I would run to the patio, open the door and take in the cool midnight breeze. I did not know what was happening to me in the beginning. But after two trips to the emergency room, I learned I was suffering from anxiety. The idea that I was sleeping and waking up child- less every day had taken a toll on my psyche, no matter how much I tried to fight the tide by keeping my routine, never skipping work or class and studying for long hours into the nights. As strong as I thought I was, I was slowly succumbing. I did not want to burden my dear and closest friends. They had their own lives, work, family problems to contend with, I knew.

But as always, God provided me with the blessing of true loving friends who attentively listened to my aching heart when it did not want to speak and wiped away my silent tears when my eyes did not want to weep. They pushed me every day never to lose hope and to keep faith that my children would wake up one day.

And at the end of each day, when the rest of the world had gone to sleep, relieved of the madness of a hurried life for a few hours, Patrick called every night to ask how my day had been, or how I was feeling. He listened to my sorrows, and consoled me with his loving words with the assurance that he would never let me go.

CHAPTER 11

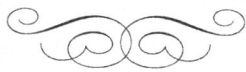

Trials & Tribulations

JULY 3, 2008

My heart could not endure the pain of removing their remembrance. The pictures stood over the entertainment set were they always had been, the albums stayed erect in the spare bedroom, and the baby pictures continued to adorn my humble home entrance. How was I to erase them from my life when they were my life? To do so would seal my fate, but I was just not ready to succumb. I continued to call Anwar since our visit the month before, but I kept getting the same message. "You have reached my broken cell phone because I went swimming with it. If you leave a message, I may get it…later; and I will call you back when I get my new phone."

My last try was at 10:15 p.m. July 1. He picked up. I was beyond belief, overwhelmed by hope and fear at the same time. I made my bold move and asked him to meet me for his birthday, July 2nd. To my heart's delight, he agreed to meet the day after. My heart jumped. For the first time, I felt Anwar was actually enthusiastic and responsive, though not engaging. I ended my conversation with *"Bhibbak (I love you), Mom."* In Lebanese culture, mother and child refer to each other as Mom. For the first time in a year, his voice, half child half adolescent rang in my heart, *"Wa'ana kamein (Me too)."* I cried, I laughed, I smiled, I screamed and I fell to my knees, and I prayed and thanked God for His precious gift. The next day, I called Anwar and sang *Sana Hilwah Ya Gameel*, a Happy Birthday tune they grew up hearing from me every year. He listened and acknowledged me with a *"Shukran (Thank you)."* My heart jumped, for I knew he loved me and that he would see me.

The next day we met at the church next to the house. I wrapped my arms around him, squeezed him hard and gave him a couple of kisses. He did not move. I knew I was in his heart, so I indulged in his smell, just as I did when I tucked him in bed as a child. I felt his skin for the first time in a year and caressed his soft cheek, still covered with baby fuzz, a few hairs were scattered around his chin. After all, my baby was only sixteen.

I struggled to hold back my tears and pretended to be cool so I would not turn him off. God guided me and we started talking. I presented his cake to him, lit a candle and asked him to make a wish. He had told me once how he would love to relocate to Whistler, Canada, in order to fulfill his passion for down-hill (DH) riding. I said, "Wish you would go to Canada," but I was hoping his wish was for us to reunite. I wasn't going to push myself onto him. What he wished for I did not know, but he blew the candle out. I had to deal with him with care not to pressure him in any way, to savor instead every precious moment however short our time together was.

I ate my piece, and he enjoyed his- chocolate cake, of course. He accepted the Japanese bread he liked and the gift I gave him, including the lucky $50.00 I had found one day while walking and had saved for a special day. And how more special could a day have been when it was his

16th birthday and I was celebrating it with him, although a day after? Still, he was anxious to leave claiming that Ryan, his friend, was in the house waiting for him. I tried not to get upset. After all, I did get to see his beautiful face and to touch his baby skin once more. I said goodbye and after two tries of saying "*Bhibbak, Mom,*" he said, once again, "*Wa'ana kamein.*" My heart danced with joy. I thanked God for the fifteen minutes we had together, and I drove back home. I did tell Anwar before leaving that I wanted to see him regularly but he said he had to think about it. That was the beginning to my journey through his heart; at least I hoped and prayed that it was.

I continued to call him once a week waiting for the right moment to ask him to meet me. In one of the conversations, he seemed irritated he could not leave the state without my permission to compete in a DH race. As a show of good will and to make him happy, I wrote the court allowing Rameh to remove him without my permission. I simply wanted Anwar to have fun and to enjoy his sport, his youth and his life, even without me in it. If it meant giving Rameh the pleasure of winning and breaking my will, as he wanted, so be it. I couldn't have cared less. I wanted Anwar to be the winner, and he was.

AUGUST 8, 2008

Trials and tribulations; that is how our relationship has been characterized. Since our last meeting, Anwar had gone through some emotional swings. He would agree to meet with me and then cancel, as though to tell me he was still defiant, still disapproved of my decision to divorce, still angry about my infidelity. He still had not accepted or forgiven me. This flip-flopping was crushing me. My heart was burdened with empty hopes, dashed time and time again until it became numb. The excitement to seeing him turned into fear of yet another disappointment, of another rejection, of another set-back.

Through it all, I could not give up, for I knew that in his heart, he loved me and wanted to see me. He had missed my tender touch and my soft caresses. But how is a teenager to assert himself and make clear he is not succumbing to his feelings? Surely he was not going to give me the pleasure of his company beyond the few precious moments that HE decided on— being the one in control. HE is to call the shots on how close our encounters are to bring us together, whether through conversation, engagement, touch, or addressing each other face to face. That, I understood, but the stab remained deep.

I tried again, and he agreed to meet me once more. The church became the default meeting location. As I patiently and excitedly waited, I saw him approach on his bicycle and was relieved that he was honoring his commitment. He said "Hi" and I gave him a big hug, touched his cheeks and his forehead and told him that I had missed him very much. He remained stiff, but that was fine with me. He was not hungry, yet still ate one Kibbeh and some Tzaziki and I did the same. We finally ate a small meal together… another hurdle crossed. Twenty minutes is all he gave me. When I begged him to stay longer, he did not hesitate to remind me that it was my own doing and that I needed to get used to it. He, after all, was already doing me a "lot of favors."

It was very hard for me to hear these words and to stay silent. I knew if I tried even slightly, it would turn him off, and who knows for how long? I was simply not going to take a chance. I sucked in my pride and sealed my lips. I touched his face again. He was growing more hair on his chin and side-burns. His baby fuzz was thickening above his well defined lips. He said he wanted to shave, and I smiled telling him how his father had little hairs like his but at a younger age. He then proudly flashed his wallet revealing his newly acquired driver's license. I tried to take a closer look, but he was quick to pull it back, as though he were hiding within it another picture, or something else he didn't want me to see.

I congratulated him on passing his test on the first try and asked him to sit next to me at the curb. He did, but he got restless quickly. His friend, who was waiting for him at the house, called him, and Anwar curiously asked if his father had gotten home. Not knowing what the answer was, I knew my time was up. Another short visit, another sweet and painful encounter. He asked me if he could leave. I smiled and said, "Of course you can," happy that he had asked. I knew he would not have stayed anyway if I had said he could not, but my heart was content that the years I spent relentlessly teaching him proper manners were not forgotten, at least not that time.

Anwar also told me he might go to Utah to compete in another race, but when I asked if I could join him, he said that I could not. "I'm going with Dad," he said. "Oh, maybe next time," I said. "I would love to watch you and to cheer you on." He took off on his bike and, as always, I said, "*Bhibbak, Mom.*" Again, as I repeated it, he said, "*Wa'ana kamein.*" When will I see him again? I wondered! I thanked God for the little time Anwar had given me that day and hoped that with each encounter, it would expand a little. I called him a week later unaware he was on his way to Utah. He gave me a short answer when I inquired about why he did not let me know that he was leaving the state as he knew to do. Irritated, he coldly responded, "I forgot." I said, "Have fun" and hung up. He will be back, and I will talk to him again, I thought to myself.

My dilemma was how to walk that thin line that was being blurred ever more with the passage of time. Slowly, I was losing the parental control and discipline that I had instilled in a young child who had turned into a very angry and emotionally conflicted teenager. I knew I was rapidly losing the little respect that I thought I was slowly regaining. I was very disappointed and hurt. I was helpless and at the mercy of his innocent mind, corrupted by a vengeful father intent on destroying every bond I had closely and lovingly knit with my son for over fifteen years.

Now when I call him again, I have to swallow my pride once more, put a big smile on my face and pretend that I am cool, reminding myself to be very careful in what I say and how I react. I knew I would be risking the same outcome in the future, now that he knew he could get away with it. Indeed, I must face the reality that he writes his own scripts, directs his own play and chooses his own characters and if I am in the cast, I must be fortunate. That is all I get and nothing more.

These trials and tribulations were manifest for both of us. Anwar would often ignore my phone calls or my voice messages. My e-mails were never responded to either. Sometimes he would behave disrespectfully, rudely and with anger, but at other times, he would be more restrained or even occasionally pleasant. His pendulum swings revealed the deep inner struggle that he refused to acknowledge. On one hand, I believed, he longed for a mother he loved very much, but on the other, he was constrained by an obligation of loyalty to a father who he believed was victimized beyond repair. Any show or sign of normalcy with me would mean that he had forgiven me for all the pain I had caused him and his father, in particular. He needed to affirm to his father that his unwavering support and commitment was to a family unit of three. No child should be put under such pressure.

Someone might argue that I should have let him go until time healed all wounds. I tried, but I could not; not only out of my arguably selfish motherly love, but also for fear that without my care and guidance, he would be damaged even more and, possibly, for a lifetime. Time proved me right, for what I knew was a direct result of this travesty. Anwar disclosed to me one day that his insomnia began as soon as I had left the house. And that was not the only detrimental health consequence he continues to suffer. Throughout my limited contact with him, I watched him transform from a very happy and loving teenager, to one always angry, pessimistic and bitter about life, caught in a past that continues to impose on and to control his future. God, however, never left him. He gave him a sport—DH riding—that dominated his spare time. Through it, he released a lot of that anger and stayed focused on school and on being a responsible teenager who never consumed drugs or alcohol. And I could not be prouder. My love for him and his sister and the values that I instilled in them were never lost, though his father took all the credit for my children's upbringing each time he posted on his social-media profile, claiming he was "the father and the mother."

Over time, Anwar became less and less interested in speaking with me or meeting me at all. My struggle to push forward became harder with each failed attempt to engage him. His excuses, rejection, or hurtful responses stirred anger, frustration and sadness within me so intense that I wanted to give up, cease all communication and attain closure, awaiting his awakening one day. But for every time I reached the bottom of the abyss, God lifted me up and kept me going. He knew that my children needed to be assured that I was never going to give up on them and let them go as they had clearly expressed, wittingly and unwittingly. And that is precisely what I did, starting with my first reunion and through all the long and agonizing thirteen years to follow.

As for Nour, she was an adult at the time of the divorce and has refused to communicate with me ever since. She was serious when she affirmed in her January 9, 2007 e-mail stating, *"Mother, if you go through with a divorce (that you'll have to fill out and sign ALL BY YOURSELF, by the way), we will not be on speaking terms. I can assure you of that. I will not want to see you. I will not want to have anything to do with somebody who can inflict so much unnecessary pain on another individual.*" I could not reach her however I tried. Through e-mails, letters, birthday and Christmas cards, phone calls and messages and texts, I tried the best I could, but her heart remained closed. She blocked my phone number several times, returned my letters unopened, and perhaps deleted all of my messages without listening to them. I had the luxury of being provided her mailing address only once, during her first year of college and only because I had to pay her tuition. To this day, I do not know where she lives or anything about her beyond what can be searched out by anyone on the internet.

One night, as I struggled to cope with my mood that shifted back and forth between hope and despair, I sat in front of my computer, sobbing, and I started typing. It was December 18, 2008, a few days after I had mailed Nour her birthday and Christmas cards enclosing a picture of me wearing a Christmas hat and a *Abayah* (Arabian tunic) and sitting next to the Christmas tree on a Persian rug pretending to smoke an *Argeeleh* (a Middle Eastern tobacco water pipe). The Christmas gifts lay meticulously wrapped under the tree as though a miracle might happen and somehow, I would be able to celebrate with them. I had just returned from having dinner with Sami and was trying to settle in for the night. What happened at that moment, I do not know.

I could never forget that night that my children assumed it was a result of my drunkenness. After all, it was not the first time they had accused me of it. I had had two glasses of wine with that dinner, which is not unusual for me when I go out. Whether or not the alcohol effect was magnified by the intense sharp pain and sorrow I was experiencing that evening, I do not know. But what spilled out would have convinced anyone that I was drunk. The truth is, under indescribable despondency, I started typing away faster than my hand or brain could transmit to a computer screen. It was a moment, I recall for the first time, that I had wanted to die; I truly did.

It was a moment that drove Patrick to call my sister, Jamileh, worried that I might commit suicide after I had called him crying until my breath gave out. My ranting e-mail to Nour had been riddled with misspelled words, improper grammar, and errors in punctuation and sentence structure as shown below. I was spilling out my feelings and thoughts which were gushing faster than my fingers could type. As expected, I never received a reply.

Is it really possible that you have been the amazing daughter whom I have nurtured with all my love and all my heart and who a year and a half later, still refuses to talk to me, to have me hold her in my arms and kiss her on the cheek and tell her how much I love her and hug her tightly and look at her beautiful face, I can only imagine for it has been so long since I have seen this beautiful face!!!!

It is just so difficult for me to imagine that there exists in this world, someone who can be so full for anger and hatred to choose to not speak or see the person they love most, their mother. I shall not fear any longer. I shall speak what I wanted for you not to hear. I have nothing to lose. I did not want to hurt you by telling you that you have been totally brain washed and manipulated by your father. But I will say that now. Now that I know that you will not speak to me until you discover the truth. I do not care anymore. I shall speak my mind, even if it hurts. I was trying to avoid hurting you because I did not want to reveal to you the selfishness of a man who can manipulate his own children to get their full support, to languish in their servitude. But what else do I have to fear? I have lost you alright and shall my mind. Is shall speak the pain that hovered and loomed over my lonely spirit for twenty-one years. I have no fear any longer for I have surrendered that you will not get back to me.... so be it. You will learn the truth one day, just as much as I did, though twenty-one years later and once you do, the truth shall reveal you and you will discover that you cannot go back.....I did, I suffered and paid the price, but I will not exchange that for anything, because there is nothing more beautiful than learning the truth.

Now. your father is hiding from you his newly discovered love and I am really happy for him. He may just understand what it means to have been in a disastrous relationship for so long and what it means, to really find your true sole-mate. He just was too selfish to risk you allegiance by telling you of his love connection, lest you may think he is abandoning you, the same way YOU wanted to believe I abandoned you.....falsely as it was and is. Yee, his newly discovered love may show him the truth. The truth that he not only deprived me from you so he can avenge my deserting him, but rather, the truth that he, in his selfishness and in his seeking your allegiance and pity, he deprived you of the motherly love that no child, young or old should be deprived of.

Let this be the proof that you shall never erase that you father, the wicked selfish son of the bitch that can say, I live by who I am and who will always be, the one, truthful person I dare to challenge the world with. I am who I am and I dare say it, unlike you, hiding behind the cloak of perfection and complacency. I fear no one because I have only God to fear. God loves me and I love Him. He gives me strength, and I carry on for the day, if it will ever come, that you will be back in my arms and be the child who I raised with nothing but pure, sincere and unconditional love that only a mother and only a mother can give. Your selfish arrogant conceited man, manipulative son of the bitch is a coward because he lives in deception and in manipulating others, he feels powerful and all mighty. But only God is all mighty and one day, when you are mature enough, you will understand, how I can type all these words with all the typos that I do, because I am a lousy typist and I am sweating with utmost distress and longing for the love I lost, the love of my children, the disgrace that you have covered me with, which, by the way, I have shed cause I have no shame. I live, I love and I continue to love with all of my heart. Not too many people in this world have this joy of loving so truthfully that they can be daring enough to express it in this terrible and totally distorted e-mail and that is full of typographical errors and crazy impromptus from the heart pouring honestly that they can only share with someone they hold so dear and so precious that who they hope will one day receive this crazy e-mail and read it over and over and over and over an over and over and realize how much they are loved and how much they are missed,........Oh Lore, when will You have mercy on me, (and when will you have mercy) on your pitiful self, Nooour

With another Holiday behind me, and the looming New Year, I regained my composure eventually as I always did. The Christmas gifts still lay idly under the tree just like my defeated spirit. How I had missed looking through my children's shimmering eyes in excitement every year as they patiently waited until Christmas Eve to unwrap their presents! I returned the gifts and sat down on December 30, 2008 to write my resolution, what I thought would be my final letter to my children; yet another attempt at closure and moving forward. I titled it just that,

My Final Letter To You

My Dear Beautiful Children:

Yes, this will be my last letter to you, so I hope you will read it now, and many times more in the future. I decided to write you one last time because the truth is that I can no longer accept your insults, total disregard for my suffering and the mockery you made out of my misery. The day has come for me to finally accept the reality that both of you have uprooted me and continue to live your lives as though I have never existed.

I shall not hope any longer. And I shall not wait for the day that you will have mercy, revere compassion and purge your souls in forgiveness because the wait serves no purpose without hope. It can only bring further despair and disappointment which I refuse to endure any longer. Take it as it is and do what you want with it, but I am telling you that I have paid the price for my decisions and have been punished all right. Still, you choose to punish me for eternity when I have so many times appealed to you, to your compassion and to the love of God that I thought once existed in your hearts...sadly, to no avail.

It is inconceivable for me to realize that hatred, callousness and love for vengeance have stripped you from your humanity; for a person without the capacity to forgive or love can be molded of flesh and blood but exists without a soul. Yee, who are you now? I never thought the day would come when you would no longer be part of my life, and I sit contemplating whether I truly knew you. So you have made your choice and are sticking to it. Lucky you are for "winning!" How elated must you really be to have inflicted the worst pain aside from death that anyone can inflict upon another!

Rejoice in your victory and jump in the lap of the leader of the pack, your wicked father—I dare say now—whose love for self, greed and egoism took him to the extreme measure of manipulating and brain-washing and intimidating his own children until he forced them into submission, unbeknownst to them. Yee, go ahead and tear this paper, delete this message, but know that it will be inscribed in your hearts and conscious forever, that this evil father of yours has lied, manipulated you, betrayed your love and trust just to gain your allegiance and sympathy. I know you will not believe me but I no longer worry about shielding you from the pain—of knowing that your own father is so conniving and selfish to do that to you—because I discovered that in pain, you gain strength and truth that make it worth enduring. You must experience pain to appreciate joy and deceit to understand truth.

It took me twenty-one years to discover your father's filth and gather enough strength to break away from his cloak. I am now free, but I pity you, for if I could be fooled for so long, and if all the people whom we have known over the years can be herded like sheep under his omnipotent devilish will like zombies in a trance, then I fear for you that you will forever be chained. I fear that your pride will cloud your judgment and reason to realize the truth. I fear that you will forever live in his shadow. Smart man he is indeed, too smart for his family's sake, but God is among us and He is watching. There is retribution in this life of ours and I pray that one day I am alive to witness your awakening.

Precious time, very precious time indeed has passed us by, not by my choice, but because of yours; never forget that. Try as I might, you refused to give me a chance. The day will come when you will look back at all the lost years, the youth, the moments that vanished without a trace and that you cannot ever retrieve, when you will really know how much I loved you and what I did to fight for you and that with each glimmer of hope, you shattered my heart and smiled in sheer delight. No letters, calls, e-mails, court orders and house and school surprise visits moved you or made you blink. You were so determined to punish and avenge your father's fake sorrow. Who was I to him but a slave who cleaned, cooked, raised my children, worked and produced a handsome pension, ironed his clothes and picked up his plate from before his nose without ever being appreciated, without any accommodation on his part for my needs which I long had stopped verbalizing after one disappointment after another, after realizing nothing was ever going to change and that your father was simply interested in what made HIM happy regardless of anyone's needs.

Where was he when you woke up crying at night and I comforted you? Where was he when you got sick and I cradled you, took you to the doctor and struggled to cope with your ailments? Where was he, Nour, when you learned your first word and read at 2.5 years of age or when you struck your first piano key at six? Where was he, Anwar and Nour, when you learned to ride your bicycles, write your first word and prepare your first book report, science project and presentations? Where was he, Nour, when you danced to the tunes of Tchaikovsky's "Nut Cracker" and Gene Kelly's "Singing In The Rain?" And where was he, Anwar, when you had your Karate meets? Where was he when you struggled to tune your violins and play duets? Where was he, Anwar, when you learned your DH riding and started to compete, pleading with him to take you, and your cries were ignored? And where was he when you went on your snow-boarding excursions or sold chocolate to get your prized Play Station? And where was he, Nour, when you needed to visit your friends in the valley, shop for clothes, books and accessories? And where exactly was he when you competed in spelling bees, swimming and speech? And where was he to comfort you and wipe your overflowing tears when life slapped you with its first lesson as your first best friend, Alice, deserted you for another?

Yee, you say, he was working hard to provide for us, day and night...as if spending few precious memorable moments with the family were too burdensome in his spare time; time that he, instead, chose to use to communicate with friends and others via e-mail locked for hours in his office...or time he spent making excuses to change oil in cars or things that could have been done by others but which he chose to do himself, not truly as he claimed to save the few dollars that he did, but to indulge in what only HE enjoyed doing regardless of the importance of spending family quality time.

And yes, lest I forget, remember the vacations that he made you feel miserable about? The ones I "dragged" you on so we could spend some quality family time together? Where was he? Yee, straggling along in resentment!

So, you think you won.... but you lost, my lovely children. Your loss is graver than mine for you will never have the joy of growing up like I did and proudly lifting your heads up high in honor because when you believe your mother is shamed, then you live in shame and people will look upon you in shame. As for me, I have none. Neither you, Nour, nor you, Anwar…not your father or the Lebanese community, here or in the homeland… not the entire world will make me live in shame. For I am proud and dignified. I have honor and integrity beyond your wildest imagination.

Never ever think for a second that I regret what I have done. My only regret is that I had a kind and soft heart that could not bear the consequences of your father's threats of killing himself unless I came back home. Yes, when we came from Las Vegas, I told him I needed a divorce; that I did not want to try to work things out because I had no interest and that our marriage was over. But he pushed and pushed and for fear for his safety, I succumbed and later paid the price for (my) betrayal. Again, when I left to live with Janice, he called a week later crying for me to come back and to take care of you because otherwise he was going to kill himself. How foolish I was to continue to be manipulated by this man.

How foolish I was for not calling the police when he beat me up and pushed me and cornered me in his office during Anwar's birthday party while you, Nour, heard my screams and my calls for help and turned your back. And when he threw me on the floor, pulled the gun and put it to my head before turning it to his, you kept the bedroom door shut only to pat him on the shoulder and in gratification say, "It's enough, you can leave her alone now." Had I stood my grounds and insisted on a divorce before I started my love affair with Patrick, perhaps you would have understood my years of misery I had lived with him just to provide you a stable home until I could no longer bear my solitude and until I could no longer fool myself that everything was all right just to make it to another day, another month, another year. Yee, that I do regret.

So you changed your telephone number, Nour, and you stopped answering your phone, Anwar. And your New Year resolution is to continue to avenge and punish. Yee, I pity your souls, for he who lives in anger will never be consoled. And he who lives cloaked in hatred cannot exalt in the beauty of forgiveness. And he who knows no love, will suffer in loneliness. And he who builds a wall will never have the courage to face reality, and he who lives in falsehood will never progress and will remain stranded and will never overcome life's many obstacles...and many you shall face one day, my beautiful children. Your path will always turn, and your destiny will unfold before you bringing goodness as well as despair, euphoric triumphs as well as utter humility.

In your solitude, I pray that you will remember me. And I pray that God gives you strength, courage, and above all, faith. I pray for Him to forgive your father, not only for what he has done to me, but for denying you the joy, peace, and warmth of your mother's unconditional love. And I pray for God to forgive you for not knowing what you have done, and for Him to give you compassion and love for humankind. Anger hurts the person who harbors it more than the one it is directed against. And I pray for Him to give you wisdom when you have no one to turn to.

Yee, the year has come to an end, and so onto another page in my life. Now I must rewrite a new chapter and bury the old ones and with them my sorrows, my fears, and my unfulfilled hopes.

Yee, it is my last letter to you so I must say, I love you, I love you and I love you into eternity. And while you have taken away all I have, you can never take away my love for you and nor my pride. I will continue to push forward and to enjoy with dignity and honor the remaining time I have in this beautiful world thankful for and proud of my accomplishments and to look forward to a brighter tomorrow, to new dreams and exciting adventures.

It is the end of the year, and I shall bid you adieu! Anwar, you no longer have to be annoyed when I call to tell you I love you or to come up with excuses to cut me off as though I were an intruder in your life. And Nour, you can stop mocking my distorted e-mails, sent in truth, but under extreme duress for not having heard your beautiful voice for over a year nor touched your skin for a year and a half. And you do not have to be revolted by my Christmas picture smoking the Argeeleh believing I am a drunken, pot-addicted whore who is out to fulfill herself. I am not who you want to believe I am. I am only a mother whose unconditional love will transcend all of your animosity, your ridicule, your accusations and your distorted perceptions of my character.

My lovely children, worry no more, for I will only call you on your birthdays and at Christmas, since my only link to your hearts is reminder to you that I am still here and that I have not deserted you. There will be no more unwrapped presents under my tree and no more birthday cards. Only two phone calls. And that is the end of my story. May God bless you and bring you back to Him!

With love always,
Mother

Every once in a while, I left voice messages and sent the children e-mails letting them know that I loved them more than anything in the world. While Anwar never responded or called me back, Nour retaliated by blocking my number. Sometimes, she forgot to renew her request to block it every 90 days as phone plans required then, so I would be lucky to leave messages. I discovered texting sometime in 2013, I believe, and would send some to Anwar now and then. He responded to a few, but the record could not be retrieved. What I was able to save were the ones since January 11, 2015. Birthdays, Mothers' Days, Christmases, came and went with neither day celebrated with my children. Nour transferred to the University of California at Los Angeles (UCLA) in 2009 where she studied Bio-Chemistry as a pre-medical student. I had no way of finding out her address, so I could not send her any letters or gifts. How I delivered Anwar's birthday and gift card for July 2008, I do not know and have no record of any reunion. But I do have a copy of my wishes to him:

My Sweet Son:

With every day that passes by, I think to myself what a sweet, young, handsome man you must have become...and I miss not being with you every moment to marvel at your growth and achievements, to smell and touch your skin and hold you tightly in my arms.

May this year bring you joy and love, and may you always encounter, but overcome, adversities so that you may gain the understanding of the beauty of life and love!

The rose in the picture personifies my love and fondness of you. I am holding it close to my heart as I would you.

I wish you days full of happiness and experiences enriched by wisdom in order to bring you peace and joy. But know that should darkness fall upon you, I will be there for you-no matter what-to console you, to support you and to carry you over the next hurdle.

I love you more than you can imagine.

Happy Birthday my lovely son....until we meet, hugs and kisses...

Love always,
Mother

AUGUST 14, 2009

And so a year had passed. My hope was running dry. Spare a couple of phone calls that Anwar decided to pick up, my e-mails were never acknowledged, including the one in which I specifically inquired if he was receiving them. I dared not tell him of my suspicion that his father had intercepted them all. I was not sure that Nour was getting hers either. I knew better than to make any accusation or to say anything negative.

But today was special. Time had stopped, and a new chapter in my life had opened, or so I hoped. Today, the painful past of not seeing or talking to Anwar did not matter. I had left it behind me, although uncertain what that moment would bring. My heart pounded as I anxiously waited to catch a glimpse of him...there, hiding in my car, shaded by the hanging tree branches above. Today, I was feeling all right. I had prayed for the entire week and I had asked God to give me the strength to withstand whatever He was going to reveal to me. I felt positive energy. After all, it was not a coincidence that Carolyn, my colleague, would share with me her son's senior pictures...Yes, those taken at the same photography studio where Nour had once had hers taken. It surely was God's way of guiding me towards this encounter.

"What a brilliant idea you gave me, Carolyn," I said, and set out to arrange my plan. I called the studio and found out that Anwar's photo session was for Friday, at 3:00. Could this happen for me, I thought? What if he does not show up? What if he sees me and pushes me away? What if he arrives and leaves before I can spot him? What if he ridicules me, shoves me aside and spits in my face in anger or utter disgust? Could I endure yet another wave of humiliation? Could I still gather enough strength to carry on hoping that he still loved me?

I thought about the encounter and decided I had nothing to lose. Pride and dignity are orphaned when one's eyes are locked into her child's. My soul awoke once again to the idea of marveling at the young handsome man I surely knew he had become. I arrived at 2:45 and toured the parking lot, but saw neither the van, nor the truck that I expected him to be driving. Good, I thought; he has not arrived. I waited and waited and when 3:05 rolled, I could not contain myself. I risked his seeing me, and I ventured outside looking for him. As I slowly approached the main lobby, I saw him in the waiting room...there in a chair awaiting his turn. I gasped and quickly retraced my steps hoping that he had not seen me. He had parked farther away, I discovered, and had driven Nour's car, the Passat. I saw him, I saw him, I cried in silence, swiftly wiping my tears away lest the arriving customers might see me.

I tied a bag of his favorite cookies around the driver's handle; my note taped on it: I love you *Habibi* (my love). *Sahtein* (Bon Appetit). Love, Mom), and hid by the adjacent parked car. The ten minutes I waited seemed like an eternity. I sat by the curb and put my head down so he would not see me as he slowly walked to his car. I heard him speaking to his friend on his cell phone. "What? Somebody left me my favorite cookies.….what the heck, they're from my mom!" I tapped his back as he opened the car door fearing that he would take off before I could talk to him. He turned and my new journey took another fork.

I embraced him. I choked with tears that told a story of pain and joy, suffering and gratification, sorrow and resilience, despair and hope. But above all, they rolled down my cheeks glimmering and sweet, for the moment had come; he was in my arms once again. He stood still, in shock but also in amazement. "How did you find out?" he asked astonishingly. I could not speak, but only smile. My hands wrapped around his still soft cheeks and my eyes shimmered. I gazed into the beauty of his pronounced eyebrows that framed his gorgeous Arabian eyes; those eyes that I had kissed ever since he had been a little boy telling him how the girls would be falling in love with them one day. I said that it was the only way that I could have seen him. If I had gone to the house, his father would have taken me to court. He said, "You should see how good I looked in a suit!" What was I to say? I was beside myself. I kept repeating, "You are soooo handsome, sooo handsome."

The moments were fleeting quickly. I didn't know what to ask or what to do. I worried that he could still shun me in his usual casual style from a year ago and tell me he had to go. To my amazement, he did not. He was receptive and appeared as though he was excited to see me. I wanted to believe he was. I told him this was the happiest day for me in a very long time. I asked him about his school, told him about a small fund I had saved for him, and asked about his plans. He wanted to become an environ-mental engineer…that, I knew, for he always cared about protecting our world. I was happy that he had bright goals, was still out of trouble, and in the company of good friends. Yes, he is still building bicycles, and saving money to buy a big truck. He had renewed his interest in dirt biking, had bought another dirt bike, and had already suffered a concussion. How thankful I was that my baby was still in one piece!

I don't know why he "assumed" I was "depressed and taking pills," which he stated as a matter of fact. I did not know other lies his father had told him. I did not know what impression he had of me or of how my life had been in the last two years. I dismissed his ideas, told him I was doing very well, moving on and pushing forward, going to work every day, attending school and getting straight A's and that I only had one semester left. To my surprise, he wanted to know what my major was, and I told him it was "political science, my life-long dream of twenty-one years." What was missing in my life, I said, was him and Nour. He said I had been in his life for the first fourteen years, and I sighed saying I would never want to change anything ....that I lived in the hope that I would be back in his life...even for one percent of it.

Then I asked why he stopped talking to me, picking up his phone or returning my messages. He said it was because of my letter...my infamous December 18 letter, I suppose, written in anguish; or perhaps my December 30 closure letter. I did not ask. He said that he still did not respect me and that I should expect to bear the consequences of my decision. He emphatically believed I was not sorry for what I had done, though I had said it many times before, verbally and in writing. Again, I responded that I was indeed sorry. He wanted me to apologize to his father, and I told him that his father didn't want to talk to me, and that my relationship with his father was separate from my relationship with him. Still, he was not going to give me the pleasure of dreaming that one day he would forgive me.

I pressed that the past was history, and while I was sorry for what I had done and that it was wrong, I could not change the past; that what we have is the future and that we can only look forward. I assured him that I was not asking him for his understanding, nor for his forgiveness or respect, knowing he was not ready. I was simply a mother who loved him more than anything. I pled with him to give me a second chance, to allow me back into his life if only by a phone call once a month. He agreed, and my heart was content.

I asked him if he had ever doubted my love for him, and he said, "No, I know you are a mother." I asked him about Nour. She was tutoring and, as expected, was performing exceptionally well in school. I am proud of both of them. I must have done something right!

I worried he would revert and not answer my calls as he did last December; or change his number as Nour had done, but he said he was not vengeful. I wanted to believe it, so I did. Confident that he had allowed me to call him once a month, I made another bold move and told him how happy it would make me feel to meet him for one of his races. He neither discouraged me, nor gave me his consent, and I left it at that.

He sat in the car as I squatted beside him rubbing his hand and arm. He has the thick Lebanese body hair now. I touched his cheeks, soft as silk, but as I slipped my fingers around his chin, I felt the scruffiness of adolescence. He is becoming a man indeed, a short five feet and six inches, by his own account.

I did not want to leave. I wanted time to stop. I wanted to touch him some more, tell him everything that was in my heart, hopelessly trying to capture in the stillness of the wind the two years that had vanished... but I knew my time was up. Fearing his dismissal and his wanting to leave hoping this fifteen- minute reunion would open his heart and allow me to enter, I knew I had to give him his space and to let him go. I wrapped my arms around him and squeezed him as though I would not see him again. This time, he wrapped a hesitant arm around my back. I said twice, "I love you" before he responded, "Me too." It would be the last time he said it. We parted, and I thanked God for his mercy.

Ten days later, hesitating for fear of a negative reaction, I called him anyway to ask him if he would be willing to meet me so we might choose the pictures from the proofs. I hoped he would agree, and if I were really lucky, he might have lunch with me. Quickly, my hopes were dashed. He did not pick up. I waited until the afternoon and called again. This time, he replied unenthusiastically. I knew the progress I had thought I made at our meeting was simply a meeting and no more. He had gone back to his old way, short and inpatient with me. He acknowledged receiving my message. I did not want to hear why he did not return the call, so I did not ask. I pressed to meet him, but he said that he had already gone to the photo studio and was not ordering any; that he did not like the pictures and that they were too expensive. In his usual manner, he quickly dismissed me by telling me "I have to wash the car," as though it were an urgent matter. I told him I would order some and send him one. He cynically replied, "Good luck with that." I did not know what to make of that.

I decided, this time, that I was not going to allow my fear of his irritation with me to put me in despair. I still wanted to indulge in the joy of having seen him and having held him in my arms....so I carried on. I shall wait the one month—September 14—to call him again hoping he would honor his commitment and answer. I shall have no expectations and no hope for anything further for now.

A handsome young man indeed. I ordered one 8x10 picture and two 5x7 which the clerk said Anwar had chosen for the yearbook. My hope was that he would still agree to meet me in order to get one, but he did not. The few phone calls that followed our last reunion only involved casual small talk. He wanted me to mail him the picture instead. Though I tried to argue that it might be damaged in the mail, the excuse did not entice him to agree to see me. Still, I was thankful that we were talking. I tried to respect our agreement of calling him only once every month, but I could not contain my feelings; and surely, he was irritated with my calls and did not hesitate to remind me to back off. I knew I was reliving the cycle of fear and uncertainty.

CHAPTER 12

"I Don't Want You In My Life"

OCTOBER 19, 2009

It was a week or two before Halloween. I had prepared Malfouf, one of Anwar's favorite dishes, and the day before, had picked up a cute small pumpkin. Anwar loved small things. How sweet it would be, I thought, if my baby would savor some Malfouf, wrapped in some garlic cloves, the way he liked it. I gathered some cookies, drew a smiley face on the pumpkin and signed it at the button with my love note, careful that his father would not see it should Anwar display the pumpkin in his room. I collected the goodies in a bag and hurried to drop it off at his High School before lunch time. To my disappointment, the school's policy was only to hold the material for pick up and not to call the student down. I knew if I had called, he would either not pick it up, or listen to my message at the end of the day after the school had disposed of the remaining bags. I took off to meet my friends for lunch in the Valley. On my way back, I hesitated, but ventured to drop off the care-package at the house. I assumed that

Rameh would be at work since it was around 3:30 p.m. and that Anwar would have returned home from school. Yet again, my journey came to an abrupt end here.

I arrived at the house and saw one of the cars parked outside and the garage door closed. I thought nothing of it since Rameh kept a few cars. I continued on to the door, rang the bell twice and without peeking through the stained glass door, I left the package on the door-mat and hurried back to my car. I drove past the cul-de-sac and decided to call Anwar to make sure he picked up the bag before his father came back from work. On the other end, Anwar's voice was angry and loud. "Why do you keep doing this to me? You cannot come to the house," he screamed. I did not understand why he would be so upset. "I was just leaving you a love-package, Mom, what have I done?" He hung up without an explanation. I was distraught, for once again, another positive gesture I had made was met with rebuke. Two hours later I knew why. A call came in from a Sheriff warning me not to trespass. I was shocked. The sheriff reminded me that he had called me a year before when I had gone to the house, knocked at Nour's window knowing she would still be asleep. It was Christmas break then, and I knew she would be home. I had tried to bring some compassion to her heart, but it was hard as a rock. She did not utter a word, but was sure to send me her worst e-mail saying how dare I "DEFILE" her property with my presence. I guess the anguish of that failed encounter had erased from my memory that call from the same Sheriff warning me to keep away or else!

The Sheriff, though seemingly amazed that Rameh would do such a thing, did what he had to do. He told me that it was Rameh, not Anwar who saw me and called him to warn me that trespassing charges would be filed if I continued to go onto the property. Still, I did not believe Rameh was home or that he saw me. My fear was that Anwar had called his father at work and reported the incident. And I asked myself if he could really hate me to that extent? I was beyond the pain, beyond disgust, beyond hopelessness and beyond despair. Still, I knew Anwar's soft heart and kindness. I knew within his soul that there was a tender loving young man who wanted to be with his mother and that he could not be vengeful enough to make that call. I knew he really wanted to enjoy the goodies that surely ended up in trash, lest his father got a hint that he cared to delight in my gesture.

It was close to 5:00 p.m. and suddenly, I was inspired to call Rameh at work to see if he was there in order to dispel any thoughts that he had seen me. I rushed to call and to my amazement when I asked to speak to him (pretending to be a customer), the receptionist apologized stating he had been laid off two months before. My worry turned to fear! How would my children survive. How would Nour continue with her schooling now that loans were hard to come by? How will Anwar deal with a depressed father, and how would he be able to attend the California State University at San Luis Obispo as he had hoped? With the economic downturn the country was undergoing and with Rameh's limited engineering skills, he probably would not find a job for months or years? He'd lose the house. Worse yet, my children's pride, and surely their father's, would prevent them from seeking my help.

I had no control over their destiny. My calls offering help went unanswered. When I called Nour, I was surprised that she had changed her phone number again, perhaps to prevent me from leaving her any message at all. I did some investigating and discovered her new number, but not surprisingly, she had blocked me again. The automatic message that I got from the operator after I called was, "This number has calling restrictions that have prevented this call."

NOVEMBER 14, 2009

I waited patiently for the month to pass so that I could have the privilege of calling Anwar as agreed. I sensed that he would not answer, and I was right. Nevertheless, I tried again within minutes and by the fourth call, he picked up, only to tell me angrily, "Don't ever call me again. I hate you. You ruin my life." He then hung up. I choked. I could not breathe. I had never imagined that he could ever utter such words. I was finished, done, totally done! I pulled to the side of the road, my head wrapped tightly in my arms, and my body shaking in my seat. I desperately dialed his number and left him a message. Three minutes passed. He rang. I muttered something, but he quickly interrupted, "Shut up and let me talk. I did not say I hate you. I said YOU make me hate you. I don't want you in my life...Every time you call, I fight with my family....because of you I cannot have a relationship." *Yee*, I quivered.

I was no longer family!

I tried to contain my profound sorrow and to say a few words, but in a broken voice, I am not sure what he could hear or wanted not to hear. "What was my crime? What sin have I committed giving you a love-package? I know how much you love Malfouf, and I wanted to show you how much I loved you," I cried. He calmed down a bit, enough for me to recover somewhat, though only for that moment. We talked for twenty-five minutes. He said that Nour had not spoken to him for two weeks because he had refused to heed her advice and block my number. And yes, his father was home the day I had delivered the package. He seems to always be there when I call. He said I must not call him several times in a row but was careful to add that when I call he couldn't answer. He never told me that his father would be there, what his father said or whether or not he felt uneasy or under pressure. I just knew. A knife cut through my heart!

My son was torn between his loyalty to his father and his love for his mother....and I wept. This time, not out of the deprivation of my son's love and of his absence in my life, but for his broken soul, for his anguish and his despair, too powerful and deep to rob him of his youth, to kill his spirit and to strip him of the joy of innocence and the normal teenage years of fun. What have I done? I wept, for I was lost and did not know what I could say or do. I did not want to cause him pain, yet I knew he needed me in his life. I wept with fear when he said that he did not care to live any longer. He tried to assure me that he valued life so much that he would never kill himself, but what is a mother to make of this? For the first time, I really wanted to let him go, but my instincts pulled me back. I am his mother and a mother will do what her love guides her to do. But I had no control over him. I knew I was helpless and could do nothing but to tell him—and to hope he believed me—that even though his mother had made a very huge mistake for which she was sorry, he was who he was, a wonderful soul; and that life was full of opportunities for him and that it was indeed beautiful.

I spoke of the past that is gone and of the future that is in our hands to create. I spoke of many a broken childhoods, and the dreams that sustained them, hope that brought them success and love that gave them joy. I spoke of not being able to change the past and that he could learn from my life—as I had learned from mine before him—and to make the choice to improve his. I said what I could in the little time we had. He only listened. I pleaded that he let me continue to call him once a month, but he would not commit. I ended my call with "I love you," but he hung up without a reply. I sensed that that was the end of our communication. I was right. But I continued to write as though they would read my life's journey one day:

My periodic calls are ignored, my messages remain unanswered, and I wonder if my birthday and Christmas cards are read or trashed. I am losing hope rapidly. Perhaps this is my coping mechanism for this loss. My faith sustains my existence but can no longer give me hope. I pray for more faith, patience, endurance and love of God, but I sit here in my loneliness thinking of a past long gone and a future devoid of the love of my life. I am uprooted. My life is no longer mine. I carry on because I must. I love life, and I love to live.

The emptiness is so vast and the only way I can deal with it is to avoid thinking of it. I fill the void with things I enjoy to do and Patrick's love fuels me. But with every passing moment, my soul burns. Images of my beautiful children run wild in my memories; their childhood laughter, their cries, their joy, their fears, their struggles...the kisses I laid upon their soft cheeks, their hair, their smell, their walk, their voices, their music, their skin, their eyes, yes, their eyes....moments when we once were a family; they all haunt me and possess me. Pictures, are all I have and only from long ago. How do they look, I wonder? My old neighbor tells me Nour is so pretty, still focused, still determined, still polite and friendly. And Anwar still hangs out with his friends, fixing bikes, stays out of trouble and away from drugs and smoking. He repaired a broken bike for a young child who lives in a trailer. His mother had lost her job. He refused to collect any money for his services, said my neighbor. I am touched by his kindness.

Perhaps, one day, these qualities that would make any mother proud will remind you of who you are and who has imparted to you values that have shaped you into the young man and woman you have become. Perhaps one day you will realize that even though I have wronged you, I pled for your forgiveness and did not leave a single stone unturned to try to reach your heart and ask for your mercy. I waited and waited and waited for you to let me in. And with every attempt, you trampled upon my soul and reminded me of my eternal sentence. Perhaps I should renew my hope rather than my fear now that Nour has unblocked my number and kept it so, even after the long message I left her on February 19, 2010. Perhaps I should be thankful that Anwar has never blocked my number and should pretend that he continues to listen to (or maybe even save) my messages for when he is down and low so that he is reminded of how much he is loved. I am still waiting for the day to come when I embrace you once more. But if this day comes too late, I pray that on my death bed, you will tell me that you have forgiven me and that you love me for who I am, not for who you have wanted me to be.

MARCH 2, 2010

I was home planning my two-month-trip with Patrick to celebrate my graduation when, suddenly, I thought to drive up to Anwar's school and leave another care-package. I did not have much time to think about planning this surprise, so I started to put together some treats-Kibbeh, Cadbury, Dove bar, four Dove hearts and a chocolate sandwich cookie with my love note taped to it. I got there around lunch time and spotted his truck. Assuming he would not pick up the bag at school if I left him a message, I parked my car close to his hoping he drove home for lunch. I was right. First I saw his friend approach, but Anwar was not with him. I tried to hide my face, in case he had warned him, but seconds later, I saw Anwar walking up to the truck. I rushed to meet him, the bag in hand. He was looking down and alone.

I got close and said *"Hi Hilo* (handsome!)." He looked up, then down and without hesitating for a second angrily scolded me saying, "Get away from me now" and proceeded to open the door. I told him I was not going to hug him so as not to embarrass him in front of his friends and asked him if I could give him the bag. He said, "No" and got into the truck. I quickly threw the bag in the truck bed as he drove off. I sensed his silent and deep anger and perhaps resentment or even hatred. Another failed gesture, another rejection, a rude reminder of the distance between us is forever becoming larger. Can time, maturity, sense of belonging, forgiveness or anything, if anything even exists, bridge this gap? I am losing hope as I see him drifting away and completely disengaged from his roots. Unlike my last encounter, I sensed he resented seeing me. He must really want me out of his life. I swallowed and waited for a few minutes to collect myself.

A few minutes later, I called and left him a tearful message, happy that I had seen him, but wondering why he had reacted the way he did. I described what was in the bag; that it had his favorite treats in it, and that I hoped he would enjoy them and not throw everything away. A package prepared with love, I muttered. I wanted him to know of the special university fund I had reserved to help him with tuition and living expenses. I suppose he was not interested then and is not interested now. I told him it was a pleasure to have seen him and that he looked great. That was all. I went home and documented my brief encounter:

I don't know how to feel or what to think. Perhaps he was still angry over my message from a week ago scolding him about his D in biology. In that message, I was tough and showed disappointment, but also concern for his well-being and future. But a day later I left a second message apologizing and offering tutoring, just as I did a year ago when he was struggling in math. Then, even with our precarious relationship, he still cared enough to leave me a message to assure me that he had brought up his grade to a B.

I was always the disciplinarian at home; that is true, but always tempered my toughness with palpable love that I know he had felt deeply. I had high expectations, and I always pushed him to reach his full potential. But at the same time, he knew that I would accept his performance as long as he gave it his best. As a parent, I believed it was my responsibility to instill in my children the value of a good education, of scholarship, of perseverance and of moral, ethical behavior. I also believe that it is this foundation, layered with abundant sweet love and affection that gave my children the confidence and determination to succeed later in life.

I do not know for how long he is going to carry this burden of anger and the heavy weight of an unforgiving heart. I want to help him because I feel he is deeply troubled, but don't know how. I have tried every way I knew. I continue to follow my instinct because I don't know of any other way to get through to him. God has not talked to me, and I am not sure if what I am doing are His wishes. I wish God would reveal to me the proper path that would lead me to my son without setting him off and throwing me back, farther away from him. So far, everything I have done has backfired, yet I continue to repeat what I know in my heart is what I should do.

Perhaps I should listen to my mind, harden my heart, and pretend I don't care. They are not around. Leave them totally alone, without calls, without cards, without I love yous and without love-packages. But I am so scared that they would think I truly deserted them in order to pursue my life; that I did not care about them. Anwar tells me that my presence in his life makes him miserable. But somehow, I am not convinced and feel he still needs to know that I am here to love him and to embrace him when he is ready. I would never want my children to forget that they have a mother waiting for the day that they will accept her and bring her back into their lives. But if somehow I really believed it would truly serve them best to leave them totally alone, I would make the sacrifice. How will I know, God, how? Please help me. I just want to do what is in the best interest of my children, even if it means my heart will be forever broken. I am not sure I have an answer to this vexing question. I pray for wisdom, for mercy, for love and understanding. God, I pray for You to help me, to take my hand and to lead my way, please.

I called Nour two days later; my number was blocked! Perhaps that was God answering my prayer to keep going and never give up. I was hurt but remained determined. I had just received this simple but true life lesson in an email from a friend titled **"Beautiful Orchids and Thoughts."** I decided to forward it to Nour in the hope that she might be inspired somehow and to affirm that no matter her defiance, rejection, or the hatred that had filled her heart, my love is unbending, and my fortitude unwavering. As usual, I did not receive any response. I did not expect any.

Nour Dearest:

It really saddened me yesterday when I called you and discovered that you had blocked my number, yet again. Nothing surprised me as I knew it was coming. I was not going to leave you a message anyway—as I had indicated earlier—lest I bother you. I was just hoping you had decided to give me access. I was wrong. You continue to condemn me for eternity and rejoice in knowing I am still serving my sentence.

Perhaps you will not read this e-mail. Perhaps you have already blocked my e-mail address, and I just don't know it. If you have not, I am sure you will now. But remember, you have to renew your request to block my telephone number every 90-days, else expect another love-you message from me. Perhaps you will change your number once again. Perhaps you will file charges against me. Go ahead; do what you please. I will not give up on you and neither will I stop trying to reach your heart in any way I can.

You are my daughter, and I love you beyond measure. It is not about winning or losing, scoring points, vengeance, retribution or shame. Love knows none of that. It just leaves you humbled by its power and in awe for its beauty. It conquers all anger and bitterness. It teaches you that forgiveness is a virtue that

*enriches the soul, calms your spirit and lets you live in peace
with yourself and make peace with whomever means anything
to you. It gives you hope, and thus, life.*

*This morning, as I read this beautiful inspirational e-mail,
I thought about you and Anwar and wanted to share these
precious thoughts with you. I hope you enjoy them.*

Take care of yourself and be well, my beautiful!

Love always,
Mother xxxxoooo

MAY 21, 2010

I had returned from a two-month vacation during which I had purposely
not attempted to contact my children. I wondered if they had even cared
that they had not heard from me. They did not. I mustered some courage
and decided to call Nour from my work phone hoping she would answer,
not recognizing the number. She did. My heart jumped and I instinctively
said, "I love you, Mom." She responded as if not to embarrass herself in
front of the laughing ladies I could hear in the background, "Hello?" I
repeated, "I love you, Mom." She hung up, perhaps leading the ladies to
think it was a mistaken caller or a call that was disconnected.

I decided I would try the same trick with Anwar. It worked. Annoyed,
he grumbled, "Oh, no, you know I don't want to talk to you. Why do you
keep calling?" He said he could not talk to me because he was driving and,
in fact, was picking his father up from the hospital after a tonsillectomy.
"Not that you care," he added. I am not sure why he shared that information with me, but I pleaded with him not to hang up. I simply wanted to
give him the chocolate (*Chocoprince*) that I had brought with me from

Lebanon. I knew he loved these treats, and I wanted him to know that I was thinking about him. He said he was not going to meet me, but that I could drop them off at school. I told him I wanted to go to his graduation. He said he did not care if I attended or not. The conversation was brief but relatively pleasant.

That afternoon, driving home, I decided to call him again and inquire about the school he chose to enroll in. He refused to give me the name lest I embarrass him and show up uninvited as I had in High School, he explained. I then asked if he was staying home or going elsewhere and he responded, "Outside." I was relieved to learn that he may finally be freed from his father's nooses. I reminded him of the 529 fund that could only be used towards tuition or school and living expenses. He said he was trying to obtain a scholarship, seemingly uninterested in my help.

The next day, I dropped my care-package at his High School, packed with chocolate *(Chocoprince, Maltesers, Lion Bar and Mars*-all his favorite), Malfouf, his framed Senior year picture, another picture of me, an inspirational book of quotes to carry young graduates through the arduous journey of life ahead and a couple of spiritual bookmarks given to me by a fine priest in Lebanon. I wanted him to remember God and hoped he would bring Him back into his life. I inserted a note to celebrate his upcoming graduation:

Habibi, El-Hilo (My love, my handsome), Anwar:

Hope you will enjoy the few treats and the Malfouf with lots of garlic, just the way you like it. Thank you for speaking with me the other day; you delighted me.

You have become a very handsome young man; Pictures don't lie, but above all, you are resilient and compassionate. Your determination and kindness will take you far, where you will meet your challenges, battle them, and eventually overcome all obstacles.

I know this because in your tender years you have endured what many people do not encounter in a lifetime. I also know this because I raised you and gave you love and tenderness. One day you will discover that that is all you need.

Live life, absorb every moment. Time is fleeting, so go ahead and embrace your journey with a smile and welcome the hurdles that will only make you stronger; and appreciate every day we have on this beautiful earth. Leave your mark!

I know you will do exceptionally well in whatever school you choose to enroll in. Hope I can visit you there one day and embrace you once more.

Love always,
Mother

A few days later, I called him several times asking him to give me a ticket to his graduation, but he never returned my calls. I managed to obtain one, however, but not without involving the school counselor, the principal, the superintendent, the school board and my congressman. I had argued that since he was a minor, I was still my son's guardian and that the school should not grant him the right to decide on whom or not to invite. Upon parental objection (from Rameh), I argued that a mother should not be deprived of such a special occasion regardless of the familial issues. My perseverance finally paid off, and I was handed a ticket, but not without a warning that the terms of the restraining order remained in effect while I was on campus. I don't know why Anwar had told the principal that there was such an order when there was none. Perhaps his father had planted the idea in his head so that he could deprive me the pleasure of watching my son on this momentous occasion. No, this time, my son was going to be the winner.

CHAPTER 13

Graduation Day

JUNE 11, 2010

Proudly they marched in their black robes, caps and yellow tassels crowning their heads. Far, sitting in the bleachers, I pointed my binoculars and saw Anwar's grand entrance, a wide smile revealing his joy. I do not remember him ever being so excited, smiling throughout the ceremony and making small talk with a pretty young lady in the seat next to his. The only time he broke his smile was when he recognized the number after I had called to wish him well and tell him I was hoping to meet him at the Quad. He did not answer, of course. Still, it filled my heart with joy to see my young man embark upon his journey, perhaps along with a cute companion, I made believe.

Every time I thought he was looking my way, I waived, hoping that he saw me. I think that he did not. He was frequently looking at the other side of the bleachers, perhaps toward where his father and Nour sat. For the first time in three years, my eyes feasted for two hours—though gazing through a lens—content he would not leave. For that time, he was all mine.

And I indulged myself, laying down the binoculars for brief seconds to rest my stiff arm. Life without my children, you see, tosses me every day with miserable reminders of never hoping for a reunion. I was lucky to be able to take some pictures, though they are blurry due to the distance.

After the ceremony, I slowly proceeded to the Quad. I did not know what to expect or if I would even be able to see him. A fine gathering place, indeed. Parents hugging and kissing their children while friends and family took memorable pictures. Years of labor had finally paid off, but certainly not without unconditional parental love and endless nurturing. I, on the other hand, was a wandering vagabond, belonging to no one, with no family to celebrate, with no child to hug, or to pose with, or to pour my love over.

I searched helplessly for him, but it was not he whom I saw. Posing for a picture with a beautiful wide smile was my child....my beautiful child.... my baby girl. Delighted to wear her brother's graduation attire and to pose for her father and his girlfriend, her moment of fame abruptly ended as I slowly approached, wild-eyed, and speechless. For the few seconds before she and her father noticed me, she, too, was mine. I marveled at this young woman who seemed to have recreated her history, was absorbing a surreal life, inventing stories of fairy tales and gardens full of every fruit one can desire...a life with no obstacles, a world of fantasy where she took center stage, her father her idol, her confidante, her god; her brother her toy; her father's girlfriend her mother. I sensed that I had been replaced. I was struck by despair. My daughter had truly erased me from her life, from existence. Yes, she is happy, it seems, but blind.

Her eyes landed on mine, and immediately she picked up her pace, angrily repeating, "Don't touch me; don't you dare touch me." I rushed up behind her and gently laid my hands on her shoulder, but she was not ready to allow an intruder to burst the utopian bubble she had created for herself. She carried on briskly, her father and his girlfriend rushing behind her. There, I stood, in shock and awe in utter silence, until they slipped out of the gate, her father turning around and giving me a brazenly stern look. My legs started to tremble, and my breath broke with silent tears. I sat on a bench in order to collect myself without truly absorbing what had just happened.

Time was running out. I had to continue to search for Anwar and to get a closer look at him. God took pity on me. After wandering for a few minutes, I saw him chatting with some friends. There I stood, smiling. His eyes met mine. He took off. I followed him as he tried to leave the campus saying, "Please, I just want to give you your gift." After a few steps, I caught up with him. He stopped. I extended my hand to give him his gift. His eyes stared at me in silence. He took his gift: a gift-card and a $100 bill upon which I had inscribed in Arabic the graduation date and the words "Congratulations, Anwar, my love, Your Mother." I smiled at him and proudly said, "*Mabrook* (Congratulations)." His eyes were tender as if they were telling me to hang on a little longer, but I dared not push it. My time was up. I said, "I love you" and I walked away.

I returned alone, as I always do, in tears, neither from sorrow nor from happiness. For the first time, I was out of touch with my own feelings. Was it pain, or joy, or nothing? I could not tell....so I wrote:

My life will carry on for another day, for another year, for another decade …alone until death releases me from this misery. And I pity you, Nour. For your callousness, your stubbornness, your convictions, pride and your vindictiveness, I pity you my child. A person without mercy is condemned for eternity and will never realize the joy reached by forgiveness. My child, I pray that one day, you will bring God back into your life and will let Him wash your hatred and cleanse your spirit. The devil must have possessed you. I pray for your release.

I downloaded all the graduation pictures I had taken of this milestone and e-mailed them to Anwar with these warm thoughts:

How proud I am of you! How delighted I was to watch you walk down the aisle and to be with you for two whole hours. I don't remember ever seeing you so happy. You were smiling all the way through, from the time of your grand entrance and to the tossing of the cap. And my heart cheered for you in absolute delight and silence. A wide gratifying smile never left my face. I waved at you each time you looked my way, but I do not think you saw me, or perhaps you pretended not to see me. It doesn't matter, for I was there. I know deep in your heart you wanted me to be there. That is good enough for me.

What a handsome young man you have become. Yet, your tender, warm eyes still revealed my precious, sweet baby boy. Look at you; you are a man now. You have earned your diploma with hard work and perseverance, and for that, you deserve great praise. I longed to wrap my arms around you and to kiss your still soft cheeks and to smell your sweetness...I wanted to have a picture with you like the rest of the parents, gathered to celebrate their children's achievements, but another rejection would have been too great to bear during such a momentous occasion. I refused to let Nour's harsh words and her pushing me aside spoil a very proud moment. I smiled, congratulated you and chose to walk away. I wanted to make believe that your eyes said it all and that you were still happy to see me. Thank you for accepting my humble gift.

Life will show another chapter to you, full of opportunities—if you learn not to ignore them—among many obstacles, setbacks and disappointments. I hope that as you go through these passing challenges, that you realize that they, too, shall come to pass and that through them, you will appreciate the joyous moments that will surely follow. In your low moments—and we all have them—I hope you remember that you can always count on me to be there for you, through thick and thin, to support and comfort you and to assure you that, yes, they too, shall pass.

I have no doubt you will be a successful man, a good citizen, and a proud father one day. And I hope you will let me be there to celebrate with you the bright future that surely awaits you. My handsome boy, my young man, my beautiful baby, enjoy these amazing pictures, though captured from afar and not from a great camera.

Love you always,
Mother

AUGUST 17, 2010

An ordinary day at work but for a fax from Anwar instructing me to pay his school fees from his 529 Fund, due the following day. Clearly, by the bold font, by the meticulous detailed information regarding his school ID, the fund account and the telephone numbers, the Registrar's address where to send the money and my name hand-written on the upper corner, Rameh's handprints were all over this fax. I knew Rameh's style of communication very well. I knew it was his way of manipulating my son so that he could get the money as if I were unwilling to pay it. Yet, Anwar denied his father's complicity, and I let it pass.

I was really surprised that Anwar would even consider my help. After all, I had offered it many times in the past, informing him of the fund that had grown handsomely, but he always said that was applying for scholarships. Nevertheless, I called and left him a message regarding the complexity of processing the transfer and of the time issues of the transaction. He returned a rude message stating that the money was easy to send because he had called customer service and was told that they simply needed my approval "So why don't you get on that for me!" he added.

I called back angry at his disrespect, and in a loud assertive voice I started to explain to him that an electronic transfer still took five days, but he interrupted and told me to shut up; that it was his money, and I needed to pay it. I was furious, and I responded accordingly. I stated I had used most of the money paying bills since he had declined my assistance. He questioned how I could spend his college fund since it was "his" money. I explained that it was not HIS money (His father had stopped contributing since our divorce). The account had carried a small balance at the time. It had been supported by both of our contributions. But it was my contribution during the following three years that had built it up to a much larger amount. He backed off. Anwar had never been so disrespectful.

I questioned his scholarship status, and he said that he had been an idiot for not applying. I said, "Live and learn. You'll have to support yourself and get a job or do whatever your sister is doing." He said, "Yes, I know." Still, I told him that I had transferred enough to pay for his fees and for the first month in the dormitory. He said all he needed was for me to pay a small amount for the registration that was due. He did not say how he was expecting to pay for the rest, and I did not ask. Nevertheless, he thanked me, and we hung up. Shortly after, he called to inquire about the details of the transaction. He seemed calmer and somewhat contrite. I told him I would send him an e-mail and repeated my willingness to continue to help him, even with the fund depleted, but not without a meeting where we could sit and discuss the details of how that might be accomplished. A fifteen percent salary cut as a furloughed state employee loomed over me.

Otherwise, I added, he was on his own because "Frankly, I am done," I said. I sent him a detailed e-mail a few hours later, but did not get a response. I gathered that he thought that I was making my contribution contingent upon his reconnecting with me, which was not the case at all.

A few days passed before I called and left him a message to let him know of my willingness to help with his relocation and in the purchase of some items that he still may need.

AUGUST 23, 2010

What happened that day, I thought, might just be the turning point in this arduous and painful journey, though I did not hold any hope. I was simply content; and for the first time in three years, I felt at peace. Early that afternoon, I returned to my desk and noticed that a message had been left on my phone. As I listened to it, tears trickled down my cheek. I did not know what to think other than I felt composed and at peace.

In a sweet voice and a respectful tone, Anwar told me that he had just gotten my message and that although he needed books, he would get them once on campus. He had all he needed. He thanked me for my gesture and actually apologized for saying "shut up." He said he should not have said that and that perhaps his adrenaline had been the culprit. I called him the same evening, but as usual, he did not answer. Still, I thanked him for his apology; said that I accepted it and repeated my wish to meet him for lunch before he went off to school in order to give him a couple of items for his stay and to bid him farewell. He never returned my call.

School began the following Monday. I took it that he was still not ready to see me or perhaps that he did not want me to think that by apologizing he was opening a door to future communication. I did not know how to interpret this unusual and totally unexpected behavior. I could only reason that God, having heard my pleas for a sign proving His existence, responded the way He always knows best. The time had not yet come. I must endure, I wrote.

CHAPTER 14

Was It Worth It?

I was already convinced that Anwar was not going to contact me for financial help. I had learned a couple of weeks earlier that the October tuition, due the first of the month, had been paid via credit card. I could only surmise that either his father had gotten a job and decided to help him or else, Anwar used his own credit card and was expecting to receive a loan in order to pay it back, through payment from some employment source. Another opportunity lost, though that may have been God's way of teaching him some responsibility, I must believe.

It was Sunday. I had prepared another care-package with love and with special attention. A blanket, fuzzy blue and warm, lay on one side. I wished when he wrapped it around his shoulders, that he would remember my warm and cuddly embraces. I wanted him to remember how he always looked forward to them every morning and at night as a young boy as he cuddled in bed with me for the few moments that he seemed never to have enough of. How I mourn those precious moments when instead of keeping him with me as long as he felt like it, I "kicked" him out of bed succumbing to exhaustion from long work days and evenings. What is lost is lost…if I had only known!

The Runaway Bunny book lay under all that, next to a wide variety of chocolates and cookies. Perhaps, this time, he will read it and realize that he is not alone; that no matter how distant, physically or emotionally, I am always close to him, waiting for his return. Behind the blanket I placed my "Was It Worth It" letter under the blanket hoping he would read it and not share it with his sister—at least not yet— and certainly not with his father.

It had been earlier in the month when I finally confronted my entire life, but most important, my entire relationship with Rameh. This had come after a brief phone call to my son from a public phone. I had hoped in not recognizing the number, he would answer and we could talk a little. After all, he was leaving in three weeks to become a university student. As I had expected, he hung up on me but not before asking me a profound question; one I contemplated for three years. He asked, "I just have one thing to say: WAS IT WORTH IT?"

I thought and thought about his question, and I decided that it was time that I told the story of my life; one that would tell the truth that I ran away from for thirty years. By doing it, I had hoped it would answer Anwar's question and would be a testimonial for his sister as well when she felt ready to read it. Writing my story was laborious. I kept changing the words, adding phrases and paragraphs, and making revisions until I felt every significant issue that I needed to address had indeed been addressed and that every word I used carried the exact meaning I had intended for it to carry. But how could you write forty-three years of your life in five pages? Even though I knew that my children might not be able to comprehend the contents fully until years later, I was still compelled to answer Anwar's question, so I did, as succinctly as I could in my letter entitled:

"Was It Worth It?"

My lovely son:

I called you and was pleased that you answered. Before you hung up on me while I pleaded with you to stay on, I had thought I heard you ask, "Was it worth it?" First, I thought I heard you say, "It wasn't worth it!" meaning that I went through the trouble of using a public phone so my number would not be recognized, only to have you hang up on me seconds later. But as I thought about it, I believe you asked a question that perhaps you have wanted to know the answer to for the last three years. And I have felt compelled to answer.

As I sit here drafting this letter, I am petrified. My fear is that I may not be able to express myself well enough to make you understand what I mean by my answer. The more I think of your question, the more complex the response becomes. Nevertheless, I owe you a response. It was interesting that you asked since for a while I have wanted to document what may in the end be the answer. I sincerely wish that whichever way you understand or interpret this letter, that you do not judge me, but only judge my actions. I neither wish for this letter to be understood as a means through which I am seeking to exonerate myself, justify my betrayal of your father and of you or to make you accept and forgive me for it. It does NOT serve to portray me—as accused— as "some sort of oppressed angelic figure who has broken free from the chains of domesticity," as Nour had described me.

It is also my sincere wish that when you start reading this letter, that you do not delete it if any of its contents upset you. I would hope that, instead, you would close and save it so as to return to it another day. Someday, I know that you will want to read every phrase in order to learn the truth. As you read on, please remember that this is MY story and MY experience with your father. It is a story of a relationship between two adults, not to be taken as a reflection of your own distinct relationship with him, and neither as a clever way to create a wedge between you two or to smear his character in any way. In composing its chapters, though, I understand that some of what I state may be misunderstood. I only ask that you recognize that that is not my intention, but more important, that there is nothing your father did or did not do that excuses or justifies my infidelity. He did not deserve to be betrayed and neither did you. No one does.

It is not my intention to play the victim, or to look for your sympathy. I simply wish my story to be understood for what it is, as truthful, from the heart and strictly as my own. You know that I cannot undo the past, wipe the tears, forget the pain, or erase the anguish. The memories will haunt us all for eternity, I know. This letter will not change that. It is simply there for you if you ever become interested to know about what I did and why. Perhaps then, you will find your answer, and I will find mine.

"WAS IT WORTH IT?" In your minds and hearts, you probably meant to ask a simple question: Was leaving our father for the sake of another man and suffering as a result because we punished you by severing you from our lives worth the affair for you? As for me, I look at the question differently. It is one which brings me to my inner self, questioning my life, examining my marriage, my youth, my desires and my disappointments. It leads me to confront my deceptions, my misconceptions, my frailties, my fears and ultimately, my quest for truth and liberty.

I struggle to define the two "its" in this profound question. Is the first "it" my infidelity and the second "it" my divorce? Is the first "it" my deception and the second "it" the abandonment of me on your part? Or is the first "it" my pursuit of love and happiness and the second "it" the anguish suffered on both your part and mine? Or, rather, is the first "it" the discovered truth, the revelation, and the second "it" the liberation of the self that no longer has to lie to make believe that life is heaven when, in fact, it was hell; that my marriage was a bond of eternal love and soul nourishment, when instead it was a bondage of servitude and self depreciation?

"WAS IT WORTH IT?" Was it worth breaking the family unit in order to go on my "sexual escapades" as Nour had accused me of? The answer is unequivocally, NO. Rather, I would ask myself, did I really leave your father because of another man? Was I so selfish to choose to risk your estrangement instead of to give up the realization of a lifelong longing for love, affection, appreciation and validation? Was that what was occurring in my mind as I indulged in my adulterous love affair unable to terminate a full fledged relationship with Patrick? No, my dear son; not at all. It was my lost life that was flashing in my buried memories.

You see, my lovely son, my story with you father began when I was a little girl, a very innocent fourteen-year-old, naïve about love and passionate about affection, a need which never was satisfied by my absent father, and never nourished by my mother. Neither is to blame. My very affectionate father, whom I was very attached to, abruptly left me at five and a half years of age in pursuit of a better life for us, making a living in Venezuela, while we stayed back in the homeland.

My desolate mother had to play both roles, the mother and the father, her heart hardened partly from her loneliness, partly from the dual role she managed to play so well, but mostly, from the lack of affection in her own upbringing, her having lived in a culture where giving love was considered a weakness. It was perceived that the deprivation of love strengthened a child's spirit and made an otherwise fragile youth tough in order to overcome the challenges of tomorrow.

When your father came into my life, I was quick to believe that he was the savior who filled that void. Sadly, he never did. But for those early years, I do not fault him, for I was immature realizing that no man can, or should, fill a void left by a dysfunctional family. I lacked experience, wisdom, and courage to overcome such a powerful need, particularly being the passionate person I am and always have been. I grew up with the inner strength that I inherited from my mother: the independent, strong-willed nature, the perseverance, the positive attitude and love of life, but my emotional immaturity always stood in my way. The fear of having no man in my life, or of losing what man I had, always held me back from facing my unhappy relationship with your father.

You see, your father and I have never enjoyed a fulfilling relationship. I know this may seem untrue and that is perhaps why what I did and the ensuing decision to divorce seemed so shocking to you. The reality of it, I discovered years later, is that I have never truly loved your father and neither did he love me. What we had, if anything at all, was what passes for love at that age, and even at that, it was only on my part. Still, I thought I truly wanted to love him, and I gave him many chances, especially after the marriage. Each time I did, he let me down, starting with when we were teenagers.

It may be news to you, but your father only loved what comfort I gave him and the security that came from my hard work and dedication, both as a mother and as a valued contributor to the home finances and daily assignments. And no, he was not affectionate. When you do not receive love, you do not give love.

What was worse, he didn't allow me to be the person I wanted to be. With him, my persona was quashed and my aspirations were put on the back burner. His needs, his lifestyle, his goals, his friends, his relationships, his opinions, his entire existence came first, and he made sure it stayed that way by belittling me, by not considering my needs, by putting me down in front of family and friends. He thought his jokes were funny, that they were acceptable, but they were demeaning to me. He conducted his life as a separate individual, not as a partner in a marriage. The times we spent together were always according to his will, whenever it was an outing he chose, or a visit among his circle of friends, never among mine.

Many a story I have written in my little journal that I kept from childhood…. since I was fourteen and he fifteen. The situations varied but the outcome was always the same. The pains that made me distant thirty years ago were the same pains that led to my divorce. The teenager who would rather spend long hours with friends, leaving the remaining few moments of the precious summer and winter vacation days to me, turned into a man whose pursuit of his own happiness, and lifestyle became the imposing reality of our marriage.

Many times I tried to express to him that we had no meaningful "relationship." He cynically laughed at the word, ridiculing my "psychological analysis" and never took me seriously. I tried to describe what I expected from him as my partner; simple things such as going out to dinner occasionally, dancing, having a cup of coffee together, watching a movie, or going on family vacations. His response was always, "I like to relax at home." On the rare occasions he compromised with me, he made sure to tell me things such as "a cup of coffee with you at Starbucks is enough for you for a month." You see, his needs always superseded mine. In fact, mine were never acknowledged, nor included into his routine. I felt lonely, unappreciated, neglected and unloved. I told him that more than once throughout the years. He heard, but he never listened.

My fault was that I conceded and continued to live my life lacking in the confidence of my strength to stand up alone without his support. It did not matter that I had a stable job from which I could have a decent living. It did not matter that I was intelligent and knew it. It did not matter that I was strong-willed, exuded confidence, strength, happiness. Yes, I was all that and more, but inside, I was dying. Your father—for the years he marginalized me—had stripped from me the confidence I needed to break away.

With all the independence and responsibility I was carrying by working, by keeping a home and by raising you, I still did not know how to make a deal on a car, how to pay bills online or how to resolve simple computer problems. All of these things overwhelmed me. I felt ignorant and weak. And in my heart, I knew he preferred it that way because that made him superior and in control. He knew by keeping me misinformed, he would win every argument, and could, therefore, keep me under his thumb.

I felt that I had no voice. I was always on the defensive and without an identity. In my ignorance and intimidated spirit, sadly, I allowed him to control and manipulate me for twenty-one years. Making that choice seemed to make my life easier to cope with, or so I believed. By doing so, I went against my own nature, against my own strong, self-confident, and assertive character. I allowed myself to live under your father's shadow, destroying my own persona.

Every once in a while, I might build some courage and try to break away. I tried seriously at least twice before (in 1994 & 1998), but the same fears which I have mentioned earlier, coupled with my desire to provide for you the most stable home possible, the best schooling and a high standard of living made the thought unfathomable. Each time, he attempted to make some changes, but he slowly slipped back into his old ways. Neither separating for two months, nor going to a Catholic marriage retreat with several follow up classes proved sustainable.

In time, I subconsciously discovered the only way that could pacify my decaying feelings and mask my inner solitude. A state of denial and numbness dominated me. Finally, I thought I was happy. To sustain myself, I pretended that my marriage was on solid ground. I convinced myself that hey, he had his roles, working two jobs, fixing the cars and paying the bills, and I had mine, working, raising the children, cooking, cleaning, doing laundry, ironing, shopping, and attending to your activities, rehearsals, performances, doctors' appointments, graduations, school functions and transportation. And I made believe that that was proper and right. Yes, my life was busy, indeed. I did not stop for a moment to think about my own life. My identity was buried under the appearance of a content marriage. But my spirit was slowly decaying.

Soon, I stopped talking about my own goals and aspirations. Mine were subsumed by his, and I really thought that that was fine. I soon abandoned my desires in pursuing the Master's Degree I had been dreaming of since my graduation from college, my hobbies of traveling, hiking, beach outings, the outdoors, camping, exploring, learning music, languages, movie watching, hanging in coffee shops, reading, visiting my friends as a couple.....and many more. I made believe that everything would be fine, if I could only do a few things at least, although by myself since he refused to join me.

Surely, and not to detract from his hard work in keeping two jobs and maintaining the home, his contribution to our finances was indeed valuable. His desire to spend quality time with me or the family, though, was absent. For years to come, he lived his gratifying life the way he liked, teaching as a "professor" (he really liked carrying that title), working as an engineer (and only through my support, putting him through his Bachelor's and Master's degrees, attending to the needs of the family while he worked and studied, a luxury he never afforded me when he knew how much I wanted to go to graduate school). He delighted in his hobbies of changing oil or fixing cars, or spending countless hours sequestered in the computer room, reading news articles, e-mailing friends or sending political essays on the internet, or socializing with his Lebanese friends, dragging me to their houses or inviting them to dinner, thus indirectly imposing on me the obligation to prepare lavish meals and countless barbeques with no help on his part. On rare occasions, he dried some dishes.

How I felt could not be described better than I did in my December, 30, 2008 letter to you in which I stated that I had served no less than as a slave who cleaned, cooked, raised my children, worked and produced a handsome pension, ironed his clothes and picked up his plate from before his nose without ever being appreciated, without any accommodation on his part for my needs which I had long stopped verbalizing, one disappointment after another, after realizing nothing was ever going to change and that your father was simply interested in what made HIM happy regardless of anyone else's needs. In short, I was taken for granted.

It wasn't long before we drifted apart. As Nour became independent driving herself to music lessons, to friends, and shopping and you became more involved with your friends and DH riding, I found little joy, in house chores or in cooking. I started going to the movies, to the beach and sometimes just grabbing a cup of coffee, all by myself. Again, I felt alone, much the same way I felt raising you as a single parent without any of your father's physical or emotional help or support. We truly became separate individuals, yet I still made believe life was good because I refused to acknowledge that I was in misery. I refused to believe I had the right to be happy apart from him.

With your independence and mine, the family unit was slowly breaking up. Less and less time was spent tougher, save the precious Sunday afternoons when I insisted on sharing a family dinner. In my solitude, my life flashed back to me. More and more, I began to reflect upon my unfulfilled desires, on my broken dreams and on my loneliness, and I realized how miserable I actually was. It was under these circumstances that I met Patrick, and my awakening began. In this man, I discovered kindness, understanding, support, compassion, forgiveness, empathy, tenderness, thoughtfulness, encouragement and acceptance. But above all, I discovered that true love is all of that and more. I caved and allowed myself to indulge in the beauty of love that had long been forgotten. I emerged from your father's shadow; I reconnected. I savored happiness.

Yeah, you argue, "If you were so miserable with my father, then why did you not divorce him before you had an affair?" A legitimate question, indeed, that I have asked myself many times. To that, I respond as I did in my October, 27, 2007 letter to you, that I wish that I could turn back the clock and do things in the proper order. I wish that I could have approached my failing relationship with your father differently. I wish that I had realized how miserable I was and simply faced it. Rather, I masked my pain to avoid more of it and to escape dealing with the fear of the unknown and the destruction of everything beautiful I had built over twenty-one years, risking the abandonment of my own flesh and blood, my source of joy in this world, you, my precious children. I really wish I could have recognized that I had been so unhappy and needed to end my marriage and had had the courage to act upon it before I commenced a relationship with another man. Unfortunately, by that time, I was in so much denial, driven to raise you at all cost, trying to make up to you what my parents did not give me-love.

But the time came, as it always does, when people must face reality and shed the cloak of deception. I faced my life and decided that I could no longer live a lie; that the truth would set me free. I admitted to my affair when your father asked me, and I asked him for a divorce. Your father refused to let go, probably due to his own fears. He insisted on trying to work things out as though everything I had done could be forgotten and forgiven, but my heart told me otherwise.

Your father's anguish, the profuse tears that followed, the vomiting, the claims of possible stomach cancer, his weight loss, his state of helplessness and despair, including pointing a gun to my head and threatening to kill himself if I did not return from having just separated for a weak, made me come back. That was my second blunder. I led you all to believe that I was genuinely trying to make amends, but I had made up my mind. I cannot tell you why I did not insist on seeking a divorce, other than that my heart was crushed watching you father's suffering, whether you believe it or not.

I tried to play the game a little longer until I could no longer live this life of deception. My well was dry, and there was nothing more for me to give. I finally stood my ground and decided on leaving, knowing that you would ostracize me. The thought of that was heart-wrenching, but the choice had to be made. The truth had to be told. Divorce was inevitable. It was the right thing to do and the fairest thing for you, for your father and for me.

You must be selfish, you shout, thinking of your own pleasures and not of us, not willing to make sacrifices and to hang on. And perhaps you are right. If it means that by sacrificing that one deserves to be dehumanized so that another can reign supreme, then I was selfish. If it means that by sacrificing that one must fall so that another may rise, then I was selfish. If it means that by sacrificing, a spirit must die so that another may flourish, then I was selfish. If it means that by sacrificing one must relive the lie and lay to rest the truth, then I was selfish. And if it means that the ultimate sacrifice is enduring a marriage of iron chains then let God sentence me for breaking its covenants.

As for me, my dear son, I beg to differ, even as you continue to punish me for eternity. I, like you, am a human who is not perfect; who will always make mistakes and hope to learn from them. But like you and all creatures, I, too, deserve to be happy.

This is my story which I have decided to share with you in the hope that it will help you find your answer rather than lead you to sympathize with me or to take sides. I know you still have many more questions than this letter can ever answer. My hope is for the day to come, when we sit as adults and have an open and sincere discussion about everything we all have had to endure; pain, that I know I inflicted upon you and for which no time or repentance can erase, but which only through forgiveness will become bearable.

So "WAS IT WORHT IT?" At the beginning of this letter I wished that you would judge my actions and not my character. Three years, I stood accused before you. Today, I stand before you bare, armed with nothing but the truth. My story told in this letter was as succinct as I could possibly make it. Read through

it with an open heart, digest every word, think critically but with
love; and you shall know the answer. I know I finally have mine.

Love always,
Mother

On Monday, I set out to go to a work-related convention in the city where Anwar went to a California State University. A faint glimmer of hope that Anwar would call back and accept my lunch or dinner invitation quickly faded as I approached my destination without a word or a response to the e-mail I had sent him a couple of days earlier. I decided to head straight to his school and drop off the care-package anyway. The dormitories appeared quiet and comfortable. I walked around hoping to catch a glimpse of him, but access was restricted to a swipe of a key card. My knocks were unanswered. I left my package at the reception desk and asked the attendant to place a note in Anwar's mail box. I also left him a phone message to pick it up.

It wouldn't be the first time I had been shut out. I walked the campus streets and alleys, across many departments and student centers and stopped for a moment at the engineering building. He must take many classes here, I assumed. I carried on looking around the cafeteria, examining every library floor, canvassing every table and every seat. The aisles gazed at me idly in haunting silence, the chairs ridiculed my glazed eyes and the walls echoed with quivering reminders: intruder, vagabond, dispossessed, disowned, leper, retrace and wipe behind you your reviled footprints.

He picked up the package a couple of days later. Still, no call, no e-mail, no acknowledgment; and I did not expect any.

As Nour's birthday and Christmas approached, I sent Anwar a package that included cards and gifts for both of them. I asked him to kindly deliver them to her, but he never confirmed whether or not he did it. Just in case he did not, I still sent Nour an e-mail titled *"A Special Wish."* It was her 21st birthday.

My beautiful young woman, Nourita:

It is so hard to imagine you are twenty-one today. Where did all the years go? It just seems like yesterday when I cradled you in my arms, laid you on my stomach so you might sleep soundly, without crying or vomiting, and I gleefully listened to you utter your first words as young as twelve months of age. How beautiful and sweet you were.

You were so special from the first moment you were born... unlike any other. I remember your pediatrician telling me so. He sensed your brightness and inquisitive gestures...your eyes.... wide and charming...told the story of your future, destined for high achievements and success. How rewarding; how proud and boastful I was of you. All my co-workers remember that too, because I could not stop bragging about you. You delighted my heart and brought me much joy as I watched you become a beautiful young adolescent...smart, well-mannered, goal-oriented, ethical, obedient, and so mature, way beyond your age.

I wonder what you have planned to celebrate your arrival at womanhood! Going drinking?....Not you. Dancing the night way?....Not you. Getting wild and doing crazy things....Not you. Then again, I ask myself, "Do I still know you?"

Perhaps you will spend it quietly with a young befitting gentleman. I know that you will always make the choice that is best for you. Perhaps you will be spending it with your family. It is always special to do so.

Whatever you do today, I wish you to do it with indulgence. You are twenty-one today only.

From afar, I celebrate you. I wish you a very happy birthday and many, many more years of good health and peace.

Love always,
Mother

PART IV

Moved On, But To Where?

CHAPTER 15

Giving Up Is Not In My Nature

JANUARY 11, 2011

As with the passage of every major holiday, I dip into a state of deep despair. Again, I pick up where I left off and resume writing my journey, not only to document hurdles that I have jumped, but also to serve as a reminder to my children, who may want to read it one day, to understand what it was that they had refused to consider and to decide for themselves whether or not their mother had abandoned them for another. My journal also served as therapy at a time when therapists could do nothing for me other than listen attentively and to empathize. Pragmatic as I am, I sought their help to devise solutions, ways by which I could reach out, novel ideas that I had not thought of, all in the pursuit of regaining normality with my children. None of the therapists had the magic bullet. I think they all would agree that I had done everything that I could have done. The only thing I still needed to do was to "live a fulfilling life, alongside my pain," as one told me many years later. I wish I could have heard that then.

Even as I carried on with my life, I still struggled to accept that my children did not want me in their lives. Instead, I fought an ever losing battle. Giving up is not in my nature. I wanted to make sure that there was absolutely nothing left that I had not already tried in order to reach out to their hearts. I wanted my children to wake up to the truth one day and to realize that their mother had fought for them with every ounce of blood that ran in her veins. Letting go would have meant giving up on them. Still, though, for the most part, I was allowing myself to grieve when the pain was intense, but I was also enjoying my life with Patrick and was forgetting myself during those special moments. I had the choice of living or dying. I chose the first.

Not wanting to over-burden any of my friends, even Patrick, with a story that had no ending, I only had myself to rely on to digest everything that was happening to me and to try to manage my grief while still savoring what life had to offer me. Praying and writing became my salvation. The nights belonged to me as I sat pouring tears onto the keyboard where no one could see, or judge or tell me that everything would be all right... because it wasn't.

"I suppose this will be my last entry. My ink has run dry," I wrote. Perhaps here, my journey has come to its end. The last chapter has been closed and this ordeal is becoming my way of life. It is said that one goes through several stages of grief until one gets closure. What closure? What silence? What is moving on? A made-up notion to ease the mind. The gap is forever wider, yet my children remain inside my being; with every breath and sigh.

Yes, three and a half years have passed by, but I have carried on, as they say. I did not miss a single day of work, I studied hard, I graduated with distinction, I played, laughed, spent ample time with friends and cherished my solid relationship with Patrick, including our travels, and our outdoor activities, an amazing partnership. Yes, I lived well and soaked up of life's wondrous journey what I could. I cry less now, not for having reached "closure," or for surrendering, but for finally abandoning the hope that was torturing me as I waited and waited, expecting and expecting and receiving nothing. Humiliation made me succumb to the reality of doors slammed shut and bolted, sad reminders that my children truly did not want me in their lives, reminders that they had erased me. They continue to live every day as though they had come from thin air.

Christmas came and went. The check I had included in my care-package as part of Anwar's Christmas gift was not cashed. I wondered how my child would smell wearing the cologne that I had packed inside the gift box which I had sent to his dormitory a couple of weeks before! Would it attract the young ladies on campus? Will he wear it every day or when he goes out at night? And will he remember me when he does? Or what will my beauty say when her friends complement her on her fashionable purse? Will she remember me? Will she be carrying it over her shoulder on campus? What will the "remember stone" I inserted in her birthday card mean to her? Will she display it on her desk? Perhaps she will toss it into the sea.

It had been five months since we last spoke on the telephone. I was desperate to know that they were all right, so I called from the work phone. Not recognizing the number, Anwar answered. Quickly I asked if he was all right. Disgruntled, he said "Yes" and hung up. I was consumed with anger and reacted accordingly. I left a message, then another and another.….

Grief and anger clouded my judgment again, freeing a harsh tongue. I rambled on about how I had not gotten a greeting at Christmas, no "Thank you" for the gifts, no word on how they were doing in school. My voice became louder with each call. "You think you are a man now," I said, "but remember you are who you are because of me." I questioned how he could ever be in a relationship with anyone since he had become no more than a robot, stripped of humanity. I told him our office was closing in a year and a half and that the ball was now in his court. He had that much time to contact me if he wanted to because, after the move, he would not be able to find me. I asked him to have Nour listen to the message too. Angry as I was, I ended my call with "I love you." What else could an anguished mother say?

I am not sure how I was able to muster the will to say what I had said, and to decide that I was no longer going to push myself onto them. Since this was nothing I had planned, I can only credit a heavenly hand for orchestrating the one thing I had not tried during those three and a half years: abruptly ceasing to make any further contact with them. I was ready, or so I thought. I had finally come to believe that there was no stone I had not left unturned, no idea or plan spared in order to open a crack into their hearts, but to no avail. They were both adults, and it was time for me to accept that. They could make their own decisions now. They no longer needed a mother's nourishment. The times I should have been there for them had already passed. The damage was done. I could not undo three and a half years of the absent care and attention I had fought so hard to provide, and which they had shunned. The hole in my heart is bigger than ever; the nine-mile distance between our homes is infinity; the road to their hearts has been barricaded. I finally came to accept that if anything were going to change this stalemate, it was going to have to come from them. I must back off. There was nothing further I could do that would break the cycle. I decided to travel with it, hoping it would lead me to shore or to wherever God intended for me to land.

MAY 8, 2011

I set out to redeem a gift card I had received the other day from a store in the mall. I passed through the packed floors, beyond mothers and daughters, families with children out to enjoy the special people in their lives and perhaps to buy a gift or two. It was Mothers' Day and the stores were showing their finest, luring children, husbands and mothers with delightful window displays and colorful advertising. I was determined not to be affected by what I saw, for it was my special day too, and I wanted to feel validated just like the rest.

My first stop was at the jewelry counter. A lady from afar spotted me and loudly asked "Do you need help?" "No, thank you," I replied, and continued browsing through the displays. She pressed on, walked closer to me and exclaimed, "Everybody needs help!" I looked at her, half smiling to hide my tears and said, "Yes, but you cannot help me." "You are a mother. Why are you here?" she wondered. Sensing my aloneness, "It's okay; I am a mother too, and I have to work," she quickly added. The shield I had built came crashing down with floods of tears. "You see, "I said, "My kids do not speak to me." Helen, who was Persian, sensed I was divorced and told me that she was too, and that she understood. Our similar cultures dictate that divorce is an abomination where blame is always on the wife; and that the children are ripped from their mothers, and that fathers retain full custody. Why I revealed myself to a complete stranger, I don't know. As we exchanged a few words, she hugged me and assured me that once my kids became a mother and a father, they would understand. Only through prayer, am I able to gather the strength to carry on, she said. I told her that I prayed every day. I thanked her, and I walked away.

Until that moment, I had thought that I was going to make it through yet another Mothers' Day. After all, it was four years ago that they had expelled me from their lives; many Christmases, birthdays, and, yes, Mothers' Days had come and gone when I had celebrated alone. Four months since I had committed to not making any further attempt to communicate with them had passed without lingering crying spells or uncontrollable urges to test their resolve one more time-albeit a couple of phone calls from a restricted number and without my uttering a word, listening hauntingly to their hellos until they hung up.

My colleagues had stumbled the other day when they wished me a happy Mothers' Day, forgetting for a second that my children and I had long been estranged. They were quick to apologize as they realized they might have opened old wounds. And they had. Yet, I smiled, anyway, and thanked them for their kind words saying, "I have gotten used to it, you know."

Until today, I really thought I had finally made peace with my destiny. To some extent, I had. A couple of weeks ago, God opened another door. Anwar's Facebook page came up when I searched for him. Every wall posting or exchange was available for me to see. Apparently, he had been on Facebook since July of 2010, but until two weeks ago, I had not been able to find any link to his name, searching for him and for Nour every day.

A small window allowed me to peak through his life and to make believe that I had been a part of it. I checked every post, every picture or link hoping to retrace his life as a student or a teenager and from that to construct how he had spent his time, how well he was doing in school, how happy or sad he was, what his thoughts revealed, who his friends were. I called it my miracle window because through it, I connected with my son, although virtually; I could finally get a glimpse of who he had become and to know that he was all right. And how pleased and relieved I was to figure out, as I read through it, that my young man seemed happy, confident, committed to learning, was surrounded by friends, still enjoyed his hobbies, but above all, had become a gentleman. All his remarks were free from any foul language, as is prevalent with young men in his age group and among some of his friends; his responses were mature and, in some respect, intelligent, as they appeared to carry interests in world events, politics and social issues. I was proud of his success and of his apparent good manners.

My labor of love had not gone in vain. Fifteen years of persistent guidance, unconditional love, devotion and care had laid the proper foundation. He will be successful and happy. I marveled.

I took a walk in my neighborhood that afternoon as I always do. Where were the joggers, the walkers, the children playing in the sports' field? There was no one, but the chirping birds filling the stillness of the air. In the distance, a couple of fathers—I assume—played ball with their sons. Where were their mothers, I wondered? Perhaps they had none to celebrate with.

The walkways were hauntingly desolate. Where did all the people go? Perhaps they were home dining with their mothers or gathered around restaurant tables like the one I saw this morning as I waited to pick up my treat for this special day, a gourmet pizza from the place next door. I thought for a moment. Do they ever think of me on Mothers' Day? Nah, what a silly thought! Life seems to revolve around them and "their family" only. But will they ever remember me when they mature, when they "grow up," when they have relationships, when they marry or when they have children? Another absurd notion! They must have been born from thin air. Nour graduates this spring and may have already been accepted to medical school, but I will know nothing! Anwar completes his freshman year in a couple of weeks, and I will know only what blurbs Facebook affords me. Another momentous occasion is missed; another chapter of their lives passes me by. A happy Mothers' Day; a happy Mothers' Day; so it is and nothing more. It, too, like any other special day, shall pass.

Yes, Christmas came and went yet again. This time, I neither sent gifts, nor called to wish them a Merry Christmas. I knew nothing about them other than from hearsay and from what little information LinkedIn gave me regarding Nour. She had graduated Phi Beta Kappa from UCLA with a Bachelor's in Bio-Chemistry in June, 2011 and was working as an associate researcher at a major pharmaceutical company, I saw. *Yee*, another milestone in her life had passed without my joining in the celebration. I had to be content being fortunate enough to order graduation pictures, containing the pride and joy that I could not share with anyone, lest they asked questions that I could not answer. What had happened to medical school? I called my old neighbor who said Nour was still applying to several schools while working.

My first phone call to Anwar in months was on his birthday, July 2, 2011. He had picked up only because the number could not be recognized. Excited, yet without expectation, I sang him *Sana Hilwa Ya Gameel*. He listened. My birthday wishes were met with resistance as he countered, "I am hanging up." And he did. Content that he still received me, I smiled and carried on. A few weeks after, he took down his Facebook page; my miracle window was slammed shut but for a few interim days when, for some reason, he decided to bring it back up during his Whistler trip. God has been listening to my prayers and has been keeping him safe. A short video he had posted revealed his Guardian Angel protecting him as he called out, "Oh my God, Oh, my God" racing at the very edge of a sheer cliff. I hoped he truly still believed in God even though he had told me otherwise. I thanked God lest Anwar did not. Through his friend's Facebook page, I realized Anwar had created another page with a pseudonym. Perhaps he suspected that I may have been viewing his posts and had thought that I would never find him under that name. Nevertheless, the page soon became inactive, and after a short time, Anwar removed it completely. My window of hope had closed again.

A year had gone by since my resolution to let them go. I realized that nothing I could do would bring them back except by their own will. What was I to make of the surprise when on January 3, 2012, as I reviewed my bank account statement, I discovered that the birthday-gift check that I had written to Anwar the year before had been cashed! Did he really hold on to it for a year and cash it because he was unable to meet his financial obligations? Or did it end up in the wrong hands? Why would he hold on to it for a year? A lot of questions spun in my head without a clue to what the real situation might have been. It is in my nature to worry, but when I am left clueless as to how my children are doing or how they are coping, my worries become intensified. And what was worse, I could not get any assurance from either one of them regarding their physical, emotional, or financial well-being. I could only send Anwar an e-mail asking if he himself had deposited the check and if he needed financial assistance. I made it clear that I was willing to help out "without any strings attached" and that he knew where to find me when he was ready. I received a "read" receipt within ten minutes, but no response. I did not really expect any. Anwar, like me, likes to earn his own buck.

MAY 1, 2012

Once more the internet led me to discover that Nour had been admitted to medical school since the "White Coat Ceremony" for new entrants had been downloaded by her department for the world to see. I paused contemplating her life and her future. The past flashed before me as I remembered that "perfect" child who could read before the age of three, who remembered stories from age two, who cried when her first-grade teacher gave her the one and only disciplinary note because she had talked in class, the girl who had cried when she got her first B, the teen pianist and violinist who settled for nothing but first chair in her youth symphony orchestra.

It is hard to believe that throughout her childhood and adolescence she did everything right, never anything to be disciplined for. She was the apple of my eye, the delight of my heart. She was the "perfect" child. She was obedient, intelligent, studious, determined and she stayed away from drugs, from alcohol and even from boyfriends who might have caused her to lose some focus. I knew early on that she was destined for success on a grand scale. But what I did not know was that her pursuit for perfection had led her to live in a utopian bubble impervious to the imperfect world around her. When my infidelity and decision to divorce threatened her serenity, she excommunicated me. The future, I thought, may not be so kind to her. I was not sure if she would be able to ride that wave of success without facing trials that could bring her to her knees. I wondered then if she would be able to cope, or have anyone by her side to soothe her heart... and I wondered if she could manage human frailties. Then, I thought that perhaps through that, she would become a real human... and that would be her ultimate success. I drafted a letter to Nour on May 1, 2012, but was unable to confirm if I had actually sent it to her then. Many years later, on February 28, 2020, I sent it, but I am not sure if my e-mail was blocked or not. I titled it:

Open Letter To Nour

My dear, Nour:

During the morning rush in my neighborhood, as I walked, I saw elementary school children, some on their bikes, some walking, and others accompanied by their parents, all scurrying to make it to school on time. Life flashed back to the memories of those special years of caring for you and of watching you blossom. How could it be that I have been excommunicated from your lives for almost five years when you were my life, my joy, and my pride? The pleasant and painful past shook me to the core as I trembled in disbelief that your heart is still shut...and it came to me that I must try one more time......just another time even though I had thought that I had not left a stone unturned.

I carried on briskly, thinking about writing even as fear gripped my soul and hope had taken permanent residence in the abyss.

What shall I tell her? How will I deliver this letter? Will she pick it up and read it, or will she trash it? Who will she share it with? Will it change anything? Will it draw her farther away than she already is? Does it matter? Does she care? Will she be touched by my love? Does she even need it? Is she able to forgive? I was not sure what would spill out in this letter. I decided fear had no room in my life because I had conquered it with love which abounds within me. I set out to write asking you "Is It Worth It?" not looking for any response.

I had struggled with answering this profound question myself when I was asked it two year ago. But when I finally did, I realized the true meaning of life, of living the naked truth, of loving unconditionally, of cherishing every moment we have on this beautiful earth, of engaging my mind, my body and my spirit in unison with our Creator. All that reaffirmed my humanity and essence. A heavy load dropped off of my shoulders. I felt peace within. In this letter, my hope is for you to ponder this question and reach YOUR inner peace on your own although you will probably insist that you already reached it long ago.

If so, know that I would be happy to believe it and to reach closure, but I don't believe it. I don't, because you are my child, and I can't believe that you are incapable of forgiveness. If I did, I would sentence you to eternal misery, for a heart that does not forgive shall bleed in pain forever. As I once wrote to you, he who lives in anger will never be consoled. And he who lives cloaked in hatred cannot exalt in the beauty of forgiveness. He who knows no love will suffer in loneliness. And he who builds a wall will never have the courage to face reality, and he who lives in falsehood will never progress. He will remain stranded and will never overcome life's many obstacles. I have decided to forgive myself as I did others, and to live the truth, thus, became free. The feeling was intoxicating. I could wish no less elation for the people I love.

Years have passed since I have heard you call me, "Immeh (Mother)." I don't know if one day you will ever realize or will want to know how my life has been for these five years. Perhaps you wonder every now and then if your plan met its target so you may rest. Well, to give you some relief, I can assure you that you have admonished everything I did to wrong you. You have succeeded in doing more than that. My roots are severed; my fruit is sour, and my land is barren. If your aim was to punish me for my infidelity even though I asked for your forgiveness, then know that your spear was razor sharp. It cut a wide and deep hole in my heart and sliced through, without a care, ravaging my soul that will never be repaired. What is lost can never be recaptured.

If you were set upon commanding the severest sentence, then I say to you that there is no greater infliction upon a mother than when she reads a laundry list of accusations, reducing her existence to some "sexual escapades" or when as a leper retracing her footsteps after her attempts—to reach out by appearing in front of her daughter's bedroom window, pleading for a word— are rebuffed with a disgusted shout, "How dare you defile my property with your presence!" Or when she tenderly touches her daughter's shoulder for the first time in three years, she is pushed away with disdain and is threatened, "Don't you dare touch me" while her father and his girlfriend sweep her away, with a stern, icy look that shouts, "Dare not; dream not that Nour will ever be yours again. She has a mother now. You have been sentenced to an oblivion from which there is no return."

But if you have convinced yourself that I must suffer for my deeds eternally, then I must differ with you. You must know that you have accomplished everything you intended for me except for three things: to strip me of my pride, of my dignity and of my resilience. If this was on your wish list, my dear child, then I tell you to cross it out forever. For through my betrayal, I have learned to live the naked truth and was; therefore, set free. Through the pain that I continue to endure, I have learned the joy of simply waking up every morning and saying, "Thank you, Lord, for I am alive." For the loneliness that permeates my life, I have learned to fill that void with exciting adventures and world travel. For the pleadings of mercy I continued to seek from you, I have learned humility. But above all, I have overcome all of that with the purest love of all: the love of a mother. Perhaps one day you will feel its limitless expanse.

But this letter, my dear child, is not about me nor is it about laying remorse or guilt upon anyone. It is merely about reflecting upon life, on its meaning and what it encompasses in joys as it does in sorrows. It is about unfulfilled dreams and disappointments, but it is also about choices, about hope and faith in believing—as I also once wrote to you—that you must experience pain to know joy and deceit to understand truth. It is about facing reality as it unfolds, one misjudgment at a time, instead of protecting ourselves in a utopian bubble, pretending life is perfect, by extracting from it anything that disturbs us, causes us pain or puts us in touch with reality, with truth, with temptation, with sorrow, and yes, sadly, with compassion. It is about the understanding that life can bring goodness, as well as despair, euphoric triumphs as well as enduring trials that bring us to our knees. Throughout all of this, we pray to maintain our fortitude and faith that all shall come to pass and that good things will happen to the good. But above all, my beautiful daughter, it is about making choices and accepting the consequences, both the good and the bad. Therein lies our inner strength.

Precious time has slipped us by. You, Nour, are a successful research associate at a prestigious pharmaceutical company and awaiting your admittance into medical school. Anwar is in his second year of engineering and doing well, I hear. I, too, have moved on. I graduated with a Master's Degree in political science with distinction, I continue to travel and to enjoy exploring and practicing many of my hobbies, and perhaps soon, I shall embark on a new career. Yet, we all have missed so much about each other's lives because of the choices each one of us has made, willingly or unwillingly.

The simple fact remains that nothing will wipe away the past, nothing will undo the pain we have all endured, nothing will leave but a perpetual living bitter memory that will haunt us every second for as long as we allow it....Yet, Nour, you continue to choose to disown me as though fearing that your determination to punish me for eternity might break your humanity, believing that if there is any mercy at all on this earth, I deserve none.

You blocked my number when I called to congratulate you on graduating with honors, but from afar, I celebrated you. You and Anwar started college and moved away, but not before making sure I remained deprived of knowing how well you had transitioned as you tasted the first few weeks of independence and experienced college life. In my solitude, I wondered if life had treated you well; if my labor of love had somehow prepared you; if you had encountered obstacles and had overcome them, if you had made new friends, or if you had any time for fun on campus. I wondered if and hoped you had fallen in love. I knew no more than an "untouchable" could, salivating over an imaginary feast, while watching from the shadows the crumbs fall off of her master's table.

So how long, I must ask, will this shadow of darkness separate us? Is there truly any compelling cause or conviction that should separate children from their parents? Is anyone infallible but God? Has anyone not sinned in his or her lifetime? Is anyone immune from making mistakes? Even murderers and rapists can dream of being freed one day. Doesn't anyone deserve a second chance, or must all sinners be condemned for eternity? If so, all humanity shall parish!

Nour, you are twenty-two-years of age now, an adult by all accounts. Have you ever asked yourself what your life might have been like with your mother by your side to love you and to support you as she did for seventeen years? Have you thought that one day you will get married and that I will not be allowed to celebrate with you lest I cast an evil eye upon your special day? Or when you are in labor one day and calling out in pain, "Akh, ya Immeh, (Ouch, oh dear mother of mine)," that I would not be permitted in the room to hold your hand and to soothe you lest I defiled you?

History is being made every day. Time stops for no one. It continues to lapse as each one of us lives a separate life not knowing when our clock will stop ticking. When confronted with our mortality or that of a loved one, must we then ponder, "Is It Worth It?" Or shall we declare NOW that life is too short to live it holding on to grudges, to unsettled scores or even hatred? Shall we take our enmity to our graves or choose instead to forgive as much as we would want to be forgiven for our transgressions that we surely will continue to make throughout life's trials? Shall we hold on to a darker past that can only stand in the way of a brighter future or choose instead to let go and let the past be the past? Shall we allow our history to determine our destiny or shall we decide to learn from our experiences, from the good and the bad, and cut our own path? Shall we choose to live uprooted as though we came from thin air, orphaned and lonely, or choose to reunite as a family because WE ARE, no matter what we think or what we feel?

The reality, my dear child, is that the blood that runs in your veins is my resilience; the smile that shines on your face is my free spirit; and your wide eyes that speak of a young, beautiful woman who endured much more than age and time can erase, glimmer with the compassion that I have for humankind. You are from me and within me. You are my child, and I am your mother who loves you more than anything in this world. You can never take that away from me, and neither can you take the eternal memories of the years I cradled you, no matter your impervious hardened heart.

For five years you have demonized me. How much longer must you pretend that I do not exist? Do you ever ask yourself why? I really mean do you ever ask yourself why my steadfastness, without stating the obvious? Do you ask what more do I want to prove or accomplish? Does this change anything? I can only believe that you have chosen your path for now for what you have rationalized as a proper punishment. I wish that one day you will realize how much invaluable time was wasted, but also, that tomorrow can always bring a new beginning. This brings us back to the question I asked you to ponder deeply, "Is It Worth it?" If you have truly read this letter with care and love, the inevitable answer—of the wise and the free spirited—will surely come to you: not at all, Nour, not at all. Believe!

Love always and forever,
Mother

CHAPTER 16

I Will Always Be Here For You

Here and there, I sent Anwar an e-mail to his school address about different things and would always get a "read" receipt, usually within minutes. Through this, I was assured that he was safe. As he turned twenty, he became more defiant and refused to answer my calls, including my birthday wishes. Concerned about his state and mental well-being, I wrote him this letter on July 18, 2012 titled *"My Thoughts Are With You, Son."* I was somewhat relieved that he read it ten days later, assuming that it was him and not his father who may well have been intercepting all of my e-mails. I had hoped it would stoke in him a sense of comfort and assurance that he would always have a mother with an open heart and open arms ready to receive him. Sadly, I received no response, as expected.

Dear Son:

I hope that you are enjoying your summer and that you're safe when on your bike, when driving or engaging in other activities. I had truly hoped you would pick up your phone—at least on your birthday—and allow me to wish you the best on your special day. I am not sure if or when there will be a day when you will finally decide that it is time. I realize that the decision is yours and that there is nothing else I can do to make you reconcile with me. Years and countless attempts, from phone calls to court orders to surprise visits to e-mails to letters and to pleadings, have gone unanswered.

Still, I want you to know, just because I no longer attempt to "impose" myself on you, I have not given up on you or on your sister, and I never will. I will continue to try to reach your heart and to make some contact whether you choose to respond or not. The day will come, my dear child, when you will realize that holding on to a painful past is a self-inflicted, perpetually-bleeding wound that can only stand in the way of a brighter tomorrow. Before any more precious time is wasted, I hope you understand and believe that for this wound to heal, it is up to us to let go and make the choice to pave our own path rather than to allow our history to determine our destiny.

You are twenty-years-old, my young man; the future is in your hands, so challenge yourself, CHOOSE to learn from good or bad past experiences, and decide to move forward. The alternative can only mean stagnation and desolation. The doors are all there for you to open, if only you decide to be bold and to knock. With all its heartaches, life is so beautiful and waiting to embrace you and continue to teach you valuable lessons that can only enrich your spirit and make you resilient and joyful, but only if you allow it. If you do not, it will only make your journey unnecessarily arduous and painful.

Son, I don't know what your life has been like for the past five years. While I know your tender, caring heart, I was not allowed to share in your life's journey or in what might have unfolded while I was excommunicated. I hope life treated you well. I also hope that at times of disappointment, challenge and hardship, you were able to confide in someone with whom you could talk to, and to spill out your feelings with someone who could guide you wisely and reassure you. I know that you probably think that you are fine on your own and in need of no one. Son, the mightiest oak will dry and shrivel in the rain if its roots, severed, cannot supply it with water.

In my younger years, I longed for a parent who could guide me through my hard times..... But I had no one, not of my own choosing, sadly. I learned all I learned from life, the consequences of which I continue to pay for. I wish for you, my son, not to have an unguided upbringing. I believe that under my care and affection I did the best I could to nurture you, to love you and to raise you in the way I knew would prepare you for life and would make you a man of character, of honor, of dignity and of integrity. I believe I succeeded. This is not to say that your strength would not weaken at times. It does for all of us because we are human and, alone, we are frail. I had hoped I could provide you with the moral support that you needed, but I was cast out....and I am still sentenced to oblivion.

You are twenty now, and surely you continue to experience the trials that anyone would. I want you to know, my dear son, that

I am here for you. My humble condominium has a special warm place for you to stay in should you decide to. I also have a college savings fund for you and another for emergencies. I have worked very hard to save some money, not knowing if and when you or your sister might need it. I have been living with a roommate for over two years, and as unpleasant as it is, it is but a small sacrifice that allows me to have financial security and to build a small fund for you.

I don't know what your relationship with your father is like; whether or not you get along, if you confide in him; if he listens; if he understands or tries; if he teaches you about life; if he shares your dreams and directs you, as parents should, along the right path even as you make your own; if he spends quality fatherly time in order to foster a bond or even attempts to replace a mother's love imperative to children's emotional growth and security. I am not sure if you are able to pay for your living expenses, for books, for your car. I hope you are working, but perhaps you have several loans too. While it is crucial that you learn to be responsible and to manage your money, I do feel I can contribute and can remove a few pressures from your life, even if it means having enough to go out and do something fun every once in awhile. We all need a break from the routine and hard work, and we all deserve a little reward now and then.

For my part, I take many vacations now, practice many hobbies, explore the outdoors, and enjoy the traveling I have always longed to do. Life is beautiful, son. I want you to marvel at it as much as possible, with its challenges and rewards. You deserve it. I can help.

I hope you are mature enough to know my offering is not a ploy to win you back. My love, for you, my son, is boundless, limitless.

More important, I want you to know that both my home and my heart are open to you. I am your mother...no stranger, I hope. You only have one mother in this life, my son, and she is here. As a consequence for the lack of guidance and nurturing in my life, I continue to struggle with many issues, although I have learned to deal with them. I struggled for decades to reach inner peace and to embrace my past. But your journey does not have to be so arduous or so long. And certainly, you do not have to face it alone, even as you think you should or have no other choice. When you need support, I would hope you have the courage to ask for it. Time is indeed precious and is the one thing that is finite. What is lost cannot be recaptured. I am here for you, at any time, or any day, at any moment. You can CHOOSE. All you have to do is to knock.

The last five years have intensified my worries. I wish to hear from you, if only to know that you are all right.

I love you, my son, so very much. I miss you ever more.

Mother

Here and there, I would find a picture or two going through countless Facebook pages from friends I knew Anwar had and from their friends too. He had become a man with a receding hairline, and with a beard. How did my baby transform into adulthood? It was only yesterday that I tucked him in bed, laid on his soft skin countless kisses, and woke him up in the morning to feed him eggs, just the way he liked them. Time seemed to have stopped for me, but not for him. Unlike other parents who watched their sons grow up, day by day, savoring the good moments and the ones that drove them insane, I was deprived of all the joy as well as the pains of his adolescence. To me, my son's image, frozen in time and space, was of that innocent boy who was caring, loving, and passionate about life. I wanted to retrieve the past, relive the beautiful years when he was mine and I was his world....but I only had memories of a past long gone. I wanted to fight this battle and retain what no one could steal from me, my engraved memories, so I wrote to him, *"Eggs Over Easy."*

My Anwar:

This morning, as I tore a piece of pita bread and picked up a bite of my breakfast egg, many beautiful morning memories flashed by me. I slipped the bite into my mouth, and I choked as I remembered feeding you eggs on Saturday and Sunday mornings—just the way you loved them—with these bare hands....way into your teen years....and I remembered as tears ran down my cheeks and my jaw struggled to chew and swallow....times I would ask you to just feed yourself...and you would always answer... "Atyab lamma bitta'meeneh (they always taste better when you feed them to me)." Somehow, the way I wrapped the pieces with the bread and dipped them in the yolk seemed wholesome to you....I say, they were filled with love.... Gladly, and with a smile, I always obliged.

Our bond was strong and I thought could never break!!! Never did I imagine you would demonize and ostracize me....not you....not with the heart I knew you had....not my boy..... not when I pled for your forgiveness time and time again and made countless attempts to connect with you at any level. I continue to struggle to accept or to believe that five and a half years have passed and that you continue to choose to cast me out like a demon, an "untouchable" leper undeserving of mercy. I choked and swallowed.

And I remembered the morning kisses I woke you up with, your sweet smell and your baby soft skin. How sweet you were my boy. NO, you cannot take these memories away from me. NO you cannot. NO.

I am human my dear son; a human who is imperfect. I have made countless mistakes in my life, and though I have shamed you, I deserve forgiveness and mercy because all of God's creatures do. I am once again, asking you to have mercy on my soul and to forgive me. I am a good person, Anwar, not a demon, not an evil wicked selfish sex-indulging whore as you and your sister believe I am...oh, no, I am not. I am simply a human who made a grave mistake and was forgiven by God, but sadly, not by you.

You have sentenced me for eternity and sent me to hell on earth, inflicting indescribable pain that I must endure until such time as you choose to commute my sentence. My Anwar, I have given all my love, passion, and hope and yet, you continue to dehumanize me and to live your life pretending you came from thin air....No, you are MY SON, MY SON, MY SON and I am YOUR MOTHER, the only mother you will ever have, so please, please, explain to me why do you HATE me so much! I gave you nothing but unconditional and pure love. Love is all I have got. It fuels my life, and it gives me hope that one day, you will return to me.

Always and forever,
Mother

Months had gone by and many more attempts to contact Anwar had gone unanswered. Still, through his "read" receipts, my heart was content to know that he was reading my e-mails and that at least he was alive. That was all I knew. It was all I could know.

However, a week before December 3, I tried to e-mail him again, but I never got a receipt. My worries intensified, and I began to panic thinking something terrible had happened. I knew that if it were the case, neither his father, nor his sister would notify me. I did not know how else to contact him. I even thought about calling his friend whose information on the internet led me to his employer's number. I hesitated, but suddenly I had a better idea.

You see, I had just acquired a landline number at my temporary desk in a new office, so I dialed his phone. Not recognizing the number, he answered. It was the first time in a very long time that he actually engaged with me, though grudgingly and for only a few seconds. I told him I was worried sick about him to which he cynically responded that he had cancer. I inquired about his schooling and if he was on track, and he said he was. I asked if he intended to go to graduate school, and he cited the failing California economy saying, "Yeah, if I can only get into the classes I need." That was all we said before he threw a bombshell at me saying, "And by the way, tell your boyfriend, or your husband to stop e-mailing me."

I was stunned. I could not imagine that Patrick would e-mail him directly without my consent or my knowledge. I argued with Anwar that Patrick would never call and that it may have been an imposter. But he insisted he "knew who Patrick was," adding "Good luck with having a big fight with him tonight," and he quickly cut me off in his usual crass manner saying, "I need to go to school." He hung up.

Frantically, I changed into my walking clothes and proceeded to power-walk, calling Patrick in order to tell him about what had happened. Sadly, Patrick admitted that he had pulled a last-ditch attempt to remedy the failed relationship with my son. He did what he did out of sincere concern for me, having comforted me countless times during my worst crying spells. I was furious, screening at him like a maniac just as Anwar had predicted. I hung up and pulled myself to the curb, sat dawn helplessly with tears pouring and called Anwar. I acknowledged that Patrick had been the one. I apologized and tried to explain. It was all in a voice message, of course.

As I picked myself up and proceeded with my power-walk, an older couple pulled their car onto the side of the road and asked me if I was okay. I said I was fine, thanked them, and carried on gasping for air as I chocked back the tears. Memories flashed in my head about the two angels who had appeared out of nowhere the day I ran outside the old house to escape Rameh's gun.

That day, Patrick forwarded all the e-mail exchanges that began October 11, 2011 and ended December 1, 2012. In all, there were no more than four, dated October 11, 2011, July 30, 2012, August 6, 2012, and November 30, 2012. They included Anwar's relatively polite exchange. Through them, Patrick had attempted to apologize for his role in the affair, to explain the strong bond and love we shared, admitting my infidelity was wrong. He described how hurt and distraught I had been for the last five years for not having my children in my life. He also questioned why Anwar and his sister hated me so much to disown me and he pleaded with Anwar in his last e-mail to call me.

Anwar's first response was, *"I appreciate your attempt to fix my relation-ship with my mom, but as much as she won't understand this, it's just going to be a very long time. I really don't have anything against you or even her, she just doesn't get it when I say I can't talk to her because every time I do I just become enraged. It's that simple. As for you having to deal with her emotional well-being, well, don't you think you signed yourself up for that when you entered your committed relationship? Not really my problem anymore, sorry. Also, your whole story about falling in true love and whatnot is touching... but you're talking to the wrong person here as I truly don't believe in any of that BS. As a result of how the divorce happened, I've become increasingly less emotional and unsympathetic toward her so I'm going to have to apologize, and politely decline the chance to forgive her. Furthermore, since I'm sure you're going to show her this response, I hope she continues to give up trying to talk to me because really it's the best thing for me; and of course she cares most about my well-being right?"*

His last was, *"Congratulations! I have now blocked you, so any future emails you send I will no longer see. Good job."* And along with that, I believe he blocked mine too.

I realized if there was any hope at all for Anwar to open up a little, Patrick, unintentionally, had destroyed it. But I also realized that this was my son's decision as I struggled to accept that all hope had vanished. That evening, as I reflected on the event, I realized how genuine Patrick's love was for me. I hoped that one day, my children would realize that too and know that our love was unshakable; that we were inseparable and that their mother deserved to receive the great love she had craved for all of her life... and to be happy for me.

DECEMBER 21, 2012

This was a decisive day; a turning point in my life. Perhaps, this will be my last writing. Perhaps this journey has come to its end and the next will be after our reunion, huh? On that day, I surrendered. I had finally come to the last phase in dealing with this unforgiving loss. I needed closure which

I finally accepted could only be attained through a complete breakaway of any further attempt to communicate with my children or to find out about their lives from any source.

On my way home, I decided to call Anwar from a restricted number. He answered. In my usual excited voice, I greeted him with "Hi *Habibi!*" His cold response before he abruptly hung up was that he was eating dinner. I decided I had had enough. I had had enough of pleading, enough of crying, enough of defeating anticipations, enough of shattered attempts and dashed hopes, enough of heart aches and of rejection.

The haunting tragedy of the Sandy Hook Elementary school massacre of twenty children and six educators on December 14 was still fresh and painful. Deranged Adam Lanza had shot and killed his mother before proceeding to murder twenty-six other innocent lives. The scale of this atrocity was unimaginable, particularly since Lanza had displayed no real warning signs. I called Anwar three consecutive times rebuking his decision to excommunicate me for five and a half years. If a son can kill his mother, then Anwar is certainly capable of the cruelty he has been inflicting upon me all these years. At that moment, in my last voice mail message, I vowed and pledged to him that he would "Never, ever hear from me again!" In retrospect, I blame myself for drawing such an unfair analogy. I was acting out of distress for what had happened.

In the New American Standard Bible, 2 Cor. 4: 6-9 St. Paul's Epistle states, "For God who said, "light shall shine out of darkness," is the One who has shone in our hearts to give the light of the knowledge of the glory of God in the face of Christ. But we have this treasure in earthen vessels that the surpassing of greatness of the power may be of God and not from ourselves. **We are afflicted in every way, but not crushed; perplexed, but not despairing; persecuted, but not forsaken; struck down, but not destroyed...**"

I ask You Lord, please have mercy on me and help me to endure.

Peace must come now!

CHAPTER 17

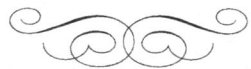

Parental Alienation Syndrome (PAS)

JULY 7, 2013

A few days ago, Anwar turned twenty-one, passing yet another milestone in his young life that I was not a part of. I had sent him an e-card and also left a voice message wishing him a happy birthday and advising him of the deposit into his account as a token birthday gift in case he wanted to buy something special for himself. I also told him that I could not pass up his birthday without calling and reminding him of how much he is loved, even though six months ago I had told him that I would no longer attempt to make contact. I reminded him that the door was always open in case he ever decided to enter. I did not receive a response. I did not expect any.

That weekend, I called my mother only to learn that Rameh's mother had left the country after an emergency request from Rameh to come to his aid earlier that week. The story was that he was bedridden with a serious back problem. I recalled how frail Rameh appeared during that court day as I waited to hear the judge decide on my visitation rights with my son. Unlike then when I had choked back tears, this time I let them flow, saddened by what I had heard, thinking that I could have cared for him and attended to his needs. If for anything, for the twenty-one years we were married, for being the father of my children, for simply being a human, like any other, deserving of love, dignity and care. But I could do nothing. He would never ask, nor would his pride ever allow him to.

The next morning, on my way to church, I decided to say a prayer and to light a candle asking God to have mercy on him and to heal him without any further suffering. As I parked my car, a strange compulsion made me pick up the phone and dial Nour. I expected the usual "We're sorry, this number has calling restrictions that have prevented this call..." as the case had been for years. But not this time.

I trembled as the phone rang instead. My thoughts raced at what message I would leave her. How to take advantage of the two minutes I had to tell her seven-years' worth of life stories and precious lost memories. I was overcome with emotions of fear, of joy, but of bewilderment. In a teary broken voice, I could only tell her how much I loved and missed her; how I saw her on you-tube playing the piano for the Phoenix Symphony, looking great and very confident. I could only tell her that I had asked her forgiveness many times and how I wished that she had it in her heart to forgive me, reminding her that, "Hatred corrodes the container it is in." I managed to tell her that the door was always open, that she should attend to her brother and take care of herself. My time was up. I said goodbye. I could not stop the tears as I proceeded to church, lit my candle, and thanked God for His kindness.

At 3:30 that afternoon, I read the last sentence of an incredible book by Amy Baker, _Adult Children of Parental Alienation Syndrome (PAS): Breaking_ _the Ties that Bind_. I had never heard of this relatively new construct though I had experienced it in every detail. A sense of relief and hope came over me. The book presented a framework to me through which I could understand, or at least, make sense of my children's behavior and decision to admonish me. It cemented my belief in Rameh's narcissistic and controlling personality that allowed him to use his children as pawns for his own gain, and to punish me for my infidelity and for leaving him. It brought to light what I had always known and feared the children would one day discover: that through his alienating tactics, Rameh molded them to hate me and even to ostracize me, believing that he had been the victim and that I had been the villain; that he was holy, and I was wicked, that he needed to be protected, cared for and loved, and I deserved to be humiliated, shamed and admonished into oblivion.

Finally, some science had backed my conviction that their father, the alienating parent, had succeeded in programming and brainwashing my children's fragile young minds, utilizing all the approaches mentioned in the book. Finally, I could hope that they were not heartless, but rather, that they had been manipulated to behave in such a way. I could make believe that they were not hateful, that they were simply closed to the truth for now and that one day, they would awaken. I could hope that they would be able to forgive.

The book outlines several modes of behavior exhibited by the alienating parent and the strategies utilized in order to effect PAS and to drive a wedge between the child and the targeted parent, some of which are included below.

- Bad-mouthing the targeted parent-in general or presenting the parent as dangerous.

- Limiting child contact with the targeted parent.

- Withdrawing love/telling child that the targeted parent does not love them.

- Forcing the child to choose/express loyalty.

- Confiding details of adult relationships with the child.

- Belittling the targeted parent in front of the child.

- Limiting contact with the extended family.

- Making the child feel guilty about a positive relationship with the targeted parent.

- Monitoring letters and phone calls with the targeted parent.

- The child's calling the targeted parent by his/her first name.

- Not allowing the child to receive gifts from the targeted parent or bring them home.

- The child is made to feel responsible for the parent's well-being, or asking the child to be the parent of the parent.

All of these strategies had been implemented by Rameh as explained in the earlier chapters.

To understand how successfully and skillfully Rameh had brainwashed my children, one has to read every document in my divorce papers, starting with the petition for the Dissolution of Marriage he filed, then proceeding to examine my petition to amend the divorce judgment in order to have visitations with my son, to grant Anwar therapy and to attempt to stop Rameh from further alienating my children and defaming my character. Reviewing Rameh's 31-page Manifesto in response to my petition is extremely crucial as well, along with all the responses and court orders that followed. All support Rameh's incessant attempts not only to smear my name, to degrade me as a human, to portray me to our children and anyone who knew me as unworthy of any respect, love and gratitude, but also to prevent the children from ever being exposed to another perspective that could sway them my way.

But before we examine all of that, I must mention that the alienation had started months before any court proceeding or even before the divorce. Rameh had manipulated the children in so many subtle ways which I did not recognize until after the divorce. From roughly November 2006 when he and I had the discussion regarding our marital problems to when I separated and returned less than two weeks later, to the time after that when I traveled to Spain and Morocco, and until the final hours before I left the house, and of course, throughout the years until now, I imagined, Rameh's poison was slowly festering within my children's souls.

PAS strategies were exemplified throughout the volumes I wrote in this journal. They were in my correspondence with the children, in the documented times they returned the gifts that I had sent them, or in the court petitions filed by Rameh in which he stated that my children had shared all of my e-mails with him "freely." Through it all, it becomes impossible to overlook the cleverly disguised brainwashing that was developing.

For the last six years, and for all the pain it would cause, I had not been able to review my divorce documents or the Manifesto. I decided that I had to be strong, to read everything I could and document—for posterity's sake—from the limited written proof I had in my possession, how Rameh had alienated my children using the only means at his disposal (them) to take revenge, regardless of the harm he would cause them. Truly, a narcissistic controlling man has to "win" at all costs. For a time, he did win, but sadly, he won at an irreparable cost: the damaged psyches of his own children.

I tried to highlight and to mark all the statements he wrote that would fit the book's description of tactics used by an alienating parent. I was overwhelmed by every statement he wrote in which he demonstrated without a doubt that he had utilized every strategy described in the book to alienate my children from me, driven by a narcissistic, controlling and cult-like personality, determined to ensure complete support and loyalty from his subjects: our children. He instilled in them the fear of facing the same fate of excommunication.

Throughout these documents, there were numerous statements and accusations Rameh had made as demonstrated in his Manifesto that I have outlined in earlier chapters. They all point to PAS strategies, from bad mouthing and character assassination, to disqualifying my contribution in raising the children, or taking care of the home, to playing the victim who deserved loyalty by his subjects, to directly and indirectly forcing my children to cut off any relationship with my family members, starting with my sister, then with my brother, and sadly, with my mother, afraid they might be persuaded by another perspective.

Rameh used many strategies including lying to the children as when they both claimed I had six affairs, or when Anwar told me that I was enjoying his father's suffering and the breakup of the family as well as the "Million" dollars his father had given me. At one time, Anwar mentioned to me that I had never apologized for my affair with Patrick or for the three or four others, and that I was "depressed and taking pills," as though to show I was lost, weak, crazy, and a pathological adulteress.

Rameh also forced on them the idea that I had abandoned my children for the sake of another man. Anwar told me once that I was enjoying raising Patrick's kids. Nour, on numerous occasions, kept referring to the life I had chosen as breaking up the family unit while enjoying my "sexual escapades." He also convinced them that I was a "ranting drunk," as Anwar wrote to the judge, saying that I am of poor character. Rameh's attempts to disqualify me as a parent and a dedicated mother came in many ways such as allowing my children to refer to me by my first name or only as a mother in quotes as in the letters they wrote to me and to the judge. They also referred to themselves as "a family" excluding me and intensifying the sense of them, vs. me. In sidelining my contribution to the household, Rameh stated in his Manifesto that after my departure, the house became in order and free of clutter when my house was always immaculate; I did all the chores, cooking, washing and cleaning. And to marginalize my dedication in raising my children further, he managed to get them to write how well they were thriving living under his roof and in his care, as though they had been neglected and unloved under mine.

There was no shortage of threats that Rameh made directly or indirectly, instilling fear and intimidation should my children not be completely loyal to him. On many occasions, Anwar told me "Every time you call, I fight with my family." He would also say my calls made him very angry, presumably because of the worry of being excommunicated for maintaining a relationship with me, the enemy. Rameh succeeded in his tactics not only by turning my children and our mutual friends against me but also by sharing with them my private and intimate e-mails with Patrick.

In order to avoid anything that could provide a different perspective for my children, Rameh was sure to cut off relationships with my immediate family and friends, leading the children to do the same. He also objected to the psycho-therapy and to my visitation petition, and convinced the family therapists to write to the court that Anwar did not need any therapy. It would not surprise me, based on Anwar's letter to the court objecting to the visitation, that Rameh had coached him to give the therapist every reason to believe that he was mentally and emotionally well; therefore, he did not need any therapy. Intercepting my e-mails, calls and letters and returning gifts, surely explain the degree of loyalty he had commanded.

Another effort that profoundly affected the children's decision to ostracize me was their father's playing the victim in order to garner sympathy, thus, to seal my children's loyalty to him. Nour became his confidante and care taker. He also claimed that he was undergoing stomach/liver cancer testing. For the record, Rameh had claimed to me before I left and perhaps to the children as well that he was at the hospital undergoing these tests, but there was no record of him when I showed up to visit. And yes, let us not forget the time he called me in desperation to kill himself if I did not return home, having been separated for less than two weeks.

He knew that through their sympathy and sorrow for his suffering and self-victimization that they would never attempt to contact me or to return my calls or e-mails. Doing so would constitute betrayal of the victim and siding with the enemy. Cultivating a relationship based on absolute loyalty and with a feeling of guilt, shame and betrayal, was the foundation from which he secured their total allegiance, much as a cult leader would do.

Rameh's incessant use of derogatory language in front of the children went to the point that they started repeating the same phrases, evident in the couple of letters they wrote to the judge and in the couple that Nour wrote to me, pleading Rameh's case better than he ever could. It is out of utter loyalty to their father and his clever manipulation of them that they came to believe that I was so wicked I accused him of incest with my daughter, an allegation or insinuation I have never made. He had simply twisted my words in a letter to Nour in which I wrote, "I fear for you in ways I cannot say" to mean incest. What I did not want to reveal to her in that statement was my fear that she would one day know her father was using her and her brother to make me suffer at the expense of their mental and emotional well-being. In further defaming my character, he made them believe that I deserved excommunication for being a "pathological liar, an avid cheater and a relentless adulterer..." who used "bigotry, abuse, manipulation, drudgery, fakeness, lies, selfishness, individualism and materialism" to indulge in my "habitual trait of infidelity."

Rameh's objection regarding the visitation, arguing he was acting on the independent wishes of my son, is another strategy he effectively used to prevent any contact with me. Another is when he threatened to call the police, (which he actually did twice) in order to file charges of trespassing with a restraining order if I dared come close to the house (such as when I attempted to talk to Nour through the window, or leave Anwar a care-package at the door). All of these are evidentiary tactics he used to sever contact and portray me as a "despicable" character, and worse, an evil mother who could actually inflict harm upon her children. He subjected them to taking the AIDS and SDT tests, instilling in them the unreasonable fear of a disease transmittal that he knew I did not have and had never contracted.

Another strategy Rameh used as revenge and to shame me and Patrick who worked in the same company was to mail his Manifesto directly to our employer instead of to my residence. He knew the mail would be opened by the mail room staff before being delivered to the employees. The content was distasteful and contained details of the divorce, of the affair and of the rest of my character assassination. I would not be surprised that some of that mail had been read and gossiped over for years. If this were not enough, he stopped at nothing, even hurting another individual whom he did not even know: Patrick's ex-girlfriend whom he was dating when he met me. Rameh wanted to ensure that she was made aware that Patrick had cheated on her with me, so he sent her an e-mail (after getting her address from my e-mails which he had hacked into) informing her of the affair, adding insult to her injuries as she tried to recover from the breakup.

In this summary, I tried as best I can to uncover Rameh's true aim—parental alienation—utilizing the PAS strategies as I understood them and without the psycho-analysis that could have further shed a more accurate and scientific basis for it. The rest will have to be through self-examination by my children, of their last thirteen years without me, and of the many years to come until their awakening.

As I continued reading the book, it became more and more apparent to me how Rameh utilized his alienation tactics through the tumultuous period before the divorce and for the years after as well. For the first time, it became clear to me that through his narcissistic controlling behaviors, Rameh had unknowingly to them, forced my children into total submission. But the book also revealed the pathetic but expected outcome: that once my children reach their awakening, they will know that their father had manipulated them. They will know that he deprived them of the motherly love and nurturing essential to every child's well-being; that he robbed them of their childhood. I feared they would be scarred for life, knowing that their father had put his own needs before those of his own flesh and blood. This is the sad truth that I have not dared to reveal to my children in order to protect them from the indescribable pain that would surely follow.

I closed the book, reflected upon its lessons, and wondered if somehow, my children might come across it one day. I wanted them to read it, but I feared their reaction and how the truth, while setting them free, would hinder their emotional development and interfere with their future relationships. Two days later, I thought to call Nour again to see if she had blocked my number. She had. I paused for a moment, not sure. I realized she had no mercy left in her heart ...then I remembered the book. I decided to push on saying to myself, she is not ready yet. Her day will come; her moment of truth will redeem her as it did mine, although twenty-one years later.

JULY 13, 2013

After much contemplation, I decided that Nour was old enough, mature enough, and strong enough to be exposed to the PAS construct. I decided anonymously to order her a copy of the book through Amazon to where I learned she was working during the summer break. I knew that she would most likely receive it, recognize it was from me and trash it immediately after reading its title. But I also thought her curiosity might drive her to read the book cover and the back reviews far enough to realize that parental alienation exists in science and in literature. My hope was that if she ever wanted to examine her life, her childhood, her relationship with her father, or the one with me, or if she wanted to gain an understanding of what she may have been going through, that she would remember this notion of parental alienation and would attempt to seek answers and perhaps even make peace with herself, with her father and with me.

I knew full well that she could completely turn this against me, believing that I was the one using the book to alienate her from her father. But that would entail her reading the book. That is all I wanted. It is the price I am willing to pay. It is the risk I am willing to take, not for the sake of hastening or bringing about her awakening and thus her reconciling with me, but rather, for the truth to be delivered and for the cloak of darkness to dissipate. My decision was an attempt to open up her mind, to break her utopian bubble, to bring her down to reality, to have her reflect on the past, to evaluate the present, to connect with herself and to hope for the future. My hope was that by raising her awareness she might avoid being a victim of PAS herself.

The book states that the awakening in all of the respondents was gradual, and that it had taken some up to forty-seven years, with an average of twenty. This would be too ineffectual and would cause needless pain to my children if they had to discover PAS so late in their lives and then to seek self-reflection, reconciliation, or treatment. I hoped that if Nour recognized PAS early enough, the damage would be contained, or somewhat mitigated. It is commonly believed that early intervention is the best cure. As a prospective doctor, she should know that.

My hope was also for her to realize that I was not using the book to downplay the gravity of my infidelity or to marginalize the indescribable pain and suffering that I have caused all of us. Surely, I hoped this would not be perceived as a clever way on my part to drive a wedge between her and her father. That was not my intention whatsoever and never will be. I had forgiven Rameh long ago and let go of all resentment for all the lost years. And while I cannot escape the sadness that will forever permeate my existence for not having my children in my life, I am comforted to know they are making good futures for themselves, that they are happy, well and thriving. In the final analysis, Nour is an adult and paving her way into the next chapters of her life. Soul-searching will become inevitable for all of us at some juncture in our lives. We hope that by then, the damage did not take up permanent residence in our hearts. I overcame; and so my hope is that she will too.

I called Amazon a month later to find out if Nour had made any attempt to find who the sender was. She had. The operator confirmed two chatting conversations on July 31st and August 3rd. Since I had given Amazon clear instructions not to reveal my identity, and the book was sent as a gift, the operator assured me that Nour was told that they could not reveal any information about the sender. I was relieved that she must have read the book since the order had been received on July 20 and her first attempt to find out who had sent it was eleven days later. I was wrong. I called Amazon again three weeks later to see if Nour had made any further attempt, only to discover that she had actually returned the book marked "Did not need it." Amazon received it July 30 and credited her account as a returned gift. I could only surmise that she figured out that it was from me and was determined to hurt me in the best way she could by returning it unread.

Surely, the pain was intense, knowing that her mind and heart were shut not just to me, but to any source that could open a crack into the truth that she thought she knew with conviction. I was left with no hope of her awakening. I carried on as I always did, wondering if she were truly a monster or just a cult follower. It was very difficult to be convinced that she was the latter rather than the former. She was an adult, I thought. Surely, she could choose to liberate herself from her father's cloak; surely she could do some self-reflection and retrace the steps of years passed and come to the decision to ask more about the lost and manipulated "truth." Surely, she was a grown up woman, fully capable of making her own choices and realizing how short life was to waste it in anger, in resentment and in holding onto a past that could only obstruct or muddy our future. But, as always, Nour never ceases to surprise me. Perhaps her day will come, perhaps never. With that, I never looked at the book again.

CHAPTER 18

Determination That Never Ceases

SEPTEMBER 12, 2013

Though excited, I got into my car not expecting anything. I stopped at Cost Plus along the way to fill a bag of fine European chocolates, just like the ones I used to buy Anwar- Malteesers, Lindt, Cadbury fingers, Loacker, and Kinder. Anwar, like me, loved chocolate, but would only settle for the finest brands. On one box of Hit chocolate cookies, I left a heart-shaped sticky note with "Anwar, so you may remember" with my drawing on it two hearts in one. I tried to disguise my hand-writing as best I could.

An hour and a half into my trip, I reached the first address where I believed Anwar lived, having investigated his whereabouts through ceaseless hours on the internet. I parked my car and walked into his street, reaching the multi-unit and multi-building apartment complex. I carefully examined the structures and the common areas, trying to get a glimpse of where and how my Anwar has lived for the past year, constructing an imaginary routine for this young man, taking his first steps to independence. I reached unit 50 where I thought he lived and knocked, not sure of who might open. I was not surprised to find a new tenant who had moved the first of August. As I suspected, Anwar must have lived there until the end of July and then moved to another complex a couple of streets over.

I proceeded to the new location, and just before reaching the complex, I was astonished to see his truck parked across the street, left for days to collect thick dust, making it impossible to see through the windshield. I knew parking at the complex was not free and parking on the street was very scarce. He must leave his truck for the week and bicycle his way to school and back, I gathered. The complex, a couple of miles from campus, was centrally located among several supermarkets and food outlets, making it convenient for students.

I proceeded to the entrance. A construction worker directed me to the rental office, where I met Jesenia. I sat down trembling at being the closest I had come to him in a very long time. I did not expect her to give me Anwar's apartment number or to verify that he lived there. Privacy laws prevented her from revealing such information. Still, I pleaded with her to give him the bag of chocolates, telling her that I had not seen my son for years. Pitying me for my helpless state, she agreed. I gave her Anwar's cell number and asked her to call him. He did not answer. She left him a message to pick up a package from the office. I thanked her and left. I walked around the large complex, checked the mail boxes for any names, asked a few of the students I saw around, but no one knew him. I tried to save an image in my head of how these units looked, peeking through some windows and open doors. Did Anwar have a decent place to stay? There was not much I could see, so I continued to walk around like a lost soul, hoping for a clue that would lead me to the unit he lived in. I was not so lucky.

Just in case Anwar did not pick up his messages, I wrote a note for him to pick up the package from Jesenia, again disguising my handwriting. I really did not want him to know that I might have left him something until he actually got it. I stuck the note under the windshield wiper, and with my finger, I wrote I love you in the dust on his windshield.

I knew that if Anwar did not listen to his messages that day, he would at least see the note the following day when he had to move the car by noon on Friday per the traffic sign where he was parked. That morning, I called Jesenia, only to be disappointed that he had not picked up the package or returned her call. She was kind enough to call him again. Around noon, my heart jumped when she called me back to let me know that he had picked up the package. I asked her if he had tried to find out who it was from and she said no, that he had told her he had seen the note. I knew that he knew and was delighted to imagine that he might think about me as he bit into each piece of chocolate, realizing how much I loved him and that I would go to the end of the earth to find him.

November 6, 2013

I retained an investigator to help me find Anwar's apartment number. On my own, I was able to find out where he lived, but the complex had several buildings making it impossible to locate his and the unit's number. The investigator met me close by. He said he was continuing to do some research and hoped to get the exact address soon. I was hopeful but guarded. I located Anwar's truck and posted a note that read:

Just remember... You will only have ONE mother EVER!! Don't ever think I will stop trying. When will this end? When will you have it in your heart to FORGIVE me, to accept my apologies

and to give me a chance? How much longer must I be punished?
I just want to be here for you. I love you forever...and ever.

Mother

From there, I proceeded to Anwar's university, desperate to find him. I peeked through classrooms in which I thought he was taking some courses, but I had no luck. It was late in the evening, but I thought of speaking to the engineering department's staff member in the hope he could tell me if Anwar was graduating or walking that summer. A kind man, indeed, the staff member could not confirm but urged me to talk to the Dean whom he described as being a very kind-hearted man who had helped families before. I was lucky that the Dean had office hours that evening, so we met. I told him the story of my son's estrangement as briefly as I could. I would never have expected to be so well received by anyone who did not know me, let alone by a Dean who ordinarily would not meddle in family affairs. Yet, the kindness the Dean had displayed was very touching and humbling. I did not want to put him in an uncomfortable situation, but I was at the end of my rope, and I did not know who else to turn to. I was grateful that he agreed to make an attempt if he determined it to be possible. I thanked him deeply, left him my business card with my cell number, and prayed for the best.

Ten days passed without a response, so I followed up with an e-mail, hoping that by giving him a few more details about my predicament, perhaps he might be able to convince Anwar to reconnect with me. I did not get a response. I wrote:

...I have tried everything. I appeal to your compassion and
humanity, while I completely understand your position and the
professional responsibility you have for the department as well
as toward your students.

I am not sure if you were able to make contact with him or what his response might have been. I know he is very angry, and I can understand, but it has been six and a half years, so I am hoping his heart has softened a bit, just a bit. I am also praying that he is able to forgive me and to accept my apologies which I have extended time and time again, but to no avail. My hope is for us to be able to communicate at least. Even if he doesn't want to see me at all, he can agree to answer the phone when I call him, even if only once a month. All I want is to maintain at least a hairline connection in order to know he is well and that I will be there for him always. If you can help me with this, I will forever be indebted to you. And if you have reason not to, I will also understand. I want you to know that I am still very thankful to you for whatever little message you can pass on to him.

A few days later, I took a long walk on the beach as I always do in times of distress. I sat on a bench to rest, and I saw a child's handwritten note in chalk on the concrete below: I love U MoM. Exactly like that. With a big heart drawn above it. Is it serendipity, I asked? I took a picture of it and sent it to Anwar with an email. I did not receive a response.

As I sat down on a bench at the beach yesterday, resting after a long walk, I looked down and saw this inscribed on the concrete: a heart and "Love U Mom." For a moment, I contemplated my fate and wondered if you truly hated me.

Then, a good feeling came upon me. One day, you will understand and learn the truth behind my story. You will then know who your mother really is and decide no longer to judge me for what I am NOT. ...and then, I thought, yes, that day will come; it will come; we will reunite; I will be your

mother—without quotes—as I always was, as I always will be.
I picked up my pace and carried on.

A couple of weeks passed and then suddenly, I received a call from a man called Nizar stating that he had been contacted by the Dean asking him to call his mother. I am not sure what exactly the Dean had communicated to Nizar, but I quickly realized the he must have mistaken a fellow Lebanese and a mechanical engineering student with my son. I apologized to him and explained what I thought had happened, letting him know that Anwar had been estranged from me for seven years. Nizar was so taken by the news and asked me to send him a picture in order to confirm my son's identity. I did and he identified him quickly as one of his classmates. Nizar has become my guiding torch, my angel ever since. He gave me updates on Anwar's progress and assured me that he was doing well.

NOVEMBER 24, 2013

As I shopped for Thanksgiving dinner, I received a call from the investigator telling me to get a paper and pen ready. My heart raced as I wrote Anwar's exact address down. The investigator was able to narrow his apartment down to about eleven and went knocking on doors with a box of chocolates as a pretext delivery. He was lucky to encounter Anwar's roommate, Gary, leaving. Gary acknowledged that Anwar was upstairs, and he said that he would deliver the package to him.

I went home not sure if I should "surprise" him or not. After much contemplation, I thought, well, it is Thanksgiving, so why not try my luck! I got there around 5 p.m., but the lights were out. I knocked but no one answered. I tried again at 6 p.m. and finally, at 7 p.m. Gary opened the door but said that Anwar did not live there. I insisted he did, assuming that Gary was in on the pretext. I did have to tell him who I was and that I had brought Anwar some gifts and had waited a long time to see him. He said that he would deliver the presents but refused to tell me where Anwar was or when he might come home. He said, "Perhaps you should give him more time." I responded, "It has been six and a half years. I traveled long and hard to see him." What happened between his father and I was between us only and the kids had nothing to do with it and my relationship with them should be separate from my relationship with their father.

In retrospect, should I have heeded Gary's advice? It became more and more apparent that Anwar was not ready to see me; in fact, he would become angry and resentful. Yet, there were the good times too, brief as they may have been, that told me of my son's longing to be with his mother, but he was being torn between his loyalty to his father and his love for me. He was fearful of asserting himself. He had a desire to be part of both of our lives without suffering his father's or his sister's wrath. Then, all I could see and feel was that my son needed me in his life in as much as I wanted him in mine, so I continued to push to see him, doing what any mother would. Perhaps time would prove me right, and Anwar would be better off for it, or it would sentence me for life for the selfishness I have been accused of, just like my children had.

As I spoke, Gary became nervous and looked outward. I turned around only to see Anwar walking in with his other roommate, Eric, with a couple of grocery bags in hand. His first words were, "So you found me, huh?" I trembled responding, "I would go to the end of the earth to find you," and rushed inside the apartment fearing Gray would shut the door. Anwar walked in. Not knowing what he would do, I said, "I am not leaving; call the police." His response was, "You know I would not do that!" I relaxed.

I could not see his features very well under the dimmed kitchen light where we sat. Yet, indeed, he had become a man, beard and all. The boy of fifteen with soft skin and slender figure had grown into a full-bodied, still short, but very mature and handsome fellow, hair thinning, like his mother, as he reminded me. He assumed it was Patrick who came looking for him with the box of chocolates, but I revealed to him that it was the investigator. He was surprised and did not appear happy about it. I had to tell him that he had left me no choice. Tears ran down my cheeks, but I quickly knew I had to contain my sentiments.

Still, I tried to hug him, but he pulled away, although not very successfully. I had to be content with what I got. I tried so hard to maintain my composure, my "cool" as they say, not to turn him off. God gave me the strength. I kept the conversation casual and presented the gifts. He appeared to like them, but was concerned about the cost. "It does not matter," I said. I had given him a Hurley jacket that I knew he would like, a shirt, an elegant sweater, a hat and a scarf to keep him warm, and a wallet with a gift card with some cash in it so he could eat healthfully. I then told him that we needed to talk. To my surprise, he agreed, but wanted to step outside, probably because his roommates were home, even though he had just told me that "They know more about you than you think."

He was quick to point out to me how lucky the investigator had been in locating his apartment because no one knew where he lived. He added that this, however, would be short-lived since his lease was ending in May and that he would not give me his new address at that juncture. I was not about to push him or to mention anything from the past. I simply wanted to relish the moment that I had so waited for. I broke down once when he refused to commit to seeing me or to receiving my calls. As I cried asking him, "How can you do this to me?" he got angry and said, "You see, you see, that is why I don't want to talk to you, not because of you, but because this is how I deal with it." I was not sure if he meant that he did not want to inflict pain on me or wanted to protect himself from further pain.

It saddened me that his way of dealing with all the accumulated pain was to block it out not dealing with it at all. Our conversion was very fragmented. We jumped from one topic to the next, not focusing very much on anything. There was so much to talk about, but not enough time. It was not the proper venue. We walked for about an hour and a half in the freezing dark night. He told me how I "messed up" and "messed up" his father "big time." "Yes, I know, what I did was wrong," I replied. "Your father and I had many problems, but he did not deserve what I did and neither did you." He said he had a good relationship with his father although he did not visit the house very often. He insisted on telling Rameh about our encounter, and actually his father rang while we were talking. Anwar had already told his father about the chocolate delivery, so perhaps they had expected me. He took the call and I gave him his privacy and space.

I asked him about Nour. He seemed to idealize her and hoped to be like her. I assured him that he was his own man and didn't need to be like anyone. I was disappointed to find out he had a very grim outlook on life. He kept saying that he had "no feelings for anything;" that he did not care if he "lived or died" although he said he would never kill himself because it would be "useless," that nothing meant anything to him, that how life "sucked;" but also that he had good morals and behaviors. I also found out he worked twenty hours a week as an engineering intern. He refused to tell me where, but it did not matter to me. I was proud that he was so responsible, was paying his $400 monthly rent, his bills, his credit card payments and had no debt besides the $10,000 student loan. I asked if he needed financial help. He was indifferent to my help. While he initially seemed interested when I reminded him of the 529 Fund, in the end he said I could do whatever I wanted and that he was already taking care of his expenses. I was content to know that my man will surely transition into life better prepared than many kids his age.

He seemed to be hard on himself, and perhaps he suffered from low self-esteem. He still did not think he was smart enough and felt he was "failing" even though he was graduating in the fall, a semester behind schedule, and only because he had been unable to secure his courses. It appeared that he still wanted my approval. He wanted to assure me that he had turned out to be what I would have expected him to be. He was right. With the little time I had, I tried to boost his morale and to tell him how accomplished he already was and how proud I was of him and the man he had become. I shared with him my view that life was beautiful; that even with all the pain, I still enjoyed my travels, my hobbies and my life because all of it had made me a better person. He could not understand why I felt life was beautiful, especially with a long commute and his own outlook that it was all about hard work and no reward. I told him that life would teach him to appreciate it and that, in time, he would understand why I said it was so beautiful.

I asked him about his love life, and he sarcastically said that he had rebuffed many girls, "Thanks to you." I told him that his fingers, while part of the same hand, are not alike and that no matter how "shitty" he thought me, every person is different. He was quick to point out to me that "I did not say that. I just said you messed up." And when I mentioned the several "affairs" he had accused me of, he denied ever saying that. He added that he "purposely" forgets things. He even mentioned the fight that broke out between his father and me on his 15th birthday but insisted that he was thirteen. I gathered that this is another way that he deals with the pain. I told him that I had it all in writing in two separate boxes left for him and Nour containing all the details of my failed attempts to reconnect with them....for posterity's sake.

I reminded him that I had sought forgiveness many times, but that he and his sister would not accept my apologies. He did not comment. He briefly mentioned how "divorce messes up children big time," and I pointed out that it did not have to, without telling him why. After all, I was not there to try to redeem myself or hint at anything that could incriminate his father. Anwar needed to discover the truth on his own. I told him that he would one day. He said nothing.

Throughout the little time we spent, I was comforted that he was respectful. And while he did not welcome me with open arms, he engaged me a little and asked about where I worked, about my graduate studies, and about what his cousins were majoring in when I mentioned them. For a while, our conversation felt like a normal one between friends or between distant relatives. It felt good. I admitted to him that I was afraid that he might shut the door and spit in my face. He dismissed my fear saying, "I guess you don't know me." I felt shamed for not trusting the boy I raised to be the respectful, kind gentlemen I had always known he was, and I thanked him.

He kept repeating that he was angry and that every time I attempted to communicate with him in the past it had made him angry. He accused me of being selfish for wanting to continue to see him and get a commitment from him. Sure, I saw a lot of anger, but I was not convinced that my visit was actually harming him. On the contrary, I have always felt that he was torn and caught in the middle between his loyalty to his father, who he believed was victimized by me, and his buried desire to maintain a cordial relationship with a mother I knew he loved so much. Not to dismiss him, I acknowledged that a mother's love can be interpreted as selfish, but that he should know it is always genuine.

Toward the end of the conversation, as we sat next to each other on the stairwell of one of the adjacent buildings, he admitted that while he was "angry five minutes ago; I am no longer." I was relieved realizing our reunion was fruitful and that he must have felt the intensity of my love which he needed to be reassured. He knew that my never having given up on him and my going to the extreme to find him, only affirmed our eternal bond. My steadfastness and my love transcended any distance or time. Still, each time I tried to get him to commit to see me or respond to my calls, he got angry and utterly refused. I knew I could no longer push the envelope. He said, "You really should leave now."

I walked him back to his apartment and restrained my emotions while saying goodbye. I invited him for Thanksgiving, but I was not disappointed when he refused me. Even though he rejected my request to hug him, I pulled him towards me anyway. He resisted slightly, but I stole a quick hug. He then lifted his arm and with a beautiful contented smile and relaxed demeanor said, "You will get a pat on the shoulder," and proceeded to do just that. I said goodbye and left. He went inside and never looked back. From his front porch, I took a quick look at his lit living room; his room-mates there watching TV, expressionless. He proceeded without picking up the gifts, left on the sofa and on the kitchen table. I picked up the pace back to my car parked in the supermarket lot across the street, overwhelmed with emotions which, to date, I cannot fully comprehend.

I drove back feeling as though I were stoned. I partly was very happy, partly afraid, partly sad, and partly numb. Surely, I was delighted to have seen him and to have spent an hour and a half with him. It was nothing like any of the other brief and rare encounters we had had over the years. After all, the last time I laid my eyes on him was in June, 2010, during his graduation. I was also worried about where this would lead, how this might affect us both, questioning if this would stir up emotions again and regenerate the bottled up pain of failed attempts, especially when I could not guarantee that our encounters would continue. And I was so sad for his anger which holds us in a perpetual state of bitterness, preventing us from progressing and from developing the strength with which to deal with life's many obstacles. I was sad about his indifference and about his unwillingness to face the pain or the reality, instead, choosing to block it, stunting his emotional growth. I was sad about his grim outlook on life that gave him no hope...and I worried about his mental and emotional well-being, knowing that I was so helpless. But I was also numb, not knowing how to react or what to feel. It was very strange for me, for once, not to be able to understand the emotions that were in play. I expected to jump with joy, filled with happiness, but instead, I somehow felt flat, and I could not explain why. It wasn't until my second encounter that I understood the cause behind the stillness.

A couple of days later, I sent him an e-mail titled: *"Proud Of You, Son,"* recapping our visit and expressing my pride and pleasure over his achievements. I hoped it would lift his spirits and boost his morale. I wrote:

Habibi Anwar:

You cannot imagine how delighted I was to see you, to talk to you and to touch you for the first time in so many years. You have grown up to be a very handsome young man, mature and responsible beyond your years....and I was so proud knowing that my man is on his way to assured success. What more could a mother ask for? Nothing, really.

You were respectful and polite. I thank you for not rebuffing me and for allowing me to chat with you for the time we had. You have become a true gentleman. I always knew that you would be. I thought about how hard your life has been. But I also thought about how this young man could overcome all this adversity, could get through a tough and challenging major while maintaining a twenty-hour job, pay his bills, his rent, his tuition and his living expenses and to be on his imminent road to graduation! And I was amazed at your great accomplishments at such a young age when other peers are still contemplating their majors, living at home or heavily dependent on their parents and indebted to the banks or the government. Well done, my son, well done.

No, I will not "stalk" you or show up unannounced. I did what I did because you had left me no choice. And no, I need not know where you work and I will not attempt to find out. You proved yourself not just to your father and me, but also, and more importantly, you proved yourself to yourself. As we progress through life, we discover that we only have ourselves to compete with and no other. This is the essence of what matters, and it's the basis of our successes and of self realization.

But life's challenges have just begun. What lies ahead will undoubtedly continue to test you. With every obstacle you encounter and overcome, you will understand why I said life was and will always be so beautiful. The caveat, though, is that we must choose to deal with whatever comes our way and not let anger and disappointments lock us into a state of resentment and bitterness. If we do that, we inhibit our potential, hinder our progress, and rob ourselves of the joy of our hard labor that makes life worth living. How can life bring us any satisfaction if we choose not to allow it to or decide not to give it a chance? How can anything?

Now, I know that you are struggling financially. And while I was very glad to know that you can take care of your needs, you deserve a little reprieve and to have some time to live your college life and to be rewarded for your hard work. I can and I want to help. The Scholarshare (529) Fund that I have built over

the last seven years for you can make this happen. I trust you
will spend the money wisely. You have already demonstrated to
me that you will.

Love you so, son
Mother

The few exchanges that followed were the first e-mails he ever responded to. They all related to paying tuition and to loans. I knew Anwar was not driven by financial gain because I know he is not materialistic at all. I believe he chose to reply probably because the issue was related to money and not to sentiments, so he could respond without feeling pressured that he was betraying his father. I remained hopeful, but guarded.

DECEMBER 12, 2013

Mother came to visit a couple of weeks earlier. I asked her to prepare some Kibbeh with the intention of saving it for Anwar. She happily obliged, as always. We labored for hours in the kitchen as I tried to help but also to learn the skill so that I may carry the tradition on for future generations. With love, I carefully packed two bags for Anwar and saved them for when I would see him next. I was going to wait to deliver the food until after I met Nour for yet another surprise of a lifetime, on her birthday, December 14. I had recently learned she had bought a house in Goodyear, Arizona a few months before, so I had decided to confront her. Uncertain of how that encounter might go and of how it might affect the delicate and fragile relationship I had just reestablished with Anwar, I decided that it would be best to visit him before my trip to Arizona.

I e-mailed Anwar regarding my visit, casually letting him know that the reason was to give him some Kibbeh. I told him I was expecting to arrive at his place by 9 p.m. His response was unpleasant, somewhat hurtful and defiant. I responded in kind with sarcasm, but mixed with love and determination. It worked. He changed his tone, gave up and e-mailed back that I could do what I wanted because he could not stop me. Finally, he might be softening up, I hoped.

Delayed by traffic, I arrived a little after 9, not sure what to expect. I rang, and he opened the door, looked at his watch and said, "On time, huh? O no, it is 9:06. You are late." It appeared to be a friendly gesture to break the ice; at least I took it that way. This time, his roommates stayed upstairs while we chatted for about an hour. I brought more gifts, a sweater, a casual shirt, another, dressier, a hat, a scarf, and some cologne wrapped in glittering Christmas paper, and stockings filled with the Christmas chocolates, just as I always have done every year. He remembered those days. I also brought him a small album containing scanned pictures from his childhood during better times. I asked him not to open his gifts until Christmas Eve and the chocolate on Christmas day, just as I used to ask him and Nour every year.

Anwar expressed his concern about my spending money, but I explained that I thought his clothes appeared worn out and needed replacing. I was glad he was careful with money, and I reminded him that I must have raised him well. Quickly, he dismissed any credit I had had in his upbringing, and I let it go. Rameh was successful in making my children and the world—his world—believe that he had assumed the role of father and mother in my absence, as if anyone could. He sold them the lie, and thus achieved his goal—the complete nullification of my existence.

Anwar mentioned how he did not like to associate with the Lebanese since they were "stupid" and fought all the time; that he would only consider going to Lebanon if the people had regained some of their senses and stopped fighting with each other. He also said he hated the culture for its ill-treatment of women, stating he did not feel he could belong to any such a society. I sympathized, but I preached a little tolerance, trying to make him recognize the reasons behind the bloodshed, steeped in a long history of colonialism that had fed sectarianism and different forms of oppression. I also shared with him that we could not forget our heritage and that we should be proud of who we are; that he was an American first and foremost, but that he could not deny where he had come from. He mentioned his father's displeasure at his sentiments toward these issues as well. Yes, he needed a lot of growing up still.

Gladly, Anwar accepted the gifts and appeared to be happy with the ones I got him earlier. I explained to him how to heat the Kibbeh properly, and I sat down at his kitchen table to talk. I informed him of the money transfer to his school account. He checked his phone, confirmed the deposit and said that he appreciated it. I asked him about his finals and his work. He said that he had done all right and that he still had a couple left. Regarding his work, he was proud to tell me that he was "really needed" for the good work he does. I said, "Sure, you are very smart," as I felt he was a bit more confident than I last saw him; and he was. While he still felt that other people were much smarter than he was, he agreed later saying he was smart, but that he does not apply himself well. I agreed and added that it was good to set the bar high, but never to underestimate one's potential or to minimize one's achievements. He seemed a bit more relaxed and upbeat. This made me very content.

Somewhere during the conversation, he mentioned how "it was so, so close." I was not sure what he meant, but I reasoned it may have had to do with my affair before ending the marriage. I said yet again, that what I did was wrong and that if I could turn back the clock I would make different choices and do things differently. He talked about how the divorce was "not friendly," and I acknowledged that I wished it had been, but that his father did not want to have anything to do with me. He knew. I tried to explain that my relationship with their father should have had no bearing on my relationship with them, but he was quick to point out, "Except we were one family." I decided he was not ready or mature enough to distinguish the separation of relationships or the issue of divorce and what had led to it.

However, there was one question that I wanted Anwar to answer: had he forgiven me? I was disappointment when he said, "No." Nevertheless, I nodded, paused for a moment and asked how his father was doing. He was happy to tell me that Rameh had lost some weight and was looking very good. I then emphasized that whether Anwar believed me or not, I actually had cared for his father, for all the years that we were married. He was the father of my children and I wished that we could have had a cordial relationship. I then took the opportunity of asking his opinion on whether his father would be agreeable to meeting me so that I could apologize to him for my wrong-doing. Anwar quickly displayed a subtle change in attitude, becoming more relaxed and content, as though a weight had lifted off of his shoulders. I felt as if he could finally take a breath of relief, even as he stayed firm and composed. He calmly said he would ask him since he felt that his father was at a stage where "he did not care anymore." But when I expressed concern that Rameh might think that this was some ploy to get the kids back into my life, he nodded in agreement.

Anwar then asked me to "fire" the investigator, but when I said I was still settling some bills with him, Anwar threatened to file a restraining order against Patrick and me. I was very hurt and I welled up. I told him that it would be on his conscience forever; that I had done all the searching by myself and only needed the investigator to get me the apartment number. Anwar said he did not like to be followed and did not want Patrick to contact him or to feel that he had to be a part of Patrick's life. I told him that I had spoken to Patrick about their communications; that he did what he had done because he was hurting for me. I assured Anwar that I would never force Patrick into his life. I added that he had left me no choice and that if he had returned my calls, answered his phone or e-mailed to let me know where he had moved, perhaps I would not have resorted to that.

I cannot explain what happened at that moment. Anwar clearly wanted to relay the stern message that I should stop using the investigator; otherwise, he would file a restraining order. I was not sure if he would actually carry it through. At one point, he hinted that he might actually decide to answer the phone occasionally, as though to assure me that he was no longer considering a restraining order after all. I am not sure if his father had planted the idea in his head, or if it was his idea, because I would never have expected Anwar to make such a hurtful threat.

I collected myself and steered the conversation toward another, more pleasant direction. I told him about my long bike rides and about how I go to the gym regularly to stay sane and to take care of my body and my spirit. I found out that he went to the gym too, so I got up and felt his biceps. He was strong. I was happy to know he was eating healthfully, as he had said. He said he builds computers as a hobby; that he cannot wait to graduate and make lots of money and move to Whistler. He liked it there, in spite of the snow. He also acknowledged having seen the Whistler pictures I had sent him. "I wanted to retrace your steps," I said. He said "Yes, and many other people's," still down on himself, I suppose. Nevertheless, I told him that I had only cared for one set of footsteps. Yet, he was happy to report that he still did not do drugs or drink alcohol, not even juice, but only milk. He asked me if I wanted my pictures from my trip to Spain which were left on the camera flashcard. I said, "No, keep them for when you want to remember what I look like." He did not react. I also told him about my upcoming trip to Iran. He was concerned and warned me not to go because "You will be killed." He was quick to realize that he had showed too much concern for me, so he added that he would not want anyone to go there. He still cared.

Time flew fast. He wanted to play some video games, and I was using up his down time when he rested after a couple of final exams. He politely asked me to leave. I asked for a hug. He refused at first, but then turned his back at me allowing me to hug him from behind. I wanted to smell the scent of the little boy I used to sniff laying on him many sweet morning kisses. He pulled away telling me that he stunk. He was not relenting; he was not ready to let me back into his life in the way things used to be. I told him that I loved him and pleaded sweetly for him to answer as he always did, "*Wa'ana kamein.*" He said he was not going to say anything, but asked me to "drive safely." I knew not to push further. I departed although this time, a bit more hopeful.

For days I could not understand or explain how I felt. Though I was a bit more confident that I might be able to sustain some sort of a relationship with Anwar, I still cried and felt confused. As I remembered our last reunion, it dawned on me that I was able to see my son in full view and under bright light and to realize how he had grown......and I knew.....I was mourning the loss of the little boy I would never see again.

Unlike most normal mother/child relationships that are nurtured over time, mine was severed abruptly overnight. I never got to experience his transition from boyhood to adolescence to manhood. I never watched him grow. His child's face was affixed in my memory, so kind, so sweet, and so loving. He had become angry, bitter, and ambivalent about everything, with nothing in between to explain how or why. Six and a half years had been stolen from me; years that I could never recapture; time in which milestones in his life had occurred that I was not privy to; emotions, high and low, that he may have experienced and that I could not console. Precious years, daily happenings were lost in space that history will never recall; moments, experiences, friends, relationships, conversations, they all have passed me by. I could not figure out what might have impacted his thinking, his dreams, his aspirations. The gap was too large to bridge. In front of me stood a man, handsome, articulate and smart, yet as I would explain to a boy, I took my time showing him how to heat Kibbeh.

What was I thinking? I don't know. Who was this man talking with me? Did I know him? Where was the child I nurtured, loved so deeply, kissed, smelled, disciplined with care so that he would become a man of good moral character and would be successful? That much I see, but where is the laughter, where are the hugs, the I love yous, the cuddling hours and morning kisses? Where is the joy that is no longer? All had been frozen in time, I realized. Yet all were lost in time. Or is everything embedded within this gentle soul resisting in order to deny me the pleasure of a love unchanged as a penance for my indiscretions and as a gesture of loyalty to his father? I do not know, and I am not sure if time will ever show me. Perhaps, I thought, after my surprise encounter with Nour, all the more would be forsaken. Then I would not only have lost the boy son, but the man son as well.

DECEMBER 14, 2013

I tried to prepare myself for the worst; that is to be escorted by the police and perhaps to be jailed. I was still reeling emotionally from my meeting with Anwar a couple of days before. Still, I prayed for a good outcome, went to bed early and got up at 4 a.m. to catch a flight to Phoenix. I arrived at 9 a.m., picked up the rental car, and proceeded to Goodyear where Nour was living. At 10:45 a.m., I arrived on her doorstep, knocked and hoped that someone would open. Through the adjacent window, I could see an older woman approach. "Who is it?" she asked. I said, "I am looking for Nour." "She is not here," the woman replied. At that instant, I recognized the voice of Fadwah, my ex-mother-in-law. "This is Futoun; open the door," I requested. She was kind enough to let me in. We hugged and cried. I asked her why she would not let me know how my children had been doing for all these years, and her response was "I dared not; you know Rameh."

Nour was asleep. Fadwah said they were supposed to travel by car to California that morning, but Nour had slept in since she was not feeling well the night before. She had finished her finals and had celebrated with a few friends and her uncle's family with some food that Fadwah had prepared for the occasion. Fadwah was concerned how Nour's reaction would be when she saw me, but it did not matter to me. I was determined to complete my mission. We talked for about an hour. She reminded me when long ago she had advised me not to leave my children and I supposedly told her that it was my life. I dismissed her statement, saying, "I did not leave my children; they left me." She assured me that Rameh was the "mother and father" in my absence and that my kids were not "deprived" of anything.

What was I going to say? I only said that no one can replace another. She asked me if Patrick had come with me, and I replied that he had not, that this was something that I needed to face alone. She also asked if I was married, and I told her that we were not ready yet, but that we were very happy together. She mentioned how Nour's uncle who lived an hour away was very protective of her and took good care of her. I asked if Nour had someone in her life. She said no, but then added that she had never asked. She offered me tea as we chatted. The Chamomile had calmed my nerves a bit so that I actually felt that I could have a heart-to-heart conversation with Nour....so I thought.

As Fadwah went to the bathroom, I looked around and took a few pictures. A nice house she has, relatively well furnished and adorned with some wall hangings from the old house. In her living room was the old brown sofa we had bought upon our marriage. On the wall behind her desk in her study was a picture of a younger Nour holding her violin, her father in the middle and Anwar to the left. It must have been taken from when I was still in the house, but there was no sign of me. That was "their family." I browsed through some books she had, mostly medical ones, except for some detective stories, and a book by Naguib Mahfouz, a renowned Egyptian writer.

At approximately 11:45 a.m., Nour's bedroom door opened. I looked behind me and there she was. Calmly and with a very straight face as though she knew I was there, she commanded, "Get out of my house." Here I thought I had been calm, but I believe her statement enraged me. I told her I was not leaving and to call the police. She said, "I will," but proceed to call her father first. At that point, I lost it and screamed at her, "Let it be on your conscience forever that you called the police on your mother." She turned to her grandmother and scolded her for letting me in. Fadwah had said nothing throughout the ordeal. As he answered, her first words were, "She is here." I shouted, "Rameh go ahead, call the police." I do not know what he told her, but I can only imagine he gave her the green light to call the police justifying it by my refusal to leave her property when she asked. She then said "Get the fuck out of my house." I was shocked to hear her use such language. I said, "I never raised you like that." She sarcastically responded, "Yeah, because everything I am is because of you." I believe it was at that point or seconds after that she appeared flustered and shocked and that is when she wiped a tear with her hand from under her thick glasses.

Before I had a chance to respond, she was already dialing 911 telling the operator, "There is a person in my house who should not be here." I became furious. I could not stop screaming, "Who are you? Are you even a human? Have mercy! You do not have a soul! And you want to become a doctor, a doctor? You did not come from thin air! What are you?" She put the operator on the speaker so she could hear my insanity. I believe the operator was scolding me at the same time, but I was so upset that I do not recall what she said. She must have asked Nour at one point who it was she was referring to, because Nour said, "It is my mother, but we are not on speaking terms." It was the first time she had referred to me as her mother in seven years, but only because she had to identify the "intruder."

Throughout this ordeal, I kept repeating, "I am not leaving, call the police." I pulled the two gift bags I had brought her and dumped the contents on the floor, telling her, "Here is what I have come for, Happy Birthday and Merry Christmas." I did not realize until the ordeal was over that I had left her Christmas card and her UCLA graduation picture in the rental car. I had carefully and with much love selected her gifts of brands she loved: a beautiful fashionable brown jacket, an Adidas T-shirt, a UCLA hoodie, Amarige perfume, Fossil wallet, a necklace with matching earrings, a White/Black summer dress and top, a scarf, and a hat. I then picked up the little album I had created from some scanned pictures of milestones in her life, put it in her face and flipped the pages as I shouted, "How can you forget. How can you forget?" She was not moved.

The fiasco lasted about ten minutes before the police arrived. A tall, husky man came inside and asked me if I had a weapon. As insulted as I was, I had to respond. "No officer, I don't." He also asked if I had hurt anyone and confirmed through Fadwah that there were no "victims." He asked me to calm down and I did, but only slightly and after the other officer took Nour outside. I kept shaking my head, "Shame, shame, shame. May God forgive you." A few minutes later, she came inside, and I resumed the screaming as the officer was escorting me out. The last thing I said was "Don't forget to file a restraining order." In defiance she said, "I will." To that, I reacted, "And you want to become a doctor? I hope you would become a mother one day so that you may know what it means to be a mother."

I took two steps outside the door in utter silence. The officer behind me, like he would a criminal, pushed me forcefully, even as I did not resist.

Instinctually, I turned around, pointed my finger at him and scolded him, "Don't push me." He threatened, "You continue with this behavior, I am going to handcuff and arrest you." Nour stood behind and said nothing, reminiscent of the time when her father was pulling my arms and shaking me around during my last days at home and all she would say very gently was, "It is enough. You can leave her alone now." I continued to walk with the officer behind me. Outside, there was yet another officer preparing a document. I asked for my purse which the officer had confiscated but he refused to give it to me. When I asked why, he would only say so that he did not have to search it. He finally allowed me to get my sunglasses.

I waited, not knowing what report I was receiving. A few minutes later, another officer handed me the trespassing letter, warning me that the next time I approached the property, I would be arrested. He said the only reason why I was not arrested was because I was allowed into the house willingly. When choosing a duration for when the no trespassing order would expire, the officer selected- presumably at Nour's instructions- "other," and wrote, "Permanently." After I signed the order, the officer handed me a copy along with my purse. I got into my car leaving behind three officers and three police cars. How violent they must have thought I was!

The confrontation had left me in disbelief, shaken, humiliated, disappointed, disowned, and reviled. I drove to the nearest shopping center and parked my car. I wept as I picked up the phone and dialed Patrick, then my mother and then my friends who had anxiously waited for a joyful reunion, even though in their hearts, they had expected this. They consoled me as best they could. I then went to my hotel, took a bike-ride downtown, savored delicious Tamales from the Tamale Festival and headed back for the night. The next morning, I walked for miles, went to church, said my blessings, and headed for the airport.

I thought I had prepared myself to expect the worst. I discovered that you could never prepare yourself for such a bleeding. The knife she held firmly in her hand had cut me to pieces, rendering me lifeless. I could never have prepared to face the sad reality that a daughter I had given birth to, whom I cradled for years, gave affectionate love, had spent a lifetime nurturing, would actually turn out to be the spitting image of her father, vengeful, callous, inhumane and sadly, without a soul, without a spirit, without a heart, without compassion, without a conscience, a robotic creature programmed to perform flawlessly as ordered.

I called the police department a few days later in order to get a copy of the police report and to lodge a complaint against the officer who had pushed me. The officer on the other line said no report had been generated, but having read the computer notes, he expressed to me in amazement and as an "Impartial Third Party" that "You were lucky that you were not arrested." When I asked what law I had violated, he said the strict Arizona laws regarding domestic violence give the officers the permission to arrest anyone on behalf of the state without bringing charges filed by the homeowner. My violations were trespassing for not leaving after the homeowner requested that I do, domestic violence, and misconduct. God must have been looking after me. I decided not to file the complaint after all.

So she proved her loyalty to her father; reaching the pinnacle of her success in humiliating me in the worst way. So she had won; so she had conquered, so she had proved to herself and to me the extent of the cruelty she is capable of inflicting.... and she rejoiced.....and all for what?....and for whom? I am deeply saddened at the loss of her. As for me, I now knew what I did not want to believe to be true. I now knew who my child was and what she was capable of. I now knew that I had reached my top and had discovered her top and; therefore, could finally attain closure. I now know that I did not lose my daughter in that encounter. I had already lost her long ago, and mourned that loss. I now know that I am free to allow my broken heart to start mending. Surrender comes sweetly. It rejuvenates me. There is no higher mountain that I can climb; no door that I can knock, and no battle that I can wage.

With every passing day, I felt stronger and stronger, thanks to the unrelenting support I had received from my dear friends and as always, from my amazing, kind and loving man, the love of my life, Patrick. Yes, God must have intended for this to happen, so I could let go; and so I did. Here is where my journey ends and hers begins.

PART V

It Is All In Your Hands

CHAPTER 19

Closure Or Not?

JANUARY 16, 2014

I had training within twenty miles of Anwar"s school for the week of January 13. I thought to make another attempt to see him, so I e-mailed him my itinerary for the week and casually asked him if he wanted to meet me for Dim Sum. A few days passed without a response. As I was checking his cycling community platform account, I saw he had recently posted that he was selling bicycle parts, listing as the reason that he no longer owned a bike and because "I need the money." Again, concerned that he may be in financial difficulty, I called him. He did not pick up on the first try, but with the second one, he answered annoyed, "What?" I expressed my concerns and again offered to help. He was short with me, telling me that every time I pay the school, it "messes up" his grant, and he asked that I no longer send any money. He said he was going to straighten the matter out with the school within the week. I reminded him that he had not responded to my e-mail. He said that he was just about to do it and then hurried to hang up. I was content that he had answered and really thought that I was beginning to make some progress in our relationship. Again, I was wrong.

I waited for that e-mail to come, but it did not, so I followed with another, letting him know that I would be stopping by. The response I received is what brought my journey with him to its end. He wrote, *"No. Again, not an open invitation to come just because you found out where I live. If you come, I will not be there."*

I drove to his apartment anyway, hoping that he would have had a change of heart. This time, though, I felt a negative energy, but I proceeded anyway, determined to get closure. His roommate, Eric, reluctantly opened the door after two knocks. He was quick to tell me that Anwar was not there. When I questioned him, he said that Anwar was at work, that he was not lying and that he was on his way to pick up some parts for Eric to sell. I choked back my tears knowing that it was the end. I paused for a few seconds, and then I mustered the courage to say, "I want closure." I went on asking him to pass the information to Anwar that I was not a bad person regardless of my indiscretions, that I loved him more than anything, and that if he wanted never to see me again, he should tell me to my face; otherwise, I was going to continue to try seeing him.

Eric nodded, bid me a good evening and shut the door. Defeated and empty, I retraced the steps to my car for what was the final attempt. I had reached my limit, and I needed to let go. I was no longer able to withstand Anwar's continual pendulum-like reaction to the attempts that I had withstood for seven years—one step forward, ten steps back.

JANUARY 19, 2014

Three days later, I sent Anwar what could be considered an ultimatum regarding our failing relationship. I titled it, ***"Our Relationship—Closure***

Or Not?" In it I expressed my feelings of disappointment, the reasons for my divorce and my indiscretions, letting him know for the first time that his father was not the helpless victim he really had convinced him that he was. I told him I was fed up with his blaming me for his miserable outlook on life and for his failed relationships, that I was no longer going to seek his forgiveness, that my crime did not deserve the punishment he had sentenced me to and that, above all, I needed closure. I briefly told him about my encounter with Nour, expressed that I had expected him to be different, to have independent judgment and to be able to decide for himself how our relationship was going to proceed, if at all. He was no longer a child, living in no one's shadow. I left it all in his hands, having tried to reach a heart that had remained impenetrable.

I ended my letter letting him know that while my arms would always be there to embrace him, I could no longer take this agonizing, undefined relationship. It was tearing me apart. If he truly did not want me to be in his life, I would make sure that he would never see me or hear from me again. All he had to do was to let me know, one way or the other. I wrote:

My Dear Son:

I am trying very hard to understand why you would respond to my kind gestures in the way you did, hurtful and cruel. I simply wanted to see you as any mother would, but I did not expect such a heartless e-mail. It was not in my imagination that you had told me that repairing our relationship "would take a long time." That much I understood, accepted and respected. But what I cannot comprehend is how is progress to be made when you continue to put up walls? This makes no sense, Anwar, and I have no explanation for your behavior other than to think that you intend to hurt me by breaking my spirit.

I am so anguished by your deliberate display of lack of empathy at a time when you had given me a glimmer of hope. At least that was the feeling I left with the two times I met you last year, even though you would probably argue you were simply being polite, afraid to confess to yourself that you are human, kind, and gentle, but plagued by your loyalty to your father and fearing his wrath should he know that you cared about me.

And while I wanted to be optimistic, I remained guarded, given your long history with me of pendulum-like moods every time I called you or made an effort to see you, starting shortly after the divorce. Enough is enough! That has to change if we are ever to reconnect as mother and son, Anwar.

I will no longer allow you to tear me as you have been. I can no longer endure the pain that comes from your yo-yo attitude toward me, and the fear that naturally follows my never knowing how you will respond the next time I make a move. I can no longer bear to wait until the day when you have a heart, when you forgive me, and realize that I did not commit an insidious heinous crime for which I deserve to be admonished for eternity. I am asking you for closure, my son, so I pray that you have some compassion left in your heart to give me that. I am done, Anwar, so done and finished with all of that. I want to let go, to live and let live as though I had no children to mourn, for you and your sister have treated me in unspeakable ways.

Enough blaming me for your anger, for your grim outlook on life, for having "no feeling for anything or anyone," for not caring if you "live or die" or for not having a girlfriend, "thanks to you," as you told me. Enough of your ungratefulness telling me "I mess everything up" when I extend a helping hand to pay part of your tuition or commit to paying off your loan. It is time for you to take responsibility for the choices you make in life and for how you live it. And yes, it is time for you to know that while I may have "messed up" your father, he was no angel either. It takes two to Tango and two to break a marriage.

For years, I worked hard with love, raising you, and attending to the house chores, working full-time, while your father completed his undergraduate degree, and then his graduate one and for all the years after. And I would not change anything, gratified only by who you turned out to be. Your father, however, was never there for me, physically or emotionally, even though throughout the years, I tried in vain to bring us closer to sustain the family unit. He simply rebuffed my attempts until my well was dry, and I had to break away. Yet, you took his side without knowing the truth. You cared not to know, to give me a chance.

It has been almost seven years, yet you choose to hold on to your anger, to nullify my existence, all after the fifteen years that I raised you; Yes, it was me, so stop belittling my contribution to your upbringing. You were not a baby when you severed me from your life, but a fifteen-year-old, full of vigor, happy, well mannered. That, my dear child, did not come from thin air and neither did you.

Still, I held hope that you were different; that you would be very upset by your sister's maltreatment of her mother who she referred to as "a person" as she called 911; that you would reflect upon the venomous lies, character assassinations, degradations and dehumanization that had been injected into both of your hearts and minds in order to sustain your alienation; that you will finally realize how unrealistic and against common wisdom the notion is that a child will be emotionally healthier and thrive better without the other parent.

I hoped that you would realize that relationships are complex and not black and white; that just like life, divorce happens, and for many reasons, infidelity is one of them, and it is not always a "sexual escapade" as your sister described it, but it happened because of unmet needs that craved expression for twenty-one years.... I hoped, I really did, that you were old enough, mature enough to examine all of that, to make some sense of it all, to reconcile with the past and then to reach your awakening. Seven years have passed, and it is high time that you do. After your last e-mail, I realized that I may have misjudged. I simply don't know you anymore, and perhaps I should not venture to speculate. How you respond to this e-mail, Anwar, will determine whether we still have a destination to reach or a fork that leads us to differing ways. It is all in your hands, my son.

It has been seven years and continuing. Do you really think I will live forever? I will soon be fifty-years-old, Anwar. Do you realize how much time has been needlessly wasted? So what are you expecting to do with all the bitterness you are harboring inside you? Where do you think this will take you? Will this accomplish anything? Will it wipe the past anyway or change anything? Surely, not! It can only breed negativity and failure.

No one has had a perfect childhood. Believe me, mine was no piece of cake. But I can't spend the rest of my life pitying myself for the absence of a father and for motherly lost affection. I married your father not knowing that it was based on an inner need for love and affection, but he was incapable or unwilling to give. For the rest of my life, I would be wallowing in pain and stunting my emotional and mental growth and would be stuck in a perpetual state of blame and misery, not owning up to my actions. Life would then be devoid of joy and would cease to bring me either satisfaction or happiness.

Yes, my dear son, I choose to let go of the past and to live life to the fullest, regardless of the deep unabated anguish in my heart. After all, happiness is a state of mind that allows you to rise above your suffering the next day after the twilight, and then the next, and the day after that, until it is dissipated or rendered insignificant through our fortitude.

This brings me back to the question of who you are and who you choose to be! Will you continue to allow the past to follow you wherever you go, towering like a giant above you, imposing on you and preventing you from proceeding toward a brighter tomorrow? Will you choose to echo your sister's and your father's sentiments and behaviors? What are you afraid of, my son? True love is about acceptance and tolerance. It does not command loyalty or subjugation. But above all, it is about forgiveness, starting with the self and examining uncharted waters without fear of perceived betrayal or alienation.

In the beginning of this letter, I asked you to give me closure. If you truly intend for me to be out of your life completely, then face up to it and tell me boldly and clearly. I guarantee you, you will never hear from me or see me again. I will do that not just for you, but for my own sanity and welfare. Now, if you want to repair our relationship, then you need to define for me how you would like it done. I tried it my way, but for your lack of communication with me about how to go about it, I failed miserably because you kept stringing me along, causing me much pain and anxiety.

How would you have expected me to deal with you when you cut me off and did not express to me your wishes, and how you would have liked them to be proceeded to reconcile, though slowly? And if you think I am imposing myself on you as you insist that knowing where you live "is not an open invitation to visit," then communicate to me in what manner, how, when and where may we see each other. I have no problem accepting that reconciliation must be on your terms, so long as you describe how it is to be carried out on a progression scale, not taking a step forward and then ten backwards as you have been doing.

Honesty and forthrightness must be respected on both sides. I don't need to have an excuse to see you by bringing you Kibbeh, Stuffed Grape Leaves and the like. I should be able to see you when you have time and when you are ready. Neither should you worry about avoiding me so as not to hurt my feelings, if that was ever your intention. I am a big girl, and I can handle it. Trust me.

Then again, if your wishes are for you to excommunicate me for what you believe is the crime of all crimes, then, my dear son, I will remain vanquished, knowing that I have no control over your decision, and I will cease all communications and visits.

From this point forward, you will have to steer your own path. You are no longer a child but a young man under no one's wing, expected to be a free-thinker, confident, determined and strong-willed. At least that is how I raised you to be.

Wherever life takes you, I pray that it treats you gently and kindly and that one day you will exalt in the beauty of love, will forgive yourself, and will live by the truth. Just know that my arms will always remain open to embrace you. All I want and expect is to know your decision, one way or the other.

Love always,
Mother.

Anwar never responded. I was done!

JUNE 27, 2014

I decided I needed to send another closure letter; this time to both children. In it, I did not ask for any response, but simply for an opening to their hearts and minds so they could examine the past and make peace with it, with themselves and with me. I wanted to know their choice so we each could live mindfully. What I got from Nour, however, was my answer, a hurtful answer. I wrote them in the hope that they realize the wasted years, the time that could never be recaptured, and move on:

We Only Have This Moment

My Beautiful Children:

For all the seven years that have passed, I have left no stone unturned in order to bring you back to me, but to no avail. The harder I pushed, the harder you pushed back showing me a part of you I did not want to believe existed....and it saddened me immensely. I searched high and low to understand your unwavering stance, but nothing made sense to me. I keep searching for answers without ever finding an excuse to justify your behavior no matter how hard I try, particularly that so much time has passed and you are now adults by all accounts, mature, responsible, confident, independent thinkers, and on your assured ways to success, as I would have expected. No, in this regard, you have not disappointed me. I have no regrets, for I am proud for who you have turned out to be, consoled that you can now spread your own wings and can fly.

As I write, I hope you do not conclude that I am attempting to justify my actions, neither to make you understand or to forgive me. I have given up on that. I just want to understand, just to believe and accept that if this is truly what YOU want, perhaps then, make peace that we will never reunite....and if it is so you wish, move on.

Surely, you are thinking, all she thinks about is her own suffering and not about the misery she left us with. Let me tell you, my children, for the millionth time; indeed I have wronged you and hurt you beyond what your hearts were capable of absorbing; surely I betrayed you and violated a sacred vow; surely I was a hypocrite in teaching you values about honesty and trust while I committed adultery. Yes, indeed, I did not live up to my promises, and I failed you...but not for the seventeen years, Nour, or the fifteen, Anwar, I was in your life raising you the best way any mother could. Vivid in my memory is your standing up on the stage at your pre-school, arms crossed over your chest, singing Celine Dion's "Because You Loved Me." As you dismiss me, it is these very years, my labor of love and undoubtedly your perseverance that continue to blossom in you, molding you into the man and woman you are today, your heads held high, I hope.

Alone, I sat countless times in disbelief that you could disown me for as long as you have when I thought you loved me and needed me. I had rationalized that infidelity would be accompanied by heightened anger and resentment and perhaps would induce a period of disconnectedness, along with unspeakable and enduring pain. I even chose to purchase a home instead of renting, anticipating you would be occupying the second bedroom when you came to see me or to live with me..... But I had never imagined you could continue to choose to keep all ties severed for seven years and counting.

Considering the passage of time, my relentless apologies and countless attempts to reconnect with you, including my proposition to Anwar to ask if your father would meet with me so I may ask his forgiveness (which I have not received a response to), it certainly makes the punishment disproportionate to the "crime" by anyone's standards, except yours...so pardon me for feeling so perplexed. This is not a case of physical or sexual abuse that warrants this kind of estrangement, I thought, but a sad reality that happens in many marriages, never justified, but generally for reasons that cause us to ponder the truth behind the deception, a defense you never afforded me a chance to present.

Then, I tried to put myself in your shoes imagining how traumatizing it must have been for you not only dealing with the divorce, and my infidelity, but also watching your father wither away in sheer helplessness as he spilled his anguish out every moment he could, trying to be consoled by you, Nour, then, a seventeen-year-old who, incapable of dealing with your own feelings, were made to become your father's confidante and counselor without any regard to the detrimental emotional distress this surely must have put you through. Or having both of you exposed to e-mails and private conversations between Patrick and me as well as incessant lies and denigrating remarks about me and my character, so inappropriate for children to hear or see, irrespective of who the "victim" or the "villain" might be.

It is these behaviors displayed by your father that I believe pushed you to subconsciously declare your allegiance to him, believing the notion that any relationship with me would represent a betrayal to an otherwise victimized father, whose actions convinced you he did nothing to deserve this. I will also have to admit to you that I cannot help but contemplate that your refusal to reconcile with me stems from your fear that you, too, will be ostracized should your father know that you had an ounce of care for me.

Had this not been the case, Nour, you would have called the police directly when I confronted you at your house last December, refusing to leave. You called your father first, reporting to him "she is here," and then you faithfully executed his orders. And Anwar, had you not been torn by your allegiance to your father and your love for me, you would not have received me politely, though with trepidation and apparent reluctance, when I showed up without "an open invitation" but then slam every door in my face.

If and when you ever decide to look deep within your hearts and to connect with your true selves unlocking seven years of pain and denial, I believe you will have reached the truth. And when you do, I pray that you will not only forgive me, but that you will also forgive your father as well. He, too, is human. Trust that no one is infallible but God, and let go. Peace and happiness will surely follow.

I have also tried to imagine the state of mind you may have been in, wanting to show your father your love and support so he might heal, while afraid that any communication with me would adversely affect your relationship with him, perceiving that you are on the side of the "enemy." I also contemplated the idea that perhaps you could not allow yourselves to ever have me in your lives after I "messed up" your father "big time" as Anwar once said, lest you betrayed a father you believed was holy and pure, while I ran off enjoying my "sexual escapades." All of these feelings were understandable and were to be expected, given his state of helplessness, profuse tears, weight loss, and the misery which he did not hide from you two as he grieved.

The truth that I wish for you to examine is that while I own my actions, I was not and could never have been in control of how my indiscretions impacted your father. I, too, realized his grief was intense and agreed to hang on when I probably should not have. Each time I tried to break away and do the right thing by standing my ground and pushing for the divorce, he became helpless, pleading with me to stay, telling me he might be diagnosed with cancer or even threatening to kill himself. I succumbed a few times when my heart told me otherwise because I truly care about your father, whether or not you believe me.

Had I stood my ground, perhaps you would be in my life now. That was my second mistake, but anyhow, this is neither here nor there. Nevertheless, you need to know why my affair lasted

*as long as it did until I could no longer bear living a lie and
needed to do the right thing for me, for your father, and for
you. Yet, my good intentions backfired as you blamed me for
not having left when I should have. You sentenced me to pay in
years for every tear he shed.*

*Well, it may now be time for you to ask your father if the divorce
was the best thing that had ever happened to him. The answer
may surprise you. You must then ask yourselves: Why do we
continue to admonish our mother? For whom and for what
purpose? What will we accomplish? Will it change anything?
And is it worth it? Perhaps, you will then realize that life is
shorter than you can realize at your young ages; it can be taken
from us so unexpectedly that it simply is not worth holding on
to the anger and resentment that can eat up our souls. But if
you are insistent on believing that you are better off without
a mother, then you have defied all wisdom. I hope you do not
realize this undeniable truth after I am many feet under. I have
two great fears that haunt me: having Alzheimer's disease and
departing this world without you by my side.*

*In all of this, I want you to know that none of your actions or
words will ever take away my pride, my dignity or the truth
about who I am. As I once wrote you, Nour, when you believe
your mother is shamed, you will live your life in shame and
people will look upon you in shame. I want you both to be proud
and resilient in the face of all adversity, else you will sentence
yourselves to a life of isolation and insecurity. I also want you
to know that there is nothing you can do or say that will ever
change my love for you. I truly wish you to become parents one
day so that you may know that a mother's love is unconditional*

and limitless. Know that I have forgiven myself and have been forgiven by my Creator. Do you believe you are greater than Him that you should not?

So I move on. But how do you ever get over the loss of your child? The truth is that you never do; you never overcome the pain; you simply learn to live with it. I refuse to allow my desolate soul to interfere in the beauty that God has created for all of us to enjoy. I laugh, I cry, I reflect, but I always live the truth that has set me free. In this finite time that we have on this amazing earth, I make sure not to postpone to tomorrow what I can do today. I travel, I hang out with dear friends, I cycle, I hike, I explore, I define my life by being proud of who I am and humbled by my history that has taught me invaluable lessons and made me a better person, a compassionate human being. That is the message I want you to receive when you see my pictures on Facebook. I keep it public for no other reason.

My hope is that when life shakes your core, you look at my pictures and read my reflective thoughts and realize that "This too shall pass." It is hard to let go of the past and not look back, but time stops for no one. We only have this moment, and tomorrow is not guaranteed; nothing is. Next year will bring a major transformation for me with Patrick as my husband; you, never leaving my heart.

If I had one wish for you, it would be for you to decide to forgive and to seek love. Look deep into your hearts and around you; when you find it, embrace it, instead of shunning from it. For as I once wrote you, Nour, he who lives in anger will never be consoled. And he who lives cloaked in hatred cannot exalt in the beauty of forgiveness. And he who knows no love, will suffer in loneliness. And he who builds a wall will never have the courage to face reality, and he who lives in falsehood will never progress, will remain stranded and will never overcome life's many obstacles.

I invite you to explore life, in all that it encompasses in hope and despair, pain and joy, suffering and vindication. This is the only way to savor its beauty. Gibran Khalil Gibran was right when he wrote, "Out of suffering have emerged the strongest souls; the most massive characters are seared with scars." So break that protective shell you have locked yourselves into for all these years, face the truth and deal with it. Life is indeed beautiful. Take it in, indulge, and pray often. You will not regret it.

At the end of each day, I reflect upon my sorrows, on my joy and on my blessings. My memories bring me back to times when you were in my arms. I can still smell your sweet scent and satiate my love with butterfly kisses on your cheeks and on your hair... and I smile, dropping a few tears, for one day, you too will learn to live the truth and freely set your sail for the voyage of life. May the wind carry you gently, and may God's hand deliver you to where you belong. I will be watching you from afar, but never away.

Love always and forever,
Mother

I wish I did not receive a reply, but what I did made me once again, question her humanity. **We exchanged our last replies:**

Nour: Do not email me under any circumstance or I will pursue legal measures for a restraining order. You should remember that I did not hesitate when you so arrogantly intruded into my house. I don't care about your explanations. You live your life and stay out of mine, especially my professional one. Any response you attempt to send will be routed to my school servers as spam and automatically blocked. I want nothing to do with you, so I highly suggest that you stop pursuing your whimsical delusions of mothering me.

Me: You are truly a lost soul! I am so sorry for you, my beautiful child. Go ahead and pursue whatever you wish. It will never change anything. However, I will guarantee that you will never, ever, ever, ever hear from me again. Should you have a change of heart, though, know that my arms are always open to you. You will know where to find me. One more thing, Nour, I must say that I am stunned by how intelligent, yet how so closed minded and ignorant you are.

Nour: Berating me for being closed minded and ignorant is a great way to encourage me to talk to you. Was there a part of stop contacting me that was unclear to you?

Moreover, she must have shared my letter with her father. It was no coincidence that at the end of the day, I received, though anonymously, a link to a video of a close relative acting in immature shameful indiscretions. And while I could not identify the sender, the IP addresses of both e-mails were very similar. As I understand it, these addresses are configured based on devices that are connected. That could either mean Nour was present and used the same computer to send her e-mails, or Rameh gained a copy of my e-mail and responded using hers. Moreover, that same link was sent to my brother, Hassan, also anonymously, and to many of our family friends and relatives back home. It is my belief that Rameh intended to shame the entire family, and me particularly, drawing parallels between my infidelity and the indiscretions performed in the video, though they are in no way nearly close.

I felt compelled to respond pointing the finger at her father and reminding her that the person is *"who she is, and I am who I am, proud and dignified. Neither you, nor you father will ever change that. No matter how hard you and he will try. Just remember, you are part of the same family, so shame on you too...LOL."* Then, I thought of the Birthday and Christmas cards that I had left in the rental car during that infamous day when I "surprised" her in Arizona. I decided to send them to her with this note to which I never received a response:

My dear child:

I decided to send you this card and the pictures that I had brought with me to give you on your Birthday and for Christmas. Nervous for what might ensue, I left them in the car. I thought you might enjoy the pictures of your momentous milestones (graduation from UCLA). For one last footnote, Nour, my last letter to you and Anwar was not an effort to present my"explanations" and neither was my "berating" you "a great way to encourage" you to talk to me. Instead, it was merely an attempt, I hoped, to open your mind to a construct perhaps yet too hurtful or complex for you to be willing to examine it. I pray you do one day so that you may understand the truth. As always, know that my arms are always open to receive and embrace you my beautiful.

Love always and forever,
Mother

I am not sure if part of Nour's reaction was the realization that her father and I would never have any chance to get back together, knowing that Patrick and I would be wed the following year. I knew the risk I was taking when I inserted a comment about my upcoming wedding, yet I felt they needed to know from me before any other. I thought that making that confession would bring me closure somehow. It did not. Instead of a joyous time spent in planning my wedding and relishing the beauty of a marriage founded on love, respect, tolerance, understanding and empathy, I started a downward spiral that almost led to my demise.

Shortly after my e-mail, I started suffering from serious insomnia, from weight loss and, from undiagnosed depression. Many a night I lay in bed awake all night. Externally, I appeared strong, happy, and content. I had tried everything possible to reach their hearts until there was no more I could do. I yearned for my children, agonized by years of loss, and now fearing that if there was hope for us, perhaps my marriage would kill it. My insomnia began, and I could not understand why. After all, it had been almost eight years, I thought; I had managed relatively well, despite my terrible pain; I had maintained my positive outlook on life; carried on with my day-to-day business; graduated with distinction; dressed up for work every day, and never called in sick for any reason other than a lack of sleep. I could not rationally explain why I could not sleep because I thought I had managed everything and had accepted everything, so why would all my fear manifest now? To date, I do not know the answer. I can only suspect that I was crippled by fear of what would happen to my limited relationship with my son if I married. I struggled to cope on my own for six months trying to focus on the wedding plans and on my job.

OCTOBER 8, 2014

With the passage of time, Anwar became more and more estranged and would not pick up the phone no matter how many times I tried to call. My e-mails to him became very limited as a result. Again, what I knew about him was the little exchanges that his Reddit platform allowed me.

I thought of calling him using a restricted number, and he answered. He accused me of being "sneaky," but I argued that he was misjudging me. I just needed to talk to him and would do what it took to do so, I explained. I asked about his health and his general well-being. He sarcastically said not to worry, "If I die, you will know." I asked about his plans after graduation and if he were going to walk in the summer. He said he was not; that he was not going to wait until then, even as I told him he had worked hard and deserved to walk down the graduation aisle, proud of his achievement.

During the conversation, I mentioned the school project in which he had been assigned to be a project manager, information I saw on the internet and which I had e-mailed him letting him know how proud I was of him. He was upset with me stating that he would no longer update that page having to tell his team members that the reason was that he "had baggage." "Wow," I replied. "What is so bad about finding information about what you are doing from the internet?"

As in the two encounters I had with him last year, the conversation was intense and consistently fragmented. I could not stay on topic as he jumped from one issue to the next, still attacking me. And when I reminded him that I was not a bad person, he insisted, "Yes you are. I would not be cheating on my husband of twenty-two years." Just being religious, he added, did not make me a good person. I am not sure why he equated my moral compass with my faith which I explained it did not stem from. "I always was a good person," I insisted. He had to tell me he was not religious and that one did not need to be to have good ethics. I agreed. And as usual, taking another jab at my infidelity, he sarcastically thanked me for not his ever wanting to be married, to have children and to spread the "bad genes" that he had gotten from me.

Anwar then expressed his amazement as to why I do not cease pursuing him as he continues to "insult" me. He could not understand why I thought he was nothing like his sister when he is "actually worse," he admitted. He was "a dick and an asshole." I told him he was not; and that I continue to attempt to reach his heart because I was a mother, and that deep inside, I knew he was good-hearted and kind. He rebuffed my statements insisting that I didn't know him. I emphasized, "You are my son, and I know you better than you know yourself."

"Pretty soon, you will have lived without me longer than you have lived with me," he muttered. I cried knowing that would mean another eight years of separation if not longer. He got angry and said I made him angry every time I called and even more so when I cried. I believe it was during that conversation that he asked me "Why don't you just pretend that Patrick's kids are Nour and me and leave me alone?" I paused for a second in amazement, not knowing how to respond. I then quickly and steadfastly told him, "Nobody, nobody will ever come before you or after you." Did he say that to test my love for him? Did he truly think I could ever replace him? Was he sending me a message that I "left" them in order to care for someone else's children? Did he really think that I had done that, as he once told me during our first reunion after the court order? What else did his father make my children believe, and what stories and lies did he perpetuate to force their allegiance? Or was Anwar just asking for an affirmation of my love and commitment? I want to think it is the latter, but I can assume nothing.

Then I asked if he was receiving my e-mails or if he had blocked me. He stated that he had told me a million times that he had blocked what he could but that somehow he continued to receive my "thousand-word e-mails which he does not read, nor does he have the ability to give them any attention since he could not concentrate, and he suffered from insomnia. I did not know what to make of his statements, but I became sarcastic over the downplaying of his intelligence telling him, "Yeah, that is why you are graduating as a mechanical engineer!" I am not sure why every time I talk to him, he says that he is not smart although there was the one time when he admitted he was, except that he does not "apply" himself well. Again, he appeared to have low self-esteem, or perhaps he wanted me to think that he did. I do not know why he does that. Perhaps it is to lay more guilt on me. I needed to know if he was saving my e-mails, telling him that one day he might want to read them, but he did not respond to my question, and I left it at that.

He expressed his annoyance that I continued to write him to his school e-mail because it was private, he claimed. I told him that he had left me no choice and that I would use another e-mail address if he gave me one. He said, "Leave me alone," when I inquired as to why he had not responded to my e-mails. I then directly asked him, "Are you saying, Anwar, that you do not ever want to see me again?" I really wanted to get an answer and get some closure as I had done with his sister, but his response surprised me! "Do not contact me unless I initiate it... So when you call me every 10 months or so.... How about that, is that good, is that good?"

I was shocked and did not know what to make of this proposal, afraid to ask if that meant he would take my calls. I did not want to hear a negative answer, so I asked, "Is there any hope?" but he did not respond. He went off on the time I had hired an investigator and had found him. He then threatened a restraining order and told me that he would never ever talk to me if I did that again, particularly after I had told him that it would be easy for me to find wherever he lived or worked. He said that I would then get him fired if I ever showed up at his work! I am not sure why, but I assured him that I would never do that, that I only wanted to see him and to know he was all right. I told him that he was stuck in the past. He became defensive and said, "So now you are blaming me!" I said, "No." I am not sure how, but he quickly moved onto another topic.

I told him that his school loan would be taken care of. He was surprised since I had not given him the money nor did I know anything of his loan information. He then added that he had the money to pay it, so I advised him to put it down on a house. I am not sure he heard me. I then told him I had a special card to give him for his graduation and that I would like to mail it somewhere since he continues to refuse to meet me. As he was not going to give me his home address, of course, he said to mail it to the house; "My father would not do anything." I dismissed his proposition telling him, "I would not do that because I know things that would blow your mind away." He did not inquire further.

It was not long before he realized that he should not allow me the luxury of an extended conversation. He abruptly ended it telling me he had to go back to building computers, but not before saying that, yes, he does it for fun, but he also makes money doing it. I said to him, "I love you" twice before he hung up. Sadly, thirty-four minutes on the phone with my son is indeed, a luxury.

CHAPTER 20

The Awakening

DECEMBER 17, 2014

could never have imagined that Anwar would have an epiphany in such a way. I had expected that a miracle, some monumental and unforeseen revelation or event would have to happen for either of my children to reach their awakenings. On that glorious day, thanks be to God, working in His own mysterious way, this miracle unfolded as would the rose release its embrace, its sweet fragrance, one petal at a time, in a heavenly order every morning at the crack of dawn.

You see, it was not serendipity that I came to know Nizar a year or so before, after the university Dean had contacted him at my request, mistaking him for my son. It is time to recognize God's power and mercy in all of this. As I have mentioned, here and there, Nizar assured me of Anwar's well-being since they shared a few classes together. However, after Anwar stopped picking up his phone and had moved away from the last address I had known, I became more and more distraught. I contacted Nizar for help.

It is no coincidence either that Nizar happened to work with Anwar on his senior project and must have been with him at the time I had asked if he knew Anwar's address. Within minutes, he scanned me a picture of a box showing Anwar's address on it. It had contained parts he had ordered for the project they were working on at the time. I am forever grateful to this man's kindness, and I hope that I may reciprocate in some way. God was already showing me the path, but I did not know it. I was just elated to know that my son was interning at a well-respected engineering corporation in Los Angeles and had been recently hired to start at the beginning of the year as a Systems Engineer.

I thanked Nizar for the information and asked if Anwar had ever disclosed to him the reason for his estrangement. I thought perhaps if he had confided in a fellow Lebanese who might understand, then Nizar could help me determine the right approach that would be acceptable to my son. I was not sure if I should keep pushing myself onto him, or if I should let him decide to come to me. I was not sure if he hated me, or if he was ready to talk at all. I kept wanting to try to visit him in case he had had a change of heart, but with each time I became more worried that by doing so, I was pushing him farther away. I thought that Nizar was my only link, the one who could help me.

I told Nizar that I did not want to upset Anwar any further, but that at the same time, I felt that deep inside, Anwar wanted me back in his life but was too proud and too loyal to his father to admit it, or that his father would then alienate him. Nizar chose not to respond, perhaps not wanting to get involved in family affairs. I respected his wishes and stopped all contact, although I was honored to attend his graduation and to meet him with his family. Indeed, Anwar did not walk, perhaps not wanting to give me the blessing of sharing his hard-earned Bachelor's of Engineering that makes every parent proud and triumphant.

I had bought some Christmas presents before I knew his home address. I had thought about mailing them to his work, but I knew that I should not, fearing that my actions might backfire. Still, I had hoped I would meet Anwar somehow and could wish him a Merry Christmas. For the couple of months that followed, I kept thinking to myself, you now have an address that you know he may vacate upon graduation. What if after that you are never able to find out where he lives? What if this is your last chance to see him? How should you proceed? I decided I had nothing to lose, so I planned to show up at his apartment on December 17, the last day of finals. I was not sure if he would have already completed them and had left in order to see his father, assuming that Nour was home and that he needed to take a breather before starting his new career a few days later. I really thought that I might miss him, but I did not want to go any earlier, fearing that he would be so angry and not be able to focus on his finals. Then, a strong intuition came upon me that I must leave it in God's hands, and so I did.

I reached his apartment complex at 7:15 pm and was lucky to gain entry following a resident into an otherwise secure building. I knocked twice. I could see light through the peep hole, but no one opened. Silence and disappointment engulfed me, but I was determined. I rang the bell again and this time a young man opened. Anwar was not home, he said. He offered to text him as he thought he might have been at the gym. I then revealed who I was and told him that I preferred that he did not. At that moment, a door to the bedroom opened and Gary, his old roommate, peered through. I greeted him as he shut the door afterwards, giving me the excuse that he needed to change. I turned to the roommate who had opened the door and said. "I am sure Gary will tell Anwar now." However, he allowed me to leave the gifts and the food that I had brought: Kibbeh, Stuffed Grape Leaves and Tzazikki. I then told him that I respected his privacy, and that I would be waiting outside.

A few minutes later, the roommate came out and said that he had texted Anwar who had told him that he was visiting a friend and would be in very late. I responded asking, "Are you telling me the truth or did Anwar tell you to say that to me?" He did not answer. "That's okay. I will wait then," I said. He then emphasized that "It would be very late." I steadfastly responded, "I have waited for eight years. I can wait."

Around 8 p.m., the roommate left the apartment with a laundry basket but returned a few minutes later, only to see me still waiting. Gary also left shortly after, while I was still waiting. None of them acknowledged me, but I did not care. I was determined to wait until Anwar showed up. The situation was getting very uncomfortable as I was in a hallway, similar to the ones in hotels, where there were many doors to other apartments. Residents were coming and going, looking at me, wondering who I was and why I was staying outside someone's door. At some point, as I paced the hallway, a woman peered though her door and gave me a stern unwelcoming look before slamming her door shut. It was not the first time that doors had been shut in my face. I wondered if someone would call security to escort me out.

I sat in the stairwell, head bowed down in deep prayer. I was thankful that I was able to deliver the presents, but had a strong feeling that God did not bring me here, set up all the right circumstances, only to disappoint me. My very dear friend, Yelena, kept my hope alive with one text after another. She pushed me to persevere and not to give up. I needed to hear that from someone who cared; a special angel God had given me throughout my ordeal and for many years after. My heart spoke to me to wait and to pray that God would make Anwar have a change of heart and make this my moment. God answered.

At 8:15 p.m., the hallway door opened and Anwar came through pushing his bicycle. I got up with a soft smile on my face, and proceeded to walk towards him. His eyes looked at me fiercely and his jaw stiffened, his teeth cringing in anger. He set his bicycle along the wall, clutched my forearms with his fingers and roughly squeezed them yelling, "How did you find me? How did you find me?" At that moment, it was not my baby whom I saw; no, it was not the soft, caring and kind-hearted gentle soul I had raised and knew he was. What I saw was Rameh in front of me, a brutal mad man, a savage beast tearing his prey to pieces while digging his teeth deeply into her flesh. I was not prepared to see Anwar's face like that, nor for him to treat me so aggressively. I remembered the time when Rameh had grabbed my forearms in the same way, had shaken me violently and had pushed me repeatedly against the office table in the garage, leaving me with serious bruises.

In a broken voice, I tried to assure Anwar that I had not hired an investigator; that I was able to find his address through the internet. He asked which site, but I did not respond, looking at him in shock, tears flowing, "Since when do you lay your hands on me?" I asked. "May God forgive you and your sister for what you have done to me." I felt broken and finished. With my hand covering my mouth rendering me speechless, but with a gaze that spoke of years of anguish, I retreated in agonizing despair. As with Nour, I was done.

What happened at that moment I could not describe, nor explain. All I know is that in that instant, instead of the angry hardened young man who stood before me, I saw my tender, caring child once more. I saw my baby boy; his eyes darkened in sorrow, yet glimmering with love, with the kindness and the softness that I had not felt in eight years. As though succumbing to the powerful inextricable eternal bond of mother and child, they spoke of innocence, of affection, and of warmth, reserved for none but for a child cradled in his mother's embrace.

Yet, even as I saw his sudden transformation and his genuine soul as I had known it, the pain of his actions was beyond anything I could bear. I was so distraught, disappointed, left with nothing. I picked up my purse and coat and walked away. He must have gone into the apartment and seen the gifts. He, then, dashed outside yelling, "And why do you bring me gifts?" or "Don't bring me gifts." I was not exactly sure what he said, but I knew he was extremely angry. I said nothing and continued to walk down the stairs, sobbing. I took a flight down and walked a few steps in the hallway before resting my body against the wall feeling I was about to collapse. Suddenly, a gentle arm wrapped around my shoulders. In a calm voice, he said, "Let's go home. Let's go home."

I was so overwhelmed with competing emotions I could not say anything other than, "You and your sister are killing me. I cannot take it anymore. May God forgive you for what you have done to me." With his arm still around my shoulders, I felt a bit of comfort. We continued to walk until we were outside. He expressed his anger over my finding him three times saying, "You Don't know what this does to me. I do not express my feelings; you do." I impressed upon him that he should express his feelings; otherwise, I would not be able to know what he may be going through during these encounters.

I said that I could never give up; that I hoped he still had a heart like mine. Quickly he cut me off boasting that if he did, then "I would have cheated and abandoned my kids." I stopped him saying, "Enough, Anwar, enough." He acquiesced adding that his problem was that he could not stand to see anyone cry. I knew. I told him he could never understand the heart of a parent. He quickly reminded me that he was never going to be in a relationship and would never know because he would never have children. I smiled and told him that not only would he be in a relationship, but that he would also have three children one day. That was my revelation!

He asked where I was parked and when I responded that I was disoriented, he accused me of trying to say that so I might spend more time with him. He still distrusted me, I suppose, but somehow he seemed to want to walk me to the car, explaining that someone had brandished a knife on campus recently. I told him that I could protect myself; that I was not afraid, but he proceeded nonetheless.

I then told him that this could be the last time I might see him. He asked, "Why? Are you going to kill yourself?" I looked at him sarcastically and then added that I would be moving to Santa Barbara where Patrick lived. "Congratulations," he said. I took it for what it was, a congratulation for my upcoming wedding. He then asked me if I had gone to Iran and if the trip was all right. I said it had been great, pleasantly surprised that he cared to engage me in such a conversation.

As we walked, he spoke about how I continue to pursue him and how he needed more time. Time is what we did not have, I suggested. After all, I was fifty years old and not getting any younger. The countdown had begun. He tried to reassure me that I would live a long life since I had good genes and did not smoke or drink, "You don't smoke right?" I am not sure why he contemplated that when he knew that I had never smoked! My look gave him his answer. I explained that at his young age, he had no concept of how quickly time was fleeting and that there were no guarantees in life for when the moment comes. We continued to approach the car, his arm still around my shoulders.

He insisted on knowing how I had found his address concerned that I would do this again and again as I did about his senior project on the internet. I took the opportunity to ask him how well he had done. He got an A but complained about the lack of effort on the part of his teammates. "I did the entire project by myself," he explained. I said that he must have learned a lot from that. He nodded, and I expressed my pride. I assured him that it was not impossible to find his address, but that it would probably be the last time I would do it. "This time, I just got lucky. A higher power was looking after me," I said. He said, "So you are religious now, huh?" I responded that I wished I had a stronger faith as he sadly kept dismissing God and berating different religions, for all the atrocities committed in their names. In time, he will learn enough, mature enough to reach an understanding.

I asked him if he had found a job, and he said that he did, but he refused to tell me where since he believed I would chase him there too. Again, I assured him I would not cross that line. It appeared that he felt relieved when I affirmed that I would not "intrude" upon his "professional life."

We stood by the car for our last words for the night. Again, he brought up my relentless pursuit to find him. He said that each time a few months passed without contact, he felt better, and then I would find him again and he would be back to square one. I acknowledged that I could not help it, that each time I had attempted to steer away, a mother's heart always brought me back. I added at least he could not say that I had left a stone unturned to try to get to his heart, yet he had kept it shut. He nodded. I said, "I just don't know what to do anymore. I just want you to be happy." He reminded me that I was crying again, and he suddenly said, "I cannot take this anymore. You win." I smiled and thought that he was going to say a kind word so I asked him, "Say you love me." He did not. Instead, he said, "I have a Christmas gift for you. I will let you back in my life, but do not overdo it." I fell to my knees.

He gently picked me up and wrapped his arms around me. I cried my heart out in joy and tightly hugged him, beyond belief. All I could say was, "Thank you." He said again, "You are still crying!" "Tears of joy, tears of joy," I replied as I wiped my cheeks smiling. I composed myself and asked, "What is this supposed to mean?" He explained, "When you call me, I will answer, but don't overdo it, and maybe we will go to lunch one day." I promised not to, and then I asked him to let me know if I ever got carried away. He said he would.

I truly sensed that at that moment, Anwar had felt a great weight lifting off of his shoulders now that he had finally made the decision to let go. He somehow became liberated, a moment I had hoped for him for a long time. I hoped all of this was true and that he was indeed feeling relief rather than anger and resentment. I do know that he relaxed, and for a brief time, we could talk naturally. Something led me to talk about his being negative, so I described how, despite my sorrows, I chose to rise above them, enjoy what life had to offer me and to push forward. This time, he did not dismiss me or ask me to stop lecturing him. He seemed to listen and take it in. He was even so excited to tell me how much his employer had offered him, an impressive 73K to start. "Wow!" I exclaimed. "That is how much I make, and I am 50." He laughed and said I should have been an engineer. The silver lining in all of this was that he had proved that he was able to take care of himself, to be independent, to pay his way through with only a nominal loan, to sustain life with roommates, and to land a great job. How proud I was of him and of his accomplishments. We talked about his living arrangement. His lease was up in May, and he may consider buying a house at some point. I urged him to do it.

I asked him if he knew that I had paid his loan off. He did, and he thanked me. I asked how Nour was. His response was that she was "perfect." I grinned saying, "And you have a life, remember?" He said he did not have a life but that he remembered how he used to say that to me when I asked him why he could not be more studious like his sister. We smiled. I told him I liked his beard and how handsome he was. He said, "Except for the balding head," running his hand over his thinning hair. He does have a receding hairline, I see, but I think it gives him character. I should have told him that.

He expressed concern regarding the cost of the Christmas gifts I had gotten him. I assured him that I managed my money well and that he had nothing to worry about. I reminded him of my willingness to pay for his *Lasik* eye surgery from the leftover 529 Fund. He said he was waiting until his vision stabilized. He then told me he had just bought himself a $600 gift—computer parts—for his hobby of building computers and I responded that he had deserved it and had also earned it. After all, he had just graduated, had landed a great job, and he continues to make some money from his hobby. I cannot be more proud of my boy.

Before we parted, he asked me to ask Patrick to stop sending him e-mails. I was surprised as I was not aware of any since the last time around two years ago. Every time I got distressed, Anwar said, Patrick e-mailed him. Anwar added that he did not want to have anything to do with him. However, he was not upset when he said that; in fact, he almost said it gently, to my surprise. I assured him that I would talk to Patrick about that. He then put his hands on my shoulders, said he would have spent more time, but that he needed to get up at five o'clock, also expressing concern for me that I had a long drive back home. I understood. What had happened during that half an hour was a lot more than I had bargained for. This time, I had no problem letting go. We wished each other a Merry Christmas. We hugged and I kissed him on the cheek. As he left running across the street, I yelled, "I love you," but he kept going. It did not matter, for this time, I did not have to hear it. I saw it in his eyes, and I felt it through his heart. In his being and mine, I knew it as the one undeniable truth. I got in my car and drove home.

How I managed to get home that evening, I do not know. I wept and wept and wept and I thanked God a million times for all of His blessings and mercy. I was on emotional overload, not knowing how I was feeling or why I could not stop crying. I sat by the Christmas tree as I did as a child in the homeland many a night, mesmerized by the twinkling lights. My tears dried and my heart rejoiced. From that night forward and until January 7, our Orthodox Christmas, the lights will remain on all night, every night.

Everything that happened that evening seemed surreal; it still is as of this writing on Christmas Day. I am still processing and absorbing the intensity of that moment, trying to understand what I am feeling. I just cannot believe that I have reached yet another turning point in my life, that I can hope and dream that my son will be a part of it.

I picked up my journal where I had left off, documenting this unprecedented, joyous reunion. Never did I imagine that he would receive me so lovingly as I saw through his eyes, let alone embrace me and tell me he would allow me back into his life. The feeling is indescribable, for the journey has been so long and agonizing that it robs the euphoric moment of triumph. But perhaps it was not victory I was seeking. No, I was not in a contest as Anwar might have thought when he said, "You win," before he added, "I will let you back into my life." It is almost as though your heart is numb when ironically you are elated; as though a sedative has quieted your excitement and made you pause and reflect instead of scream without a care like a mad woman. It is as if you have finished a marathon, but came in so far behind, that the cheering crowd had packed and left.

But, could it be that instead, I was fearing a setback? Could he change his mind and not pick up the phone as he said he would? Could he really be so cruel to do this to me again? I would be torn to pieces, never ever to recover. As I refuse to believe he could, an element of fear still lurks....and a sense of guilt and betrayal haunts me, for how can I not trust God to see me through after he has carried me so far? I struggle to believe even though my heart is at peace sensing good things to come. Forgive me, my Lord. I am weak and my faith is weaker. I ask for Your protection, Your love and above all, for You to show me the way and to guide me on the path of faith and righteousness.... I pray to You, my God.

Or could it be that I am coming to terms with the loss of the eight years that I was locked out; time that I can never recapture, time when I could not watch him grow, time where I could only watch his momentous milestones from afar, time when I was deprived from any interaction or visits so that I couldn't gradually observe his transitioning from the soft boyish loving teenager to the young man, with a beard, with a scruffy voice, time when I could not hug him, or kiss him, or caress his cheeks, or tuck him into bed and tell him every second of every day how much I loved him.

What is gone is gone forever. But I have tomorrow, the day after and the day after that. I will be back in my son's life and in my daughter's too, I believe. Life is a miracle. God has given me a second chance.

I e-mailed Nizar to let him know what happened and to thank him for the miracle that God had worked through him in order to allow Anwar to make peace with himself somehow and to let go of his anger as we reconnected one step at a time.

CHAPTER 21

You Lift Me Up

My insomnia became profound right after the reunion. Though it was the best day I had had in eight years, finally feeling my son's compassion, and touched by his gentle soul that committed to opening a small window into our relationship, the fear and anxiety started slowly to settle in. I did not know how to approach him, how often to call him or to ask to see him without pushing him the other way. I wondered many times if he would reject me and shatter my hopes again.

My worst nightmare, however, came as I approached my wedding day. Internally, I was torn between moving on and the fear of my children's eternal estrangement. I remember forcing myself to eat just so I would not collapse. I could not understand what was going on with me. I knew I was never a great sleeper, but never had I experienced such serious and perpetual sleep deprivation. I remember getting ready for work every morning, not wanting to take a shower, to get dressed or to drive to work. I remember sitting at my desk, so nauseated that I had to leave work early on many days. On many others, I called in sick for lacking the composure to drive. I remember multiple visits to doctors and therapists who only wanted to give me medicine which I hated depending on. I refused to allow a substance to control my consciousness or my being. No matter how much my closest friends tried to convince me that the prospect of marrying another man was causing all my symptoms, I rejected their comments. After all, I was the happiest woman on earth, about to marry the man of her dreams. I struggled to cope on my own for six months, trying to focus on the wedding plans and on my job.

Here again, I was in denial, refusing to give in to my fear that if there were ever a chance that my children would someday reconnect with me, the marriage would absolutely destroy any such prospect. Seven years of relentless rejection, humiliation and alienation would become the eternity. My fate would be sealed forever; a new life, 180 degrees different from the one before, would transform every aspect of every day I had lived for fifty-one years. I searched high and low for any natural remedy, including yoga, meditation, sleep strategies. Nothing worked.

What I had left was only my close sister-friend, Salha. Every day, without a fail, she called to check on me. She listened to me, comforted me when I was at my lowest and boosted my determination when she recognized I still had the will to conquer. She counseled me better than any therapist could, not only because she truly felt my pain, but also because she knew me well enough to have faith that I would overcome. She understood my frailties, and she encouraged me; she cried with me but lifted me up; she recognized my grief but refused to let me surrender to it; she agreed that my life would be turned upside down but reminded me of the joy of living in the moment, letting go of what is beyond your control, leaving it all in the hand of our Almighty, loving and merciful God. Indeed, as He always does through His Own ways, God delivered me once more.

In time, I accepted the certainty that fear was the culprit and I slowly changed my mindset. I prayed more, meditated more, continued to exercise and socialize with friends, went to work every day and looked forward to my new beginning. My insomnia, while still very much with me, stopped interfering with my life. It became a part of it as much as everything else I had had to accept. I carried on with the wedding plans, sent the invitations and booked our honeymoon trip. My brother, Hassan, walked me down the aisle on June 28, 2015 as the few celebrants and our families looked on with gladness. In the ballroom, my spirit and body danced fervidly to the tunes of traditional *Dabkeh* and Belly dancing songs. I lifted my champagne glass toasting all the guests, touched by the unforgettable memories of how each and every one of them had left an imprint on my life. I put the glass down after my speech that had given a glimpse of my broken heart, and I thought about my children and prayed that they would accept me one day and would be happy for me.

May 17, 2015

It took five months after my last encounter with Anwar before he allowed me to see him again. In the interim, I tried to restrain myself from calling or texting so as not to turn him off, out of respect for his wishes "not to overdo it." As hard as it was to control my emotions, I limited my calls to intervals of three to five weeks. He seemed content with that, and I learned to accept it, and cherish every communication as a step in the right direction. During these times, but not without struggle, I kept our conversations basic, short and sweet, knowing that if they got emotional, he would be quick to remind me to "just be normal."

Mother had arrived late this year in advance of my wedding. Hoping to delight Anwar with special treats from her loving hands, I asked her to make some Kibbeh which was Anwar's favorite foods. On the 15th, as we put the last tray in the oven, I thought to call him in order to see if he would allow me to visit. To my surprise, he agreed to meet me for lunch at TGI Friday's. Two days later, I loaded the ice chest with Kibbeh, Stuffed Grape Leaves, Tzazikki, Stuffed Zucchini, Spanakopita, Labneh, some Arabic bread and Easter cookies, with some chocolate, of course, and proceeded to drop them off at his apartment. When he met me downstairs, I approached and gave him a hug. He remained stiff as though to remind me that he had not forgiven me. I was proud to know that he shared his apartment with three others so that he could save some money. I did not spend much time browsing, but it appeared he had managed well, living within his means, lessons which I had passed on to him.

I offered him a ride, but he chose to drive separately, and that was fine. As we ordered our food, I was yet again surprised by another lesson he had learned—proper table manners, a taste for fine foods and for a balanced diet, but I said nothing. He even showed me a picture of some Sheesh Kabab that he routinely barbecues for his roommates. My child could indeed take care of himself, I thought.

I was delighted to know his plans to save for and to buy a house, though as an investment, to hear him express his hope for a promotion and to dream of later moving on so he could have time and could make space for his passion for DH riding. As I inquired about the insomnia he had mentioned during one of our telephone conversations, he did not appear willing to share his struggles. We talked about his move the following month to live with his father's friend who lived close. Everything was pleasant and somehow natural. I asked him about Nour, and he said that she was "perfect." I maintained my composure, played it as casually as I could, and when it was time to part, I thanked him for meeting me and gave him a tight squeeze. This time, he put his arm around me and seemed a lot more relaxed than when we had just met for dinner. It was as though he was relieved that I did not bring up hot topics that could provoke or upset him. I blew him a kiss and told him, "I love you." He responded, "Bye, Mom!" How pleasant it was to hear him call me Mom. That was more than I could have hoped for. I smiled, replying, "Bye *Habibi*," and drove off.

My life is indeed turning, I wrote in my journal. The date marked our first reunion for the first time in eight years with HIS permission instead of through unwelcome surprises. It was also the first time that it left him relaxed rather than apprehensive as he had been. I knew then that he would agree to see me again without worrying that I might antagonize him or make him feel guilty, angry or any of those sentiments he had been carrying around for too long. I hoped that this encounter had brought him some peace and calm in his life and had helped him to shake his anger and negativity and perhaps to relieve his insomnia. That, I may not know for years to come, but I hoped and prayed that we would continue to move forward and to rebuild our relationship, one call, one visit, one text at a time.

November 29, 2015

Yes, it was another six months before I saw Anwar again. During that time, I made a few attempts to meet him, particularly one in order to celebrate his birthday, but he always had an excuse—in Mammoth, or with his father, etc. If I pushed the envelope, he was quick to remind me to "cut it out," interpreting everything I said as my way of trying to make him feel "bad," no matter my intention. He rebuffed every assurance that I did not want to make him feel angry, guilty or upset. A mother shouldn't have to explain what is natural. Rather, my concern was for his well-being given his inability to shake off the anger that I sensed with every text.

As he continued to have serious insomnia, telling me on one occasion that it started as soon as "you left the house," my heart was crushed. What was worse is that Anwar never would allow me to engage in any conversation relating to the divorce or its aftermath. Not once did we talk about any of the whys, the hows that could have brought some healing. I could only send e-mails hoping they had been received and read. I shared with him the strategies that I had utilized to help me over time, but ultimately, I knew that he would have to face his past, our past, deal with it, and move forward if he were to get better. I let him know that I would no longer ask to see him; that he would have to make the choice himself, not out of guilt, but out of love and out of a true desire to reconnect with me. I also assured him that my arms would always be open to receive him. Sadly, I also knew that his bottled anger is what will continue to impact his mental state adversely, intensifying his insomnia, among who knows what other symptoms.

All I can do is pray for his epiphany, for his release.

Our conversions were limited to very few phone calls and to random texts that I always initiated. There was nothing substantive about them; rather ordinary day to day talk, except for the one time when the conversation led me to tell him that he had a heart when his sister did not. I brought up how Nour kicked me out of her house and called the police on me when I surprised her on that infamous day. That is when he said something to the effect that he really did not have a heart and that in actuality, "Nour had cried her heart out" at that time. I was in disbelief and did not ask him to elaborate. I wish I had, but I doubt he would have, as he may have slipped trying to defend her. I became speechless trying to understand what I had just heard. To this day, I don't know if I believe it or not, so I remain neutral. A part of me wants to believe that she has not lost her humanity, that she had acted out of fear, pride, self-preservation, or to shield herself from the pain of the discovery of what she really feels and why. Yet another part of me thinks that her loyalty to her father and her hatred towards me have sustained her resolution to excommunicate me forever.

As another Thanksgiving came and went, I decided to contact Anwar in order to offer some food I had been saving for him and to give him his Christmas gifts. Why do I continue to do that when time and time again I have promised Anwar not to? Why could I not realize the state of anger and resentment he felt upon seeing me or communicating with me and just spare him the pain? I can only say that in my heart, I was not convinced that my limited presence in his life was causing him all of his grief. Rather, it was bringing it out from a buried past that Anwar had refused to deal with; a past that I could not change, nor could he.

In fact, I would like to think that our brief encounters gave Anwar the assurance that he is loved beyond measure; that he was not abandoned, that his mother did not choose Patrick or his children over him; that every failed attempt to reach his heart is reminder of my relentless effort to convince him that I would never give up on him. I would like to think that through all of that, deep inside, Anwar rejoiced enough, became content enough to develop some inner strength. Sadly, my children might not have had to endure such suffering if Rameh had played a positive role instead of putting indirect pressure on them to cast me out completely, relishing the attention that fed his ego, and the victory that crowed his narcissistic self.

Anwar was visiting his father that weekend so we agreed to meet at the church by the house. It was not a pleasant occasion as Anwar kept putting me off asking me to not leave my house until he contacted me. It got late, so I drove to the church, called him upon my arrival, but still waited for about an hour before he finally showed up. I was not happy, but tried to suck it up as much as I could. Still, I sounded my resentment and told him that that would never happen again. He defended himself by saying that he had told me he was having dinner. I argued that he could have just picked up the gifts and left. His answer was that he wanted to keep the peace. I asked if he was having dinner with Nour and he said, "No, with Dad's friend." I suppose Rameh has a girlfriend now who may have prepared a special meal to impress Anwar. I truly hoped that Rameh did indeed have a girlfriend so he could perhaps loosen the nooses that had choked my children's necks for nine years. I guess I underestimated the extent of his vindictiveness. Girlfriend or not, his grip continued to control my children more and more every day.

Our reunion barely lasted ten minutes. He looked so fine without his glasses and with a thick beard. He stated that he had recently trimmed it, then flashed a picture from his phone with his full beard, proud of it much as his father used to be at that age. He loaded the food and the Christmas gifts onto the truck. I hugged and kissed him goodbye. He said, "Bye, Mom." as he had been saying lately when we talk over the phone and after I tell him I love him and goodbye. A step forward but not much more.

JANUARY 21, 2016

I had planned to visit the relics of Saint Sharbil—on loan from Lebanon—displayed at the Maronite Church in Los Angeles. I wanted to say a prayer for my friend who was battling cancer and also to make a *Nidr* (a promise to God) for when Nour and I reunite as mother and daughter. I had been communicating with Anwar about some snow pants I had bought for him. As he was going snowboarding that weekend, I thought to meet him for dinner and give them to him, along with a jacket I had bought earlier. To my surprise, he agreed, though expressing amazement at the distance I would be traveling. He also inquired about my selection of an expensive restaurant, and I answered that I had chosen it because it was elegant and was close to his apartment.

I arrived a little late due to the traffic. Anwar looked as handsome as ever waiting at the table. I kissed him on the head as he said, "You look nice; did you have a conference or something?" "Thanks, just work clothes," I responded. We ordered our food and engaged in the usual small talk. It was difficult for me to remain calm and composed, but I knew I had to, so that I would not turn him off with my nostalgia. He mentioned his heightened stress from work and said he was considering leaving engineering altogether to become an "athlete!" or to do something else that he had not yet figured out. I emphasized hard work would pay off, urging him to hang on until he found another job. He sounded bitter and angry as usual, upset that he was being a slave to the job with little money or time to enjoy life, to rest, or to have fun, even as he still enjoyed DH riding and dirt-biking on weekends and was earning a decent salary.

An hour and a half flew by very quickly. As we walked outside, he saw my car parked next to his. Even though I had not noticed his truck as I drove into the lot, he still assumed that I purposely parked next to him. I gave him the pants and jacket and a big hug sending it to Nour. He responded that he does not hug people. As we parted, I assured him that I would not impose myself on him, but simply wanted to have a "relaxed" relationship with him; one where I would not feel any trepidation each time I called.

MARCH 18, 2016

Nour was expected to graduate in the summer. As I browsed the university's website for information about her graduating class, I was pleased to discover what they call a "Match List" of every student's chosen specialty and where they would be completing their residencies. There for every proud parent to see was my daughter's name in the middle of the list as a Medical Doctor who will spend the following five years in residency in general surgery at the U.S Naval Base in San Diego. I bought a navy cap from the nearby store and snapped a picture of myself saluting her.

I attached it to my e-mail with the caption, "Congratulations Lieutenant Haddad. Very proud of you, daughter!"

The next day, I went back to the same site and discovered the list was missing. I inquired with the Associate Director of Public Affairs who was in charge of the postings. Her response shocked me. "We were advised by our Admissions office that a student objected to having her name published, so we took the list down." "Was this student Nour Haddad?" I followed up. As expected, privacy laws prevented her from disclosing that information, but she did refer me to the Associate Dean of Student Affairs. I pleaded my case with the Dean imploring her to tell me if it was NOT my daughter who made the request, just to calm myself down, but I got a similar response. Cornered and despondent, I texted Anwar, but he had no answer for me either. I needed to know if my daughter still had a soul. I wanted to believe that she did, that she still had enough compassion not to punish me in any way she could, so I sent her an e-mail titled:

What Have You Become???

My dear Child, or what should I call you?

I need to know from you directly if you had asked the Match List be taken down so that I could not have access to it....Did you Really? Really? Really? When all I wanted was to congratulate you and to tell you that I could not be prouder! Can a surgeon succeed without compassion? Can a child intentionally be orphaned? Can a heart beat without a mother's womb?

As expected, she never replied. A couple of months later, in May, the graduation ceremony was downloaded to the university website and shortly after, it was posted on her father's Facebook page. As I watched my child receive her medical degree, waves of happiness and sorrow surrounded me.

There she was, again, successfully accomplishing yet another major milestone in her life, and all I could do was to celebrate her from hundreds of miles away. No hugs. No kisses. No words on pride and joy. She will always be my child, no matter the time or the distance. I reminded her of that in a beautiful short poem by Rumi:

I choose to love you in silence...

For in silence I find no rejection,

I choose to love you in loneliness...

For in loneliness

No one owns you but me,

I choose to adore you from a distance...

For distance will shield me from pain,

I choose to kiss you in the wind...

For the wind is gentler than my lips,

I choose to hold you in my dreams...

For in my dreams you have no end.

JUNE 3, 2016

For the year and a half that had passed, Anwar and I mostly communicated via simple text messages and occasionally with a phone call, on my part, of course. Except for a brief meeting at the church behind the old house to give him his Christmas gifts and some food, we did not see each other. In fact, with the passage of time, he was slowly reverting to his old ways, not picking up the phone or texting back with a word or two and only after several attempts on my part to communicate. Our conversations, if any, were general and brief. I became more and more distressed, concerned that the few blocks I had built over the years where starting to come down.

His hard-line stance continued for the remainder of the year as he stopped answering the phone altogether. Occasionally, when I asked to see him, he texted back that he was busy. Many times he was curt and hurtful. In one instance, upon my return from Europe, I tried calling him several times, but he did not answer. Concerned, I called his work line late in the evening, not anticipating that he would be there. I just wanted to hear a voice message or something to indicate that he was still working, that he was well. Though I did not leave a message, he must have been there and seen my number through the caller I.D. He texted shortly after, "I am fine. Stop treating me like a kid. Don't ever call me at work."

Hurt as ever, I responded, "Wow! All I wanted was to see how you are doing and give you the chocolate that I told you I would bring from Switzerland. So sad you continue to treat me this way. I will no longer allow it. Blessings to you, and may good tidings come your way."

I was distraught realizing that with the passage of time, he was becoming more and more disengaged, and had no desire to rebuild our relationship. After all, I had not been in his life for nine years and he had grown completely accustomed to life without his mother. In as much as I wanted to withdraw completely, as usual, I was unable to. As Christmas approached, I picked up my texting, sent him pictures and greetings and asked, yet again, to see him. None of my texts were responded to.

PART VI

A Journey That Never Ends

CHAPTER 22

Acceptance

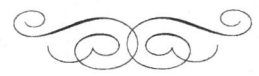

I cannot explain what happened or why Anwar had a change of heart at the beginning of the year. I had texted him to ask if I could send his Christmas gifts to his work place and he agreed. Since then, he has started responding to every text, and commenting on pictures I sent. Some of his texts conveyed funny sarcasm and subtle humor. He even shared with me his plan to go to Switzerland and joked about finding his "future ex-wife" and staying there. Through Godly intervention that I cannot explain, it was clear he was relaxing so much more that I felt confident he would not reject me if I asked to meet him for dinner. So I did, and he agreed, though not to the elegant restaurant I had suggested. Panera was the place, ordinary enough not to give me the impression that a formal dinner would memorialize it as special.

It had been fourteen months since I last saw him. I anxiously paced back and forth in the parking lot attempting to appear calm and praying that God would help me stay composed and not to say anything that might turn him off. How is a mother to react upon the sight of her precious young man, casually walking towards her as though he is meeting an old acquaintance? I smiled, embraced him tightly, but I knew to quickly release my arms upon his stoic greeting. Nevertheless, I was determined to carry on and bury any hurtful thought. We sat in the lounge chairs and started talking.

He was still suffering from insomnia, though he had accepted it. His sleeping two to four hours a day made me very concerned. I suggested he take Magnesium or try the medication I took for a few months to regulate his cycle. He was adamant about not taking anything, even as I emphasized that none of that was addictive. He told me he did not want to be dependent on anything and reminded me that Magnesium was a metal! I found out that he did not have a special person in his life recalling five years ago a girlfriend who broke his trust. He did not want to elaborate, perhaps not to draw analogies from my story.

He told me about getting pneumonia after a steroid injection for two herniated discs, about his plans to move to Washington in a year so that he could afford to buy a house with a garage. Offering to care for him in case he needed back surgery in the future, he declined, stating that his father would take care of him.

As we settled in for dinner, he opened up a little more about his plans and about his personal life, though mostly through prompting from me and in response to my questions. At some point, he commented that I was trying to "catch up for eight years "to which I responded, "No, what is lost is lost forever." I teared up, but quickly regained my composure, fearing I would upset him. He mentioned he had bought a truck, that he had saved 20K, and that he would have looked for another job that he actually enjoyed, like working for Honda, if it had been in California. He shared with me that he changed positions from a systems engineer to a test engineer so that he did not have to endure the undue stress and to deal with the bad boss he had; that by being a test engineer II, he made up for the pay differential.

Clearly, he felt that he had no work/life balance since he works long hours, through lunch breaks, and gets home too late and tired to go to the gym. He was not convinced that weekends and vacations would bring about that balance. Still, his face looked rested and beaming with excitement as he showed me a short video of him on his bike, taken by a professional. I felt that he had opened up enough to maybe agree to show me where he lived, but my asking obviously put him out of his comfort zone. He did share, however, that he had his own room and bathroom in a house with four roommates, but that he paid more in rent for the privilege of using the garage.

I asked him if he ever took drugs or drank alcohol, and he denied that he did either. I was so grateful and proud and mentioned that it had helped that neither Rameh nor myself had tried drugs and that we drank alcohol only during social occasions. He agreed. I then started talking about how I had raised him and Nour with discipline due to which he turned out to be a fine man. He said he was because "I could do whatever I wanted." I reminded him of the value system I raised him and his sister with which did include some restrictions, crucial to good character. He then told me about his friends going wild in college, but that he had not. Thanks to the stability we provided in the home, I said, and he nodded.

He mentioned that he had had no money growing up, and I emphasized that while I had provided everything they needed and had given him a small weekly allowance, this had helped him become independent and responsible, building his nest egg at such a young age. It seemed to me as though he was content with the path he had chosen for himself and somehow proud of his upbringing, though careful not to attribute any of it to me. I let it go, gratified and proud of his character and early success. I wanted to remind him of the five tenets I used to tell them they could not violate, and the others that were permissible, but I was not sure it was the right time.

For the record, should they ever read this memoir after my passing, may they be reminded of my love and discipline that shaped them. Often I told them they could not 1) drink and drive, 2) have unprotected sex (if they must have it, that is), 3) to let it always be THEIR choice to have sex and not be pressured by a partner or be taken advantage of, 4) never consume drugs of any sort, 5) never lie and if they did, they must confess, else the lie doubles. It is from the prism of this last tenet that they see me as a hypocrite, perhaps through today and forever. I also routinely reminded them that college was not an option, but a given; that what people say about them does not change who they are; that performing at less than their maximum potential is unacceptable; that in life, they will surely make mistakes, but that they had better know how to learn from them, and to bear all responsibility for their actions. It is ironic that my trials have given them their first test. It remains my wish that they learn from these valuable lessons which I taught them and to realize and deal with the consequences of their choices, though not as harshly or as unforgiving as life has dealt them to me.

The conversations were small, but sincere. I thanked him for making this coincidentally Lebanese Mothers' Day, celebrated on May 21, so special. Slowly, the conversation became more intimate. I asked if his father would be ready to make peace and to receive my request for forgiveness, to which he responded that he would not, "Just as I did not give you that forgiveness." I paused for a second and said, "I hope that someday you will," before we were interrupted by the waiter. I changed the subject.

I was pleased that for the first time he actually asked me a few questions himself; about my mother, my siblings, my job, and my retirement, commenting that I must have accumulated "hundreds of thousands of dollars." I wondered if his father had given him that idea. I then asked about Nour. His response was brief, "busy." He does not visit her, I learned. He did mention that she gets a meager salary while in residency. I joked about showing up in San Diego, if she would receive me. His response was, "Good luck with that." I mentioned my visit to her in Arizona and how hurtful it was for me when the police officer pushed me out of her house. He said that the officer was doing his duty and that I was acting erratically, or something to that effect. Bewildered, I stared at him in silence for a few seconds. He then changed the subject, perhaps recognizing he was adding to my pain.

As we carried on, I expressed my desire to speak to him by telephone once in a while, but he emphasized that he would only respond to texts. He said he was always too busy, and texting back allowed him time to respond when he had a free moment. At some point later, he told me that he was "here for a reason you will never know." I said, "No, I know; it is because of the commitment you made to me when you said you would let me back into your life. He nodded, and I thanked him, praising him for his integrity and for being a man of his word.

I was pleased to see him maturing, being responsible and level-headed and having a plan for his future. As night started to fall, I realized it would be best to say our goodbyes and for me not to impose on him any longer. I gave him the food I had prepared for him, we hugged and he said, "Thank you, Mom." I blew him a kiss and drove off. How sweet it is to hear "Mom."

JULY 25, 2017

Our relationship was mostly limited to cordial, but guarded texts to which he always responded. I tried in vain to meet him once for lunch, but he claimed to be busy as usual. Nevertheless, he was pleasant and a bit more reassuring that the lines of communication would stay open. That did not last for long. As I pushed for a meeting on July 25, he rebuffed me rudely stating that I make these requests every week. I, then asked if I were an imposition and he responded, "Kind of." Hurt and disappointed, I texted him about being fed up and letting him know that I was moving on. He dismissed my sentiments saying that I say the same thing every time, "This isn't about you. Stop being so selfish," he concluded.

For me, that marked the end of our relationship. I thanked him and asked him to stop his insults. He then inquired about what I wanted to talk to him about, to which I did not respond. I had wanted to discuss how I could partner with him in buying a house, but after his rude behavior, I changed my mind, feeling disgusted, hurt, defeated, angry disappointed and without any hope left. I knew then that it was over. All that I had built had been destroyed as I was thrown back once again into this cycle that I could no longer allow to torment me. I think it was at that point that I had finally reached acceptance, that there was nothing more that I could do to change his heart; that reconciliation must truly come from him, and that I was totally powerless. And so it was. I closed this chapter and tried to live my life surrendering to a fate, that perhaps, I may never have my children back. I asked God for His help in giving me resilience so I could carry on the rest of my life, comforted by their good health, by their successful careers and by all the blessings in my life that I could not ignore.

JANUARY 10, 2018

My phone rang late that afternoon. What compelled me to answer, I do not know. After all, I had not been picking up any calls from numbers that I did not recognize due to the many solicitors that had been calling me incessantly. A doctor from Kaiser asked to speak to Anwar having called and been unsuccessful in reaching him. I verified his number with her, but inquired about her call, worried about his condition. She said that it was about blood work results, or so I heard. I really panicked at that time because doctors do not generally call unless there is some abnormality, some bad results. I pushed for more reassurance, but all she would say was that "It is nothing I did not expect."

Later that evening, I called Anwar twice before he picked up. He sensed the panic in my voice as I asked him about his blood work and why the doctor had called me and if he was okay. He asked me to calm down telling me it was not blood work, but his MRI result showing he had two herniated discs—from DH riding—for which he was considering back surgery before he dropped off of my insurance due to the age limitation. I calmed down a bit and we had a pleasant conversation where at the end he agreed to let me know when his surgery would be scheduled. After a few text exchanges, he told me it was going to be on January 29. I offered to help, but he refused stating that Nour and his father would manage things.

I contemplated life's hard reality that my son was going to undergo surgery without me by his side; without my comforting touch, without my warm gentle voice reassuring him of a quick recovery. Still, I felt compelled to be there but considered the backlash that Anwar might face if his father or Nour were to see me. I was torn between what I needed and wanted to do and what I was not sure would be in my son's best interest. I prayed for God to give me a sign and to guide me in making the right decision. In the nights that followed, I had two dreams. In the first, I was coming down the stairwell in my home and saw Nour in the kitchen. Without a word, we embraced as tears ran down my face. In the second, I was by Anwar's bedside as he asked me, "Why should you care?" Strengthened by God's guidance, I set my plan to go to the hospital and to find out where the surgery was to be performed.

JANUARY 29, 2018

My heart raced as I drove to the Kaiser hospital in Downey. I did not know what to expect and feared Rameh and Nour would make a scene if they saw me. With a flowering Spring bouquet and a red vase for well wishes, I entered the recovery reception room, only to be stopped at the front desk. Kaiser does not allow flowers into the recovery rooms, I was told. I left a note on the arrangement, hoping someone would give it to Anwar upon his discharge, then I proceeded to enter. In the middle of the long hallway with several beds hidden behind curtains for privacy, there he was, alone in his hospital bed, blue gown, tubes, heart monitor and a thin bed cover marked his first hours post op. He appeared to be sleeping as his eyes were shut. I looked at the nurse who assured me all went well and that he was still groggy. I smiled and laid my palm on his forehead. He opened his eyes and asked, "You came all the way here?" "Of course," I responded. "I had to be by your side...hopefully your father and Nour will not give you a hard time." "I really don't care!" he responded.

I kissed his forehead and caressed his cheeks. He became once more my baby boy and I became his mother for the first time in eleven years, and my heart leapt for the serenity I had not felt in an eternity. He was all mine and under my wings, though just for that enchanting moment. About ten minutes later, as I stood on one side of the bed, caressing his hair, I looked up, and there was Rameh on the other side. Nour was by the foot of the bed. He gave me a stern look that spoke of vengeance, hatred, vindictiveness, and everything his wicked soul represented. Calmly, I said, "I beg you, don't say anything for Anwar's sake. He is my son as he is yours." I turned to Nour, but could not read her facial expression. I quickly turned my head back to my son, preoccupied about him and his recovery. With that, the nurse reminded us that only two people could be present. I said I would leave soon, but Rameh and Nour decided to walk out. I was relieved to know that I could spend a few more precious moments with my child. He was calm and composed. I pointed to the gifts I had brought him and his sister and reminded him to pick up the flowers that I had left at the reception desk. No, he did not need any more clothes, but did like the blue sweatshirt since it matched his truck color and I knew that it was his favorite color anyway. I hoped he would take the gifts home, along with the get-well card and to give Nour hers, a handbag and a watch to celebrate her successes.

My visit lasted about 45 minutes, a lot longer than I expected. I knew that I had to leave. As I kissed him goodbye, he asked, "Did you leave lipstick?" I wiped his still soft check, told him I loved him and walked away. As I stepped away from the bed, Rameh approached, Nour a few feet behind. I asked him if I could speak to him for a minute, but he gave me the same stern look and gestured swiftly with his head, no. I asked again, and got the same response. As I passed Nour, I turned and looked at her for one last time. Without hesitation, she kept her head straight, purposely ignoring me with the stoic look that reminded me once again that she had relegated me to oblivion long ago. I walked out of the hospital surprised not to have shed a tear, thankful to God for that beautiful encounter and for the strength that he had given to me to maintain my composure.

MARCH 1, 2018

In the weeks that followed, I texted Anwar to check on his progress, and he cordially responded. He even let me know that he was staying at his father's house while recovering for four months and that he would be searching for a new job. Later in February, as mother prepared Stuffed Grape Leaves and Kibbeh, I called to ask him if he needed some. He did not pick up the phone, but to my surprise, he called me back a few minutes later. I told him I could bring him a variety of his favorite foods. He questioned if the containers were disposable, which I affirmed, recognizing his concern that he may want to discard anything from me without having his father know that he had brought my food into the house. His response was that he would think about it, and I left it at that, asking if he could let me know later.

As many days and texts later rolled by without any firm responses, I called. He was short, annoyed by my insistence. He told me that he did not need the food, but I sensed that he had reasoned his father would throw a fit if he saw so many containers in the refrigerator. I confronted him about that, and he asked me to stop. When I continued, he hung up. I was very disappointment and texted him that I raised him to be a gentleman, never to hang up on his mother. His response was, "I've got one rule and you continue to break it. Note that I occasionally answer your calls as a favor, not as an obligation. I don't like talking to you. Being a gentleman has nothing to do with anything." I was so disheartened for this break in communication, lack of respect, and halted progress. I texted him back reminding him that I would not accept his behavior, wished him luck and a "goodbye forever," until he decided to be "a man and have an adult conversation." He ridiculed me stating, "K, talk to you soon, same conversation every couple months LOL," to which I responded, "Nope."

A couple of months later, I received information regarding his insurance, so I had to resume my texting though I kept it relevant to the subject matter. I sent a Christmas card and care-package to his work. I also sent him some pictures of my trip to Austria and Switzerland, and he made short, but kind comments. Through his "Reddit" platform, I learned that he had started a new job in Seattle. I was relieved that when I asked him about it, he stated that he was happy and had no stress. I hoped his life would be relaxed and his attitude and mood would change to being less angry and negative and more hopeful for brighter tomorrow. I hoped that his quality of life would improve and, with that, his health and his insomnia. Later in December, through his father's Facebook page, I learned that he and his sister were at the house, probably for the upcoming Christmas Holiday. I offered to meet him, even daring to have him ask Nour to join us, hoping that my miracle would be fulfilled. "Not so fast," he responded, "Not really comfortable meeting up at the moment."

JANUARY 13, 2019

A year had gone by since his surgery and all we had shared had been a few texts. My calls were not answered but I would let it go. On that day, however, he picked up. Hearing his voice for the first time in over a year made me emotional. Tears started flowing. He heard my cracking voice and got upset saying, "You torture me when you call and cry. You have other people you can talk to. I am not the one. I am not like Nour. You have issues with her. I am not her. I will talk to you if you compose yourself and be normal." The problem, I responded, is that our relationship was NOT normal; that if it had been, and if he had dealt with the past, he would be at peace. He responded that "No, I don't want to deal with it."

I wanted him to be happy. I tried to explain that if I cry, it is because I am human and as a human, I made mistakes. And while I did not want to burden him or to make him feel sorry for me, I did not want a relationship in which I am feeling that I am constantly walking on eggshells each time I call him wondering, will he pick up, will he respond? "I always respond if you text. Better to text," he responded.

He then calmed down and brought up the divorce settlement, to my surprise. Apparently, he had been misinformed about the money I received and how I had spent his college fund. I tried to explain, but time did not permit, nor was the venue appropriate.

I then asked him about his sister and how she had probably blocked my number and was not receiving my messages. While he did not deny that, he added that she was fine and on deployment oversees which is why her number did not work. I asked him to tell her that I love her and that she is always in my heart. As with many other conversations, this one was fragmented also. He kept jumping from one subject to the next without giving full attention to each or to my responses. At one point, he mentioned he was at the doctor when I had called him, but refused to tell me if it had been for a routine appointment because I "panic." "You don't need to know about my daily life. What if everything were normal and we were away and independent?" Why does he tell me these things? Is he craving attention? Or does he delight in troubling my soul?

I responded that I wanted to know that he was fine, happy, and success-ful, but that he does not even tell me that, or even where he works or lives. How sad, it was, I said, that when people ask me about him and his sister, I can only respond that they are fine, afraid to engage in a conversation where they might ask questions I could not know the answers to, having been locked out of their lives for twelve years. Tearing again, I said, "I am finished. My mom is eighty-two and when she passes, I can say I spent good times with her and have good memories. With you, I should be **making** memories still, but all I have **are** memories."

I did not want him to hang up and feel sorry for me, so I explained it was just one of those days; that I was strong and would push on, but I was also weak for being left without them in my life. I ended the call by assur-ing him I was fine; that I was sorry and did not mean to upset him. I then jokingly said, "Perhaps you will invite me to go up there one day and we can go biking or hiking." We said our goodbyes and that was it. It was the last time I heard his voice.

A couple of days later, I revisited our phone conversation and felt I needed to clarify his misconceptions or whatever his father may have told him regarding the divorce settlement. I was puzzled and a bit unsettled over the remarks Anwar had made to me regarding the payouts from the 529 Fund and from the house settlement I had received. I contemplated sending an e-mail to clarify what I thought he already knew since I had sent him e-mails regarding these transactions before, but also to shed light on that other part that he may have been misinformed about or misunderstood. I truly hoped that he believed that it was not my intention whatsoever to make him feel obligated to me ever, or that it was a ploy on my part to obtain his support. If anything, this e-mail could set our relationship back years, I thought. Nevertheless, I felt compelled to put the information out for him to see. Also, it was my intention to bring to light the terms of the divorce settlement since he appeared to believe any money his father had given me was not due to me or out of his good will.

I sent him an e-mail thanking him for the call and stated my concerns. Assuming that his e-mails were intercepted, I also texted him to let him know I had sent him a very important e-mail for his review. He said he would read it, but never acknowledged that he had. What ensued, however, were abrupt and rude e-mail exchanges that to this date, I cannot understand. I wondered if my e-mail had set him off, but I have no way of verifying that.

In my e-mail I explained all the details of the transactions relating to his and his sister's tuition/loan payments that Anwar seemed to think they came only from accounts that Rameh contributed to when the majority of them had come from me. For his concern that his father had given me "half of the house" as though it was money I was not entitled to, I had to explain that I had contributed equally to the finances of the home and had actually agreed with Rameh not to sell in order to spare the kids another trauma. Unlike what Anwar might have thought, it was Rameh's choice to buy me out so that he would not have to deal with me in the future. I also enclosed all the divorce documents stating that his father had drafted them and that

> "I had signed them as they were because as I did not want to argue and was in utter distress having been pushed and shoved repeatedly against the office desk in the garage, bruised and threatened with a gun put to my head in the bedroom a few days earlier. I am still traumatized by this experience fearing your father would shoot me dead. Still, I chose not to file charges when our neighbor Warren asked me to. Your father would have landed in jail for it. So don't think he was giving me charity."

I ended my e-mail stating, "You once told me that you had ignored all of the e-mails that I had been sending over the years. I have copies of them all, for one day, I hope you and Nour will want to learn the truth. Forgive me if this has brought you grief, for that is not my intention. I could not have fathomed sending such an e-mail, risking the precarious relationship we have had, had you not made those statements to me the other day. I just had to put it out there to set the record straight. That is all."

FEBRUARY 25, 2019

I texted him since I had not heard from him following my attempts to call him twice the day before. He responded that he did not have the "energy" to talk. I tried to downplay it, but when I tried a couple of days later, he texted me that he still had "No energy to talk this week." I became concerned for his health, given his history of insomnia and his visit to the doctor a few weeks before for which he had not disclosed the purpose. I asked if it was because he was busy or due to the insomnia and he responded, "Both;" that it was not related to his job and that he was going to try and get a sleep study. I offered to talk, to be there for him whenever he needed me, to share my experiences in life, my own insomnia struggles, anxiety, loss, or whatever, just to give him some comfort. But he texted, "Still don't want to talk to anyone, and before you say I'm being mean to you, I'm really not talking to people right now." That is when I became extremely concerned not only for his physical health, but also for his mental well-being.

I was not sure if he was descending into depression, and it killed me that I was helpless to console him during what appeared to be a very dark time in his life. I was desperate to know if this was a passing issue or if it had deeper roots that could lead to a serious mental illness. The unknown was driving me crazy, worrying about worse things to come. I hesitated to call him not knowing if that would aggravate his situation, so through a few texts, I would send him words of encouragement and of love and to check if he were feeling better. But still, a month later, he had not gotten the sleep study and did not want to engage, responding to one of my inquiries, "Just don't want to talk about anything to anyone."

This was not the typical anger I had grown used to. His attitude and responses were very different. I truly sensed something serious had happened. I could not understand why he did not want to talk to anyone and for so long, so I inquired about it and offered to help. He responded, "Please leave me alone." I tried again a couple of weeks later, really worried about him, but again, his reply was "You're ridiculous. I am fine, please leave me be for now. Stop Worrying." How easy for him to say that. How was my aching heart going to be calmed when I could know nothing and could only assume the worst? Again, I was so helpless and desperate that I thought to call his father, but quickly changed my mind, worried that this might aggravate Anwar more. I just did not know what more I could do to help him, afraid that anything I tried could lead him into a downward spiral. I prayed that God not just be his Father, but also his Mother when I could do nothing, say nothing, but simply surrender to His almighty power to see His child through.

His 27th birthday was coming up. I packed the snow hat I had brought from Budapest and a couple of elegant shirts. I also packed Nour's gift and asked Anwar to deliver it to her: a Hippocrates Oath plaque that I had bought in Cypress, hoping she would hang it in her office someday. I included a copy of some baby pictures to go with the card that described the sentiment of a parent reminiscing over how quickly the time had gone transforming a baby into the man he is today. As I read it, my own journey flashed back at me; and I recalled the good times that had flown in an instant; the days, weeks, years that were gone and could never be reinvented...and I wrote him a little poem about what I would change if I could relive my endearing moments with him:

I would let you cuddle longer in bed...

Instead of letting the exhaustion later make me regret...

Yee, the things I had to stress...

To lovingly bring you up and lead you to success...

Yet through it all I hoped, you felt my tender touch,

My warm embraces you never rebuffed,

My sweet kisses I thought you loved so much...

Love, Mother

With that, I also enclosed the lyrics of The Living Years song by Mike + The Mechanics that has resonated with me very much, though as a mother. As I interpreted it, the artist is regretting not having been forthright with his father, while alive, about troubling issues and disagreements that had led to their estrangement. And the son laments not being able to fulfill any of the dashed hopes his father had had, now that he had perished. Through some introspection, the artist envisions his father as his own son is born, finally understanding why their disjointed conversations or "crumbled" letters could not bring them peace or closure. He recalls the frustrating wasted time spent in laying blame, quarreling or holding on to a past that only darkened the artist's future. No matter how his father tried to brighten his outlook on life, hoping to impart his knowledge that nothing was constant, and asking him to keep an open mind to new perspectives, the son kept his eyes closed. What could have been conceived while alive, but chosen not to, the shadow of death will forever strip the son from reaching the peace and the gratification that come with reconciliation and forgiveness.

Since I did not have Anwar's home address, I could only send his gift to his office. However, not certain he was still working for the same employer, and respecting that he did not want to talk to me, I called his work number, verified he did and hung up. An hour later he texted me inquiring why I had done that, and I explained. He texted that he appreciated the gifts adding, "But as I've always told you, I don't want gifts." Perturbed, I responded, "God, why do you hate me so much?" He snapped texting, "Dude, this isn't about you."

Here again, I was very frustrated, not knowing why he was treating me like this after we had made some progress; why he was distancing himself ever more and insisting on shunning me; I needed him to explain to me why, beyond just displaying anger. After all, it had been twelve years since our divorce, yet with the passage of time, his anger was intensifying instead of abating. I asked him to "talk to me, so I could understand" letting him know that I was sending the gift that I had bought before "deciding to let you go as you wish." Sarcastically, knowing that I had reneged on my commitment so many times in the past, he responded, "Yeah you've clearly made that decision probably twenty times and continue to do what you want instead of what I want. That's the problem."

I paused for a long time and decided to let him know why I could not stop and why things would change from this point forward. "Yes, I have struggled every time, for my heart is weak, and my love is everlasting. I have asked God to help me through this, and I trust that He will. I pray that you change your mind someday and realize that life is too short." He got the gifts a few days later; thanked me via text, and informed me that he would give Nour hers. I texted back, thanking him for doing that.

I pondered his last words and questioned what he really wanted. Did he mean that he wanted me to leave him alone? That he did not want to talk to me as he had said many times? Or that he needed more time? Is twelve years not long enough to dampen the anger? No, I was not expecting time to heal all wounds, but I would have imagined some softening given the long passage of time, his maturity level, experiences that have happened along the way, employment and responsibility, hardships that he may have had to overcome, euphoric moments and disappointments he may have endured, or, life as it is for all of us, in its ups and downs, successes and failures, enchanting moments and disparaging ones too.

I am more determined than ever, that truly, there is nothing else left to try other than to let him come around himself when he grows up. This chapter is now closed with much pain, which, while it hardened my broken heart, left me with no hope for salvation or redemption. How do you live life without hope? To console my soul, I must believe that without hope, you have no expectations, and without expectations, no disappointments, and without disappointments, you are more apt to focus on life in the moment, mindful of your finite existence and the sorrows that serve as the cornerstone of your faith and resilience.

CHAPTER 23

Reflections: Where Do We Go From Here?

here was one more thing still weighing on me, and that was coming face-to face with Rameh and asking for his forgiveness. I had asked Anwar a few times to ask his father if he would meet me so that I could whole-heartedly give him what he and anyone who had been wronged should receive, but he never got back to me; one time thinking his father would refuse anyway. I did not know how I should approach Rameh or what the outcome might be. I worried he might use anything I said against me, having history as my example. I hesitated for many years and then stopped thinking about it until one day, while driving back from a meeting, I was about to pass the exit to the house. It came upon me to stop and to deliver my apologies. I trembled in my seat, but I still decided to exit nevertheless.

I parked my car by the curbside and proceeded through the entryway to knock. Through the stained glass door, I saw Rameh sitting on the sofa talking on the phone. My hand shook as I rang the doorbell. I believe he saw me. He opened the door with a frown saying, "What is going on?" I said, "I just need to talk to you for a few minutes." He said, "Wait!" and disappeared for about five minutes. Here I was in front of my old house where I had spent years with my children as their mother, where I had cuddled and cradled them with love, had watched them ride their bicycles, roller blade, skateboard, receive their friends and grow up with much good discipline, ethics and high moral character. This is where I slept with them every evening and woke up with them every morning, celebrated their birthdays, built science projects with them, watched them as they practiced their violin or piano, prepared for them healthy nutritious meals to sustain their long days at school. This is where my heart beats were engraved upon every wall, writing the story of their lives. Here is where my babies remained babies. Here is where they were mine, and I was theirs. Here is where Rameh stole them from me and stole me from them. Here is where my memories where being rewritten every day through Rameh's narrative. I gazed around the premises as I stood waiting, a stranger indeed to all that was lost. And I wept, for all that is no longer.

Rameh came out and proceeded towards the curbside, clearly not wanting to have me close to the entrance or to stand in clear view of Nour's bedroom window that overlooked the spot. It was the same window that I had knocked on ten years ago, pleading for her to talk to me, but she had remained silent. Her car was parked outside the garage. I sensed her presence, but unsurprisingly, this time too, she stood silent. I told Rameh that I was sorry; that what I had done was wrong. He said that it was long ago and over with; that he had moved on; that he understood that I was not happy. I said, "Yes, we were incompatible, but that does not justify my infidelity." I even stated boldly that I had thought that he did not love me either, but perhaps he had thought that he did. He did not respond. I don't know why he brought up that it was not my first time cheating on him. I was caught by surprise, but I did not want to argue with him or to dispel his lies. This was neither the time nor the place for any such discussion. I believe I said that he had not deserved it. "I came here, Rameh, to ask for your forgiveness." "Who am I to forgive?" he replied, clearly avoiding having to grant me the mercy. I insisted that what I was asking for was not just for him, but also for me, but got the same reply. I knew at that point that he was not going to grant me any peace.

Without being questioned, he surprised me by saying that it was the children's choice not to talk to me, to which I responded that if the tables had been turned, I would have encouraged them to have a relationship with their father. I was very careful not to provoke him. That was not my intention. I simply wanted to ask his forgiveness, and that was it. He was sure to remind me, or perhaps assure me that the kids had not been deprived of anything, that he had become both the "father and the mother." I thanked him for taking care of our children, but I did remind him that when I left, they were fifteen and seventeen. I believe he understood that what I was inferring was that they were not babies who needed nurturing day and night. I then inquired if either of them were in a relationship. He said Anwar had been in the past but was no longer interested, pursuing other things these days. As for Nour, he gestured as though she were in a relationship, but I could not confirm. I had hoped my children had discovered the beauty of love and of loving. I wondered if their hearts were still capable of exalting in love's enfolding wings.

I then told him that I had been checking his Facebook page. He said that I had followed him once and that he could have blocked me years ago but chose not to. I thanked him and asked him to continue to post pictures and stories about the children through which I could get a glimpse of their lives. I ended our brief encounter by thanking him again for allowing me to talk to him and asking him to pass on to the children how much I loved them and that they would be forever in my heart. He said he would do so "and more!" What he meant by that, I do not know, and I did not ask. I certainly did not expect, now that he had been avenged, that he would make peace with everything that had happed and would encourage our children to reconnect with me. I was right. Sadly, Rameh is a man who will take his grudges to his grave. Perhaps this would be what will take him to his grave. I wish he had realized the futility of it and the bitterness that it brought. It is these sentiments, I am afraid, that he passed on to my children, darkening their hearts and their spirits, leaving them prisoners of their own passions.

So what is it to be destitute? How do you get there? Throughout these chapters, I laid out the story of my life, of my struggles that marked my childhood over which I had had no control, and which led me to many wrong choices that I later made in my adult years and which, yes, were within my control and from which I never shied, assuming full responsibility. During my lowest moments, I had not wished to live any longer, even as I was relishing the beauty of loving and of being loved as I had dreamed of for decades. The void in my soul felt impossible to fill; the gaping hole got bigger with the passage of time, not narrower, as is usually the case for a despondent; the pain turned to anguish many times over as my hopes for better days continued to erode. Every attempt to reconnect with my children had been rebuffed; their hurtful rhetoric or action intensifying evermore.

I reflect upon a time when alone in my car, I cried and cried after Anwar yet again rejected my requests to meet him during that week while I was in training close to his apartment. Hope was sucked out of my spirit, leaving me lifeless. For a few moments, I truly wanted to crash my car or to be killed in an accident somehow. I drove aimlessly for a long time.... but somehow God guided me back to my hotel. Other times I cried myself to sleep wishing that I would not wake up....but I did wake up every morning. There were days and nights when grief seemed to take permanent residence within my mind and body.... but I carried on the next day and the one after that as the weeks turned to months and months turned to years.

Was it resilience, I asked?

Surely, many will interpret my resilience as selfishness, particularly as time and time again, Anwar made it clear to me that not only does he not wish to communicate with me but also that my calls make him angry. Surely, they will argue that I was only pursuing what I needed to do to satisfy my ego, or to fulfill my own desire to reconnect with my children at their expense, further traumatizing their already fragile psychological state. Or even boldly say I was seeking my children's love to satiate my own longing for a love lost many years ago, using them to fill the void of my own parental neglect. Sacrifice, to them is to endure a destructive marriage for what they believe will be in the children's best interest, not to escape to the comfort of another man's arms. All I cared about, they will say, was to satisfy my own needs without a care for my children's desire to truly break free from me or from the constant reminder that their mother actually had cheated, had lied and had abandoned them for another.

To all my detractors, including my children, I say, I do not blame you. I have questioned my drive also and wondered if I had been selfish. But can a mother be that? Can a mother not forgo her own desire to have her children in her life if she's convinced that it would destroy or harm them? Not doing so would be inconceivable; for a mother would sacrifice her life without any hesitation or conditions in order to see her children thrive and prosper. But if these mothers do exist, I surely pray that one day, my children will realize I am not one of them. So, why did I keep pushing and pushing instead of letting go as everybody tells you to do desiring to live mindfully in the moment? Why did I continue to fight until my last breath as though my breath was the infinity? Why did I not just live my life, as though my children were somewhere in a faraway land, until the gentle winds blew them back to shore?

I can only say that I continued to seek my children simply because I am their mother, the only mother they will ever have. I did it because I felt they needed me as much as I needed them. I did what any mother would do, and that is to fight against all odds so that her children will one day reach their peace knowing that they were not abandoned. Truly, it was their choice, not hers, whether through their father's manipulations or through their free will, to ostracize her. Truly, their mother's love was, is and always will be unconditional, unwavering, and everlasting.

Perhaps the way I approached it was not the best way, but I did not know what else to do or how to do it. I consulted family therapists, but none could provide me with answers. Overnight, my children were no longer my children. I was uprooted and dumped with no ability whatsoever to partake in their lives or to have any knowledge of how they were doing, coping, grieving, or recovering. And I became helpless behind a fortified barrier that they built up with their father, built with massive blocks that no earthquake could shake down.

I really wish that my children had allowed me the opportunity to sit with them and to have a discussion about all of this, about what they were going through, what they truly wanted or needed me to do besides just putting up with everything and living a lie just to maintain a "family unit." I wish the family had joined in the therapy that I petitioned the courts for. I wish the court could have enforced the visitations. I wish that my children could have given me a small window into their hearts and minds so I might have gained a sense of their suffering, something beyond their state of bliss that their father reported to the family therapists, to the social workers and the judge. I wish that they had told me the truth about their well-being, being apart from me, instead of pretending that they had conquered everything through their father's dedicated love and attention. I wish that I truly believed that they would have been better off with him instead of being "forced' to belong to a "mother" who they were told is a "pathological liar, an avid cheater, and a relentless adulterer."

But I was afforded none of that. I did what I did driven by a motherly need to protect rather than to harm them. Sadly, they believe the latter to have been my driving course. Still, what I reflect upon every day is the haunting thought that I may have "tortured" my son throughout the years, as he once said, for pursuing him endlessly against his wish. I tried to have him speak to me about his anger; I wrote him many encouraging e-mails and texts; I tried to glean the extent of his anger that seemed surreal given how long it lasted; I pushed and pushed to get him to let it out and to find ways to deal with it so that he could release his pain and move on. That is the only way I believed he would have any peace and thus closure in order to open up his horizons for a brighter tomorrow.

Sadly, he dismissed me each time, choosing to deal with it by NOT dealing with it. In doing so, I may have negatively contributed to his depression, his anger and his resentment although I don't know if he suffers from any of that now. If this is the case, I pray to you, my son, to forgive me for I did not intend to cause you any pain or suffering; no mother would. I only wanted you to be happy. I was just not convinced that happiness would ever come your way if things stayed the way they were and you remained unwilling to let go or to embrace life for all the beauty that exists when we choose to allow the light to shine through. If I misjudged you, please forgive me.

As for you, Nour, for thirteen years I tried to enter your heart, but you were determined to keep it shut forever. In one of your earlier e-mails you stated, "You probably think that I don't love you and that I hate you because of your harsh and unmerciful actions toward my father. No, mother, that is absolutely not true. I love you, and I certainly do not hate you." That is when you still referred to me as your mother, without quotes. Today, I am not so sure you still hold these sentiments starting with blocking my number, to your harsh accusatory e-mails, to calling the police in order to have me kicked out of your house or simply by choosing to ignore any e-mail, call or voice message I was able to leave you, or better yet, to share them with your father. Know that when you lie on your pillow at night, distressed from a long day of patient visits, of surgeries, and perhaps of death, be comforted that I have long forgiven you, that my love will always shine through you, from you and to you even after the day I am no longer on this earth.

And you, Rameh, know too, that while you have never forgiven me for having wronged you, you, too, have indeed wronged me, so I wish you would stop playing the victim; you have no clue of what it means to lose your children for thirteen years and continuing. Nah, partners die and are often replaced, but no one can ever step in where your children have departed. I wish you would swallow the pain that comes to all of us and to many more couples in the world and make peace with the choices that you, too, made in our marriage. You may then find a life enriched by the vigor of a true love that you never had for me, but one that you and every human being deserves. So stop living your own lie and stop feeding it to our children. It is time that you shared the truth with them so that they may have a genuine perspective of what led to our estrangement and to the one you fostered between them and me.

For my part, I have forgiven you long ago, and thus I have reached peace. I wish that you could reach yours by recognizing your role in stunting our children's emotional maturity, and then to make amends with them by asking for their forgiveness. Once they reach the truth on their own, they may not. I will then pity you for the loss that, only then, you can call it "cruel and unusual punishment" causing you "tremendous agony," not by my infidelity or by the subsequent divorce.

I look at my resilience through my internal frailties, my struggles and my experiences that have shaped my life, making me a better person, more than ever in touch with who I am, proud of my perseverance and fortitude, confident that there is nothing worse that can happen to me which I could not overcome. The inner strength I have built over the years has made me impermeable to any pain that can destroy me. No, it did not make me immune to pain or suffering; rather, it taught me, as one counselor said, "to live a fulfilling life alongside my pain." This is the highest level of resilience anyone can ever reach.

So how do you enjoy life when your life is shaped by pain? You do it by surrendering to it and by letting it take you to where you need to be. That is not to say you are defeated. To the contrary, it is only if you have developed or found your inner strength to make the CHOICE to surrender that you are able to shape your future instead of letting your agonizing past determine it for you. In fact, if you chose the latter, your future would be very predictable, one that locks you into a state of misery from which you cannot escape. When you choose to surrender, you learn to live life WITH hope not FOR hope. That is to say to enjoy the best as well as the worst. That is to enjoy every experience, regretting none, for all become learning lessons that will make you grow and will enrich your mind and your spirit.

I am no psychologist, and I have not read a single self-help book. But based on life's being the best teacher, I finally learned that living WITH hope is to live in the moment mindfully, without any expectation. For me, it means not to count the days, the weeks, the years, and all the time that has passed me by waiting for my children to wake up and to reconcile with me. I lived for thirteen years waiting FOR a hope that never came. For all these years, riddled with disappointments, with shattered hopes, and with unspeakable suffering, today, I live, I laugh, I cry, I love, I cry some more, I live again, all WITH the hope that they will be back in my life someday. I no longer set timelines, read guidebooks or create a mindset that this will inevitably happen. This kind of hope can lead to disappointment and despair and it truly deprives you from living a fulfilling life. I have tried all of that and more, but with each step forward, I took many back, causing me intense grief and suffering. So I CHOSE to overcome, I CHOSE to be happy over being sad and sorrowful. One really has only these two options.

Throughout the worst of it, I made myself get out of bed every morning, wear my makeup and business attire and head to work. I carried on my daily exercise routine, I hung out with friends, I attended graduate school in the evenings, and I studied hard in order to graduate with distinction, much as I had pushed my son to reach his full potential and to graduate with excellence. I cherished my loving intimacy with my life partner, my amazing husband, Patrick, by going on outings and memorable vacations, savoring each and every experience that enriched my mind and made me even more connected to this earth that we all belong to, that we all share in its intoxicating beauty, but also in its inextricable sorrows suffered by so many destitute people. And I thanked God every day for His compassion, the blessings that He had bestowed upon me as His humble servant and yes, also upon MY FAMILY, I daresay, for their health, for their success, and for living in a country of abundance where what we take for granted is considered a luxury for the majority others.

Throughout these chapters, I have expressed extreme passions, many of despair, but others of hope and contentedness. If that is what the psychologists call closure, then perhaps I achieved closure. If going through the phases of grief is succumbing to the reality that we all must accept, then I have grieved, and am now free to make a new reality, the one that God has written for me. If surrendering means abandoning hope as I have perceived it throughout my ordeal, then I have surrendered to a past that has passed and I am ready for the future, guided by the light of my faith, cradled in God's loving arms that have carried me across rough waters, floods, storms, and across barren lands too. And for that, I have my God, my kind loving husband and my dear friends who have never left my side to thank.

Thirteen years have passed with no glimmer of hope that I will ever have my children in my life. They ARE MY children and they ARE MY life. I will have lost them when I have lost IT. They are very much alive within every beat of my heart and every breath I take. They dominate my existence. They take center stage. Everywhere I go, wherever I turn, their images, their laughter, their tears, their "love you too, Mom," travel with me, attached to my soul. No time or distance can ever take them from me, nor can the memories that engulf me. I have transcended their animosity, their revilement, their estrangement, their rebukes, their humiliations, their accusations, their false assumptions, their ingratitude, and their unwavering loyalty to a father that shut their hearts to the truth, locked the door and threw the key into the abyss. No, Rameh. No, my beloved children, I shall never give up on you, nor surrender to the fate as you want for me. You do not control my destiny. Only God does.

Not too long ago, one of my friends re-posted this quote by Mareez Reyes on Facebook. I thought it was very fitting,

"One of the hardest lessons in life is letting go...

Whether it is guilt, anger, love, loss or betrayal...

Change is never easy.

We fight to hold on

And we fight to let go."

As for me, my beautiful children, I love, I cry, I forgive, I live mindfully, I hold on to God and I move on. This is how I define happiness. I hope you, too, will find it someday and be freed to live fulfilling lives alongside your own pain.

May God continue to look after you, bless you and return you to Him.

Acknowledgments

This book is dedicated to my beautiful children. Know that there is no degree of pain, sorrow, or suffering that will ever shake my love for you. A mother's love is unbending and eternal.

I especially want to thank my dear friends, Salha and Yelena, whose support was unrelenting. Through the hardest periods of my life, they have stood beside me every step of the way, crying and laughing with me. They have shown me sincere love, much needed at times of uncertainty and despair. They made me continue to have faith in humanity and to accept that times have changed, that we live in an era when children are not as closely connected to their parents as they were during our generation, or as we expect them to be. One day, when the time is right, perhaps when they have children of their own, they will undoubtedly return to my arms, *Inshallah!*

Special thanks to my dear friend, Celina, whose daily prayers God must have answered. Her unwavering faith set the example for me to never question God or the goodness He brings to our lives, but rather, to surrender to Him in times of joy and pain, living every moment in His Presence, through which our salvation is assured.

Last and without reservations, I thank my amazing husband and life-partner, Patrick. After 43 years of waiting, of forgotten hopes and dreams, I had found the love that I had come to believe could never exist. We say, "God closes one door but opens another." Through that open door, Patrick held my hand through the agonizing passage of recovery. A man of very few words, his empathy, his acceptance, his kindness, his understanding, his warmth, his affection and compassion, spoke a million words. He engulfed me with his love; he was my shield when I was vulnerable; he took on my pain every time I needed a shoulder to cry on, and he lifted me up when I had hit rock bottom. He enriched my life with the adventures of traveling, of exploring and of connecting with our world with all its beauty, reminding me of how grateful I am for all that is to come, the good tiding as well as the bad.

About The Author

Futoun Haddad was five when her father abruptly disappeared from her life, emigrating to another country in order to earn a living for the family. She never fully recovered from the trauma. In 1975, when she was eleven, a bloody civil war broke out in her home country, Lebanon, which further aggravated her sense of insecurity and danger. Shortly after, her mother joined her father overseas in order to assist him in the business, leaving the family behind and visiting only intermittently. Haddad was left to be cared for by her then nineteen-year-old sister while enduring the fallouts of many more wars, foreign invasions and never-ending skirmishes, fighting, brutal killings, and bombings. At twenty, Haddad left for the U.S. in order to pursue a BA in Journalism. Upon graduation, she married her childhood Lebanese boyfriend and became a naturalized citizen. Her struggles that had begun when she was a child became manifest throughout her adult life: marriage, divorce and the ultimate alienation of her two children twenty-one years later. In 2010, she received her MA in Political Science/International Relations, and she married the love of her life, the subject of the alienation five years later. They live happily in California now. **Cast Out: Holding On To God** is her first book.